Letters to

This is the picture Win sent to her husband, Don, whilst he was in the desert. He made a frame for it out of a petrol can. Part of the words 'petroleum fuel' can be seen on the back. (1943)

Letters to Lamar

Win Wyatt

First published in 2005 by
Lusby Publications
159 Minard Road
London SE6 1NN

© Win Wyatt 2005

All rights reserved

ISBN 0–9550448–0–4

Set in 11/13.5pt Bembo
Designed and produced by Sandie Boccacci
Printed and bound in Great Britain by
Antony Rowe Limited, Chippenham, Wiltshire

I dedicate this book to my family.

If any profit is made from the sale of this book, I would like it to go to Breast Cancer Care.

This is the picture that was used with my byline in
The Lamar Daily News (*1940*)

Contents

List of Illustrations
ix

Foreword
xi

The Family in 1940
xv

1939
1

1940
7

1941
101

1942
145

1943
199

1944
237

1945
275

1946
323

Postscript: 15th June 2003
333

List of Illustrations

Win in 1943, picture framed by Don using part of a petrol can	ii
Win in 1940, picture used with her byline in *The Lamar Daily News*	vi
Alfie aged 5 months, March 1940	27
Alf and Doris	48
In the garden at 23 Dumbreck Road just after Don joined up	108
Grandad Smith in the garden of 23 Dumbreck Road, 1941	122
Edna, Alf and Peggy (the dog), 1941	123
Wedding Day, 15 June 1941	129
Wedding party, 15 June 1941	129
On honeymoon in Bournemouth, 1941	130
Don, 1940	139
Family group, 1942	175
Concert programme, 1942	191
Memorial to victims of Sandhurst School bombing	202
Memorial to victims of Sandhurst School bombing	203
Donna on her wedding day, 1943	208
Don's favourite picture of Win, 1943	214
Jeanne, Edna and Paddy at Bath, 1943	220
Airgraph from Dick Nevius to Don Wyatt, 1943	223
Don, 1943	230
Don, 1943	231
Win in ambulance uniform, 1944	254
Patricia, born 1944	262
Alf, Doris, Alfie and David	271
Picture of Donna, damaged in bombing	296
The yellow suit that came in the parcel from Lamar, 1945	321

Foreword

On a summer's day in 1933, a 12-year-old schoolgirl in Lamar, Colorado, U.S.A., wrote an essay as part of a school exercise to an unknown schoolgirl of the same age in London, England.

This letter was received at County Hall and passed by the powers-that-be to a school in Eltham in South East London. Here, another exercise took place: all members of the class were told to write a reply to this letter, and the best would be forwarded on to Lamar.

This is how the correspondence between Donna Marie Pivonka, as she was then, in Lamar, and Win Hellewell, a 13-year-old from Eltham, started. How could we have known then that in the year 2005, some 70 years later, with both of us now widowed, the friendship and correspondence would still continue?

By 1939, when the schoolgirl letters had developed from school activities to news of boyfriends etc. as the girls grew up, Win found herself with lots of newsworthy items to fill her letters as the Second World War started. Donna, at her end, passed these letters to her friends to read. It must have been so hard for those folk in that little mid-western town to realise just what was going on in war-torn Britain. Soon the existence of the letters became known to the editor of *The Lamar Daily News*, and Donna allowed them to print these letters, minus the personal bits, so that they could be read by a wider audience. At one time the editor actually wrote to Win and asked if she would send articles direct to the paper, but remember we were in the middle of a war, security was tight, and she worried about censorship. Knowing that her letters were subject to the censor's scrutiny, it was decided that the articles would continue as before, in letter form. This way, pages and pages were printed throughout the remaining years of the war. All sorts of things were discussed from clothes rationing, which started the week before Win's marriage, to the bomb damage around her and the loss of work colleagues. The naïve girl of 1939 grew up fast in this war-time atmosphere, especially with a husband overseas.

During the course of this time the residents of Lamar collected money and sent parcels to England, full of luxuries that were impossible to buy, for all members of Win's family. Imagine what nylons, lipstick, a summer suit and knitting wool must have meant to a girl in her early twenties to whom these things were unobtainable.

Donna sent several packages of copies of the newspapers, and, filled with embarrassment to see all her innermost thoughts there in print before her, Win consigned these to the loft. There they lay until some five or ten years after the war, when she read them again. Unable to visualise that these were to become part of history, and that any feeling of embarrassment would dissolve with age, and wanting to get on with post-war life with her safely returned husband, she consigned all the newspapers to the bonfire and promptly forgot them.

Many, many years later a parcel was received from Faye Johnson in Arizona, whose mother had posted cuttings of all these letters to her whilst she lived out the war years on the west coast. Faye discovered these in a shoe box and realised that here was a slice of history, and thinking that they deserved to be read by a later generation, sent them to Win Wyatt, as she was by then, in England.

Seeing these letters again after all those years, they were now read more objectively, and it looked as though it would be criminal to ignore this second chance.

So thanks to Faye we set to, my daughter and I, and burned the midnight oil typing up all these letters from the cuttings. Many had got lost crossing the Atlantic during war-time, but with the help of a load of originals, preserved by Donna, we were able to fill in some of the gaps.

So this book eventually evolved, and although I am happy to see it in print for my children, grandchildren and my darling great-granddaughter, I hope there may be others out there who will want to buy it and read it, and contribute to Breast Cancer Care as a result.

I remember, before Faye's copies arrived, on one of the war-time anniversaries my son asked me what I did on V E Day. I told him vaguely, I couldn't really remember, I thought I danced in the street. Then Faye's letters arrived and I was able to read every detail of how I spent that day, and all the memories came flooding back. It proved to me that memories of an 80-year-old are not all that reliable, but these letters are comments on events in most instances the very day or the day after they occurred.

The Family in 1940

At 23 Dumbreck Road, Eltham:
- Dad, Alfred Thomas Hellewell, aged 52.
- Mum, Maggie Alice Hellewell, aged 52.
- My brother, George Hellewell, aged 27. (George later left to join the Army.)
- Me, Win Hellewell, aged 20. (In 1941 I married Donald Wyatt and became Win Wyatt. I lived at '23' throughout the entire war.)
- My sister, Edna Hellewell, aged 17. (Edna later left to join the Air Force.)
- My sister, Phyllis Hellewell, aged 11. (She spent most of the time right from 1939 until very late in the war away from home, evacuated to various places of safety in the country. She did return home for brief periods between venues, and was actually at home for good at the latter part of the war.)

At 21 Dumbreck Road – next door:
- My brother, Alf Hellewell, aged 29.
- His wife, Doris Hellewell, known as 'Dot'.
- His son, Alfred Ernest, (Alfie) born in Wales in October 1939.
- and later, his son, David, born in Wales in October 1941.
  These two children lived next door for most of the war, save for brief spells out of danger in Wales, when things got very sticky.

During the early part of the war there was an occasional extra occupant at '23'. Grandad, my mother's father, lived alternately with us and with his other daughter a few miles away. This explains the sometimes long gaps between mentions of him as a member of the household.

Since the death of my brother, Alf, at the age of 92, in 2003, there is no longer any family connection with either 21 or 23 Dumbreck Road.

Just four of the people who inhabited these two houses during the war are alive today. 'Baby' Alfie is now in his sixties and retired, as is David who was born in 1941. Edna and I celebrated our 82nd and 85th birthdays respectively in June, 2005.

1939

THE PHONEY WAR

The last few months of 1939 and the early months of 1940 became known as 'The Phoney War' as nothing very dramatic was taking place.

The first few letters therefore reflect this state of affairs as seen through the eyes of a typical 19-year-old of the time. Judging by our present day standards she was a very naïve, young 19-year-old, exhibiting the strong patriotic fervour of her time.

Although I am pretty certain that I wrote to Donna immediately war was declared on 3rd September 1939, this letter does not appear to have survived. The first letter written post the outbreak of war is dated 20th October 1939, which is still pretty early on, and this is therefore the date on which this book begins.

20th October 1939

My Dear Donna,

Hello, hello, AZ★★★★9/4 calling with all the latest news from the Home Front.

First and foremost, the most important piece of news – Alfred Ernest Hellewell arrived on 6th October, weighing 8-lbs, and according to his father looking a very chubby kid, with blue eyes. You can imagine the excitement at home, Mum and Dad are grandparents for the first time, and my young sister Phyllis was tickled to death when we wrote and told her she was an Auntie. She has been looking forward to this baby for months, and has told everyone about the baby 'we are' going to have. The baby has become common property in the family, and everyone refers to it as 'our' baby. We have not seen him yet, as Doris is away in the country. The latest news of him came in a letter about a week ago – he has gained 4 ozs. He is to be called Alfred Ernest: Alfred after his father and his paternal grandfather and Ernest after Doris's father. I think I can safely say he will soon be known as 'Alfie'.

Secondly, that bottom drawer of mine is now extended up one to the second from the bottom. My, what a lot of stuff! Last week Don and I went out and bought blankets, sheets, table cloths, towels, tea towels, pillow slips, bolster cases, and some gay working overalls. Prices have gone up already, and they will be sky high in about six months' time. It will be bad enough having to pay top prices for furniture and curtains, so we are trying to get some of the things we will need, now. We did not rush to get married at the beginning of the war like some people, and we are not going to wait until after the war (if it lasts until June) like so many others. We are just going to get married, how, and when we've always planned to do. After all it will take more than Hitler to make us change our plans. I expect we will know by then whether or not Don will be called up. If he is, that may make a little difference. I wouldn't be much good to the country, sitting at home all day in an empty flat, I would be doing more good at my job.

I am hoping against hope that Don's job will be a reserved occupation, because if they say his job is more important on the home front he will not be able to join up. It is not going to be easy though even if he is exempt, I can't imagine Don being content to stay at home, when all his pals are fighting. From my own point of view I want him to stay at home of course, and I pray and pray that he won't have to go, but I should feel awful if through me he lost all his self respect. His job is important here, civilians have got to be fed, but men never think they are really doing their bit, unless they are in the firing line. Why even at this moment, his young brother is in the Army 'somewhere abroad'. That isn't for the benefit of the censor either, that really is as much as we know about his whereabouts. Don doesn't say anything, but I know he is worried about him (he is only 20), and I can understand because from my own experience I know that my own safety counts for nothing, when someone who means something to me, is in danger.

1939

Phyllis is still staying in the country, the whole of her school were evacuated at the beginning of the war, and they share the village school with the locals. I missed her terribly at first. When we had the first Air Raid Warning (it turned out to be a false alarm), I jumped out of bed and ran to get Phylly. I even got as far as stretching out my arms to pick her up, before I remembered that the bed was empty and she wasn't there. It is not quite so bad now, we are getting used to being without her. Sometimes, when we are playing some sort of game in the evening, we say 'Phylly would like this', or 'I wonder if Phylly is in bed yet'.

This war has made us far more united as a family. We always were of course, but we are in so many evenings together now, that we get together and play 'Monopoly' or 'Pontoon'. Whereas before we were out most nights of the week, and if we were all in together, we wanted an early night or something. We have heard so much about 'Black-out blues', but really, I don't know what they are like. I have such stacks and stacks of wool all ready to be made into trousseau jumpers, or pullovers, or baby things for Christmas presents, that the long evenings hold no terror for me. It is worse for the boys, they just cannot be contented sitting at home with a book like we can. Actually though, I am only in two evenings a week more than usual, those are the evenings my girl friend and I used to go for long walks. The other evenings, I see Don, and we go to the pictures as usual, or have darkness for nothing in the front room. Once a week I stay over at his house to save him a journey home in the dark.

Let me give my impressions of the black-out. It's intriguing. I always thought it would be just the same as any evening in a dark country lane, but believe me, London in complete blackness is a never to be forgotten experience. Houses loom up in front of you in dark black shapes, they are all you can see, save the sky. You notice the sky in the black-out more than you have ever noticed it before. Somehow, unconsciously you keep your eyes on the stars, and the moon (if it is out). You hear more too, you cannot see people, but you hear voices and your ears become sensitive to any sound that isn't normal. Last week, Don and I were getting off a bus, when he heard a little cry. It was so faint that I didn't hear it, but he said he knew it was something out of the ordinary. He went back across the road, and it turned out to be an old lady lying in the middle of the road. She had had one foot on the bus, but the conductor thought it was all clear, and the bus moved before she had time to get on. Every time I think of what might have happened, if Don hadn't heard that faint little sound, I shudder. A car coming along would never have been able to see her. When I am with Don or anyone else, I don't mind the darkness, I just walk along the same as usual, but when I am on my own I carry a torch, and when I hear footsteps approaching, I shine it on the ground to let them know I am coming, it saves many collisions. I flash it as I walk across the road, but really this isn't necessary because if you wait until you can't see even the tiniest flicker of light, you know the road is clear.

My girl friend has an important Government job, and has been evacuated 'somewhere in England'. She didn't want to go, because it is not like children, grown-ups don't mind about their own safety. Still, the work is important, and she had to go. She has been home for a couple of weekends, and we have been out to celebrate. With all these people away from home, life seems to be one long orgy of letter writing these days, and I am sorry to say I have to write some of them by hand, because time at the office will not permit.

I am writing to you, without waiting for a reply to my previous letter, because I couldn't see much sense in waiting, perhaps in vain, for an answer to a letter that might never have reached you. I have got a new idea now, I have taken a carbon copy of this letter, so, if this one goes to the bottom of the sea, you will stand the chance of getting the carbon copy later on. I will post the carbon in about three weeks' time. So, if this letter you are reading now is a carbon, the original has been lost. If on the other hand you are reading the original, maybe you will receive a carbon copy as well. It sounds a bit complicated, but I hope you get the idea. That's what we do with all our business letters to U.S.A. so the idea isn't entirely my own. If you write to me, don't wait more than a reasonable time for a reply, will you, for I am bound to answer pretty promptly. I am anxious to hear how you are doing (we're doing fine by the way) and whether or not this rotten war is affecting you.

What did you think of Lindberg's speech over there? With all due respect to the fact that he is a fellow countryman of yours, I have no hesitation in saying that over here we thought it waff. General opinion has it that Lindy would do well to stick to his own vocation, and leave politics to those that understand them, and Canada's affairs to Canada, who up until now has always been able to decide for herself what to do, without any help from a bitter busy body. He is bitter, that is the only excuse you can find for him, you can't blame him for that, but we were certainly most indignant about his speech.

Well I think I seem to have told you about everything of importance at the moment. Last weekend a lot of the girls from the club whose jobs have taken them off to the country came home for Saturday and Sunday, and the tandem section came into its own again, and we had a jolly good day. The only complaint was that two gas masks in the bag on the back made extra weight to push up the hill. Never mind, better to be safe than sorry, but they are a curse, we have to carry them with us everywhere. Touch wood, I haven't left mine at home once yet, but lots of people have, and have breathed a sigh of thankfulness when they safely reach home again at night without needing them. You feel like a little school child, going to school with your satchel on your back, though some of the cases are very gay. Mine is in black shiny cloth, it goes with anything, and it is also waterproof, which is a great blessing, when you remember all the rain we have been having lately.

What do you think of my Identity number? Gives one an air of individuality, don't you think?

Cheerio for the present, let me hear from you soon, won't you?
Tons of love,
from,
    Win xxxx

Throughout the letters, reference is made to 'The Club', so I think a short explanation will help with the understanding of this phrase. 'The Club' was, to give it its correct name, 'The Lee Cycling and Athletic Club'.

In 1935 my brother George, seven years older than myself, joined this cycling club, I think the athletic side of the club had faded out some years before. Members were all cycling enthusiasts in the days when it was safe to cycle around the country lanes bordering our part of South East London. In the main, the men members rode single bikes, whilst most couples opted for a tandem, with the girl on the back. There were a few exceptions of girls who rode their own single bikes.

Most Sundays throughout the year saw us gathering at a meeting point, and spending the day cycling around the Kent countryside. The men also raced, 25 miles, 50 miles, 100 miles, both for club events and district events which involved other clubs in the area, mostly larger than ours. These events always started very early in the morning, and if you were not racing yourself you went out as a 'helper', handing out food and drink at certain points especially during the longer races. I remember one memorable weekend when one of our members took part in a gruelling 24 hour endurance run. I don't know what position in the district he ended up as, but I know we all turned out to see him finish.

On the Sunday runs, we usually stopped at a pub for bread and cheese and a lager, and teatime was a real event. For 1/6d (less than 10p in today's money), we all sat down at selected venues to a feast of ham, salad, bread, jam and cakes. Usually, after the table was cleared there would be an hour or so of card playing before we headed for home.

On Bank Holiday weekends, we used to go to the coast and stay over night, usually to Hastings, or at Whitsun, we always took the boat over to the Isle of Wight and stayed in Sandown.

At Christmas 1935, George invited all his new club friends to a party at our home, and it was there that I met Don for the first time. At the next club meeting after the party, Don asked George if he would ask me for a date on his behalf. George's reaction was 'My sister? She's only a kid!' I was at that time fifteen and a half – the half being very important at that age. However, Don wasn't put off and we did in fact have our date and the rest as they say is history.

Six months later Don exchanged his single bike for a tandem and I became a member of the club.

At this time our greatest friends were another couple, Sook and Doris. I never really knew how Sook or Sooky got his nick name, but in later life it was dropped and he became 'Dick'. Although, like Don, Dick is no longer with us, Doris and I are still in touch, and have remained friends throughout our lifetime, sharing many holidays and card-playing evenings.

1940

1st January 1940

My Dear Donna,

I received your very welcome letter just before Christmas, and a more acceptable Christmas present you couldn't wish to have sent me.

At the present moment, half past two on New Year's Day, I am feeling a bit under the weather, having got into bed at four this morning, risen again at half past six, and arrived at the office an hour and a half late because of the dense fog. Still, I will go back to the beginning and tell you about Christmas.

On Sunday we spent a quiet day at home with just the family, my brother and his wife and baby, and Don. On Monday, one of the couples in the club, Sook and Doris got married. That only leaves yours truly as the one remaining single girl in the club, but not for long I hope. Anyway, all the club turned up in force to witness the occasion. She was married in a brown two-piece, consisting of a brown frock with a high neckline, and two little golden reindeers at the throat, a brown coat of the same material with huge fur lapels each side. A brown velvet hat with a massive veil, brown suede shoes and gold gloves. She wanted to be married in white, but Sook wouldn't hear of it, he only wanted to have a quiet wedding. He didn't even want to get married in church, but I think they compromised by Doris giving up the white dress and Sook agreeing to be married in church. He was no ordinary bridegroom I can assure you, no shaking at the knees for him, like the bridegroom at the wedding the previous week. (You remember I told you in my last letter that I was going to be a bridesmaid to one of the girls at the office.) True, it may have been the six whiskeys Sook knocked back before the ceremony that gave him his false courage, but I have never heard 'I will' said with such vigour and firmness before. After the wedding, we went to the Wedding Breakfast at the bride's house, but it was after the breakfast (which incidentally we had at half past three in the afternoon) that the fun began. Dancing, singing, games and laughter the whole night through. Don doesn't dance, but I managed to get him to dance all the waltzes with me, and I think he enjoyed it. I don't know where the time went to. I remember looking at the clock at three o'clock, because somebody started to play 'Three o'clock in the morning'. Anyway, I finally went to bed at 7 o'clock on Tuesday morning, with the bride. About half an hour later, Don and Sook came up, as their game of cards had faded out due to the sleepiness of the remaining guests. I offered to sleep on the floor with Don, but they wouldn't hear of it, so all four of us crammed into one bed. I don't know what my Mum would have said, but I can assure you it was all above board, Don having replaced his best trousers for an old pair of Sook's, and myself in an old frock of Doris's, only minus my stockings. We had breakfast about eleven on Tuesday, and dinner at four, then we thought we had better go home, as we had promised Mum that we would spend Boxing Day at home.

On Wednesday we went to see 'Let us Live' and 'Naughty but Nice', much to Don's mother's disapproval, she thought we ought to have an early night. Don worked until 12 at night, and was up at half past five, every day during the week before Christmas, plucking turkeys and getting all the other good things ready for Christmas.

My only regret about Christmas is that as we went out, we missed our Christmas dinner, but Don brought a turkey with him last Sunday, and so we had Turkey, Christmas Pudding and Mince Pies, like a real Christmas dinner on New Year's Eve. After dinner we went on to Sook and Doris's again, and were very much surprised to see all the gang that were there at Christmas, and more besides. The procedure was much the same as Christmas: Dancing, Singing, Games. We greeted the New Year with 'Auld Lang Syne' and 'Knees up Mother Brown'. Although the war was far from our thoughts, I think everyone offered up a silent prayer that this bright New Year might bring peace to our dear land once again.

The funniest part about it was when we tried to get home. It was a terrible night, one of those really 'Pea soup' fogs that the film people imagine hang over England all the winter. Both fogs and the black-out are bad enough apart, but to get them together, well you couldn't see your hand before you. We had not worried very much because as usual I was going home with my brother, and Don was going straight to his home, instead of making two journeys. We always adopt this arrangement when 'the crowd' are out late. About half past two we rang for a taxi and were surprised to hear that they had all left their receivers off, because they didn't want to come out. New Year's Eve is always considered the taxi man's paradise. You can't blame them really for not coming out, they are independent now as they can easily use up their petrol ration in good weather, without coming out on a bad night. You see, we don't all own cars over here, and if we miss the last bus or the last tram, the only thing to do is to get a taxi, or walk, and it is usually, walk. It is only Christmas, New Year or some very special occasion when the pocket runs to a cab. I could have got a tram part of the way home, and it meant walking the rest with my brother, or I could walk all the way home with Don. Needless to say I chose walking with Don, especially as he would have to walk on his own otherwise, and my brother stayed the night. We could have stayed too, but Don had to get up very early.

It took nearly an hour and a half to get to his home, and four o'clock was striking as I got into bed. Don changed his clothes and dressed ready for work, and with his dressing gown over the top, slept in the dining room all night, whilst I had his bed. Poor chap, he had to get up after an hour or so, and he was freezing. That's one thing about his job, the hours are so long in the first place, and when you are your own boss, you have all the responsibility too. He is often very tired, and since the war he has had to fight like the devil to keep his supplies up. There is no shortage of meat, but he can't just go up to market and buy what he wants now, he has to take what he is given, and dash around all over the country to try and get just that much more than the other man, that makes business successful.

Tuesday 2nd January 1940

We had that early night that his Mother was so anxious about on Monday night, and got to bed about ten.

By the way, I haven't told you about some very important news. It is three weeks ago now that it happened, and I am so used to it that I forget who I have told and who I haven't. About a fortnight before Christmas, Don and I got engaged. We went up to town, bought the ring, and then went on to the London Palladium afterwards. I must tell you about my ring, it is gold (I am old fashioned enough not to like platinum) with five diamonds. One large one in the centre, two slightly smaller ones on either side, and a slightly smaller one still on either side of that. It sparkles and shines, and at first I was very self conscious about taking my glove off in public, in case it looked as though I was doing it purposely. I am quite used to it now though, and don't notice it on my finger. To go back to the celebration. We bought the ring, and I had it put on in the railway carriage (it was conveniently darkened due to the black-out), and we went straight to the show at the Palladium. It was a smashing show, and I laughed from start to finish. After the show, contrary to the usual procedure of going out and getting tight, we went and had a jolly good blow-out, and then went home to Don's house where they drank our health.

I sleep over at Don's house quite a lot these days, and it saves him having to see me home, and then having an hour's journey himself in the black-out. He stays over at my house over the weekend, but during the week I stay two or perhaps more nights at his house, because the shop is only just around the corner. Rationing started this week, and I must say it hasn't affected our family the slightest little bit. Our bacon ration is more than we usually have, sugar is just about a pound less, and butter is less of course, but we are fast getting used to dripping on our toast, and margarine when we have jam or something else on our bread. Those three things are the only ones rationed at the moment, besides petrol of course, but meat rationing will start in a few weeks' time. I am not worrying about that either, with a butcher for my husband-to-be, I don't expect to starve. We don't mind about it at all, if rationing is going to make it easier for our brave sailors and merchant seamen, then it's O.K. by us.

By the way please excuse the change of ribbon in the middle of a sentence at the top of the page, only I had to stop this morning and do some letters, and the boss happened to mention that my ribbon looked as though it wanted changing.

11th January 1940

Contrary to my original promise of making all mention of the war taboo, there are one or two things I really must mention.

Firstly, I am sure you will agree with me that the courageous Finnish people well deserve the success they have so far achieved in the 'David and Goliath' war of theirs. At first the cry was 'Poor Little Finland', but now we take off our hats to a great people, may they come through this struggle victorious, as we shall, ours.

Secondly, all honour to the gallant neutrals, who despite terrible danger from mines and torpedoes, still brave the seven seas to bring us our food and supplies. I couldn't help feeling proud the other day when I heard that in a Dutch newspaper, someone had said that Germany had as much chance of stopping Holland from sailing the seas, as she had of stopping Britain. We have always been on the best of terms with these small countries, but now we respect them. They have shown courage that it is easy for us to show with all the might of our Empire behind us. They have nothing save their grim determination not to be downtrodden by the tyrant.

There is not much else to tell you that you don't know already. I expect you have heard of the latest tactic of bombing and machine-gunning fishing boats and their crews. I ask you, what possible material help can the enemy hope to get from these cowardly actions? When they sink a submarine of ours, we are naturally shocked by it, but they are vessels of war, out doing a warlike job, and even though they did not wish to do it, it is quite within the 'rules of war' for them to be sunk – but fishing vessels? It makes you think sometimes that there can't be a God to allow these terrible things to happen.

23rd January 1940

Last night Don and I went up to town to see George Black's show

'Black Velvet', and boy was it good. We had not booked or anything, but we decided at the last minute that there wasn't anything worth seeing locally, so we splashed out. We were lucky enough to get two seats that had been cancelled. Usually, you can't get a seat before months of booking. Have you heard of Vic Oliver? He was in it. I have heard him on the air and thought him pretty weak, but he is different again on the stage. This is one of his gags – 'Jack and Jill went up the hill, they each had a dollar and a quarter, Jill came down with two dollars and a half – do you think they went up for water?' There was one very funny scene taking off the censor's office. He held a newspaper up and demanded who gave permission for a certain article to be published. 'Look at it,' he stormed. *It's a Long Way to Tipperary*. We don't want the enemy to know it's a long way to Tipperary, we want them to think it's quite near'. So it went on, all nonsense like that. He held up a sausage and described it as 'Hitler's secret weapon'. Adolf old boy you are causing us a Hell of a lot of trouble, but you are giving us a Hell of a lot of laughs as well.

By the way, talking of censors, your letter to me was not censored either.

You ask if Don has been called up yet. No, luckily I still have him with me. He is due to go May-July, so of course that washes out all our plans for June. He absolutely refuses to get married before he goes, having got some crazy idea into his head about it being unfair to me, and selfish of him, and lots of other nonsense that makes me wish I could shake him, and at the same time makes me respect him. Really, when I look at it sensibly, I know he is right, that to wait until he comes back is the only sane thing to do, but it is so hard. These six months were going to be so crammed full of lovely things, all the spending and preparations. At first I thought myself very hard done by that the war should spoil my wedding, but now I realise that there are plenty of people worse off than me.

In your last letter you asked me to explain the black-out to you, and a harder thing to explain, I can't think of, but I will endeavour to do my best to enlighten you. Firstly, the reason is this, the glow of London, i.e. street lights, lights at windows of all the thousands of houses, cinema lights, theatre lights, railway stations, car headlights etc., can be seen from the coast by air. Not individually of course, but a glow that shows up London from all the neighbouring countryside. It would be too late to turn off all these lights after enemy raiders had been spotted, they would already have seen the glow, and know what direction to fly. Whether or not they would get there of course is beside the point. Also, there would be bound to be people that in the excitement of the moment would forget to put their lights out when the alarm was sounded. So, as a precaution, all lights are extinguished from sundown to sunup. There are no street lights, no neon signs over the cinemas or theatres, no lights showing from any household window. (Even a tiny chink, brings the Air Raid Warden knocking at the door with 'Put that light out'.) Even cars are only allowed to show the minimum of light. There are special lamps for headlights which throw a little light on the road, and none up above. Even traffic lights are reduced to just a tiny red or green cross, but it is surprising how they show up in the blackness. Some nights are worse than others, when there is a full moon you can see as clearly as daylight. It is funny, we never used to notice if it was lighter one evening more than another, but now we count the days to the new moon. We were done out of it at Christmas, there was supposed to be a new moon on 26th December but as I mentioned before, we had a dense fog. The best way I can get you to realise the black-out is this. Walk down the busiest street in Lamar, and let your imagination run riot. Look at all the brightly lit shops and houses, and imagine them as nothing more than big black shapes. Look at the cars and trams and buses (that is assuming you have trams and buses) and imagine that instead of their blazing headlights, all you can see is tiny particles of light, which shines out like a searchlight in the complete blackness. Look at all the people around you, and imagine instead, hundreds and hundreds of flashlights bobbing about. Don says it is like navigating, you don't steer by objects, you steer by lights. If you see a torchlight coming towards you, you move over, because you know there is someone holding that torch, although you can't see them.

 I forgot to mention above, my younger brother is due to go Sept.–Oct. but my elder brother does not have to go until next year, and we hope all this will be over by then. Don's brother, who has been in France since the beginning of the war, is due for leave any day now, and each letter is eagerly scanned for the word that is going to send their whole family into ecstasies. There is no end of things they are going to do 'When Eric comes home.' He is Don's mother's youngest son, and naturally she is crazy with fear that Don may have to go too. Dad was my brother's age when he joined up in 1915. What an insane, crazy world is this we live in! Will our children be doing the self-same thing, twenty-five years from now? Will our prayers that our efforts to create world peace be in vain, like our parents' were? Will all the lives that were lost, and all the hearts and homes broken, be for nothing, like the last lot were? We willingly fight for our Country, yes, after all if it is worth living in it is worth fighting for, but it all seems so pointless, so unnecessary. Still, who am I to question what the powers that be desire? Is it really, God's will that all this should happen? I am not religious, heaven knows, but I always had faith that no matter what happened, right was always bound to prevail in the end, and it will, but what a terrible price we have to pay for it.

Enough of this, what am I trying to do, make you think I am morbid? Believe you me, and this is the honest to goodness truth, I have seen more laughter, more genuine willingness to help others, since the war began, than ever before. We just don't talk about it out loud.

Despite the fact that it is a hundred to one chance that it will come off, I am going ahead with my plans for June, so that as soon as it is all over, we can be married and start again without having to wait. I had a lot of things for Christmas to add to the 'bottom drawer'. An ironing board, wine glasses, a dressing table set, a pair of chrome candle sticks to match, a butter dish, a dressing jacket, a set of chair backs and a settee back, some towels, and a funny little tea caddy spoon all covered in Chinese writing. Since Christmas I have myself bought new shoes, and more undies to put away. There is no end to the things that are 'going up'. You can't get a stock of all of them, so I am just jogging along, buying something every week while I can. 'Stock's as good as money' seems to be the motto these days. By the way, Don bought me a new winter coat for Christmas. It is black, and has a lovely soft grey fur round the neck and halfway down the front. He says, one day, if I'm good, when the war is over, he will buy me a fur coat. You can bet I promised him I would keep him to that.

This letter seems to have trailed on long enough, so I think I will finish it, and post it, and then start again.

Cheerio,
Let me hear from you soon,
Tons of love,
    Win xxxxx

10th February 1940

My Dear Donna,
You will probably be surprised at hearing from me so soon after my last epistle, but I wanted to send the match cases I forgot to enclose before, and also as I have a slack half hour, I thought I would take the opportunity and write. Slack half hours are very few and far between these days, so we have to make the most of them.

Hold on to something tight and listen, I went out last weekend and bought six dresses – just like that. They are for my 'torso' of course, and I always dreamt of going out and doing that, and I wasn't going to be done out of it, war or no war. Of course it is rather a weak attempt at optimism, for goodness knows when we will be getting married. Nevertheless 'Stock's as good as money' in wartime, and clothes will be terribly scarce and expensive, next year, when all the stocks have gone. It is impossible to lay in stock of everything you need, and it was only because I had already saved the money for the purpose of buying clothes for my trousseau, that I was able to do so. Stocking prices are going sky high already, but one consolation is the fact that everyone is in the same boat. If no-one wears silk stockings then it isn't so bad. Before the war you could buy fully fashioned stockings at 2/- a pair and even less. That is less than half a dollar. Now, you can't buy fully fashioned under 3/11d. That is nearly a dollar. You can still buy stockings cheaper than that, but they are not fully fashioned, and of course they don't look or wear so well. Still, san-fairey-biscuits, why worry? After all, who wants sailors to risk their lives bringing things like that across the water? Those that are made in England are needed for exchange of vital materials. So, next winter will probably see us all in woollen stockings. What a game! Still it's all part of the war effort. Ordinary coloured wools, khaki, navy, black, white and grey, are easy to get, although they are a bit dearer, but coloured wools for jumpers, greens and blues and pinks etc., are getting scarcer and scarcer. I have bought enough wool to keep me occupied for many a long day, and even if I never make another jumper, I have enough to last me for the duration, so I'm not so badly off. I have just finished knitting a helmet for a sailor. I don't know who he will be that will wear it, but I would like it to go to a sailor on a mine-sweeper for, if possible, these face even graver danger than the rest. Please don't let anyone try and kid you that we are short of food. This is not so; we have enough and more for everyone, and it is because we want this state of affairs to continue, that we are willing to go without luxuries, but even that we haven't had to do yet. If you can afford the extra coppers, you can still buy most things you wish.

I want to buy some more shoes, pyjamas, and a few odds and ends, and then I shall have a pretty good outfit. If IT does come off this year, I shall get a navy edge-to-edge coat, and an extra special frock to wear with it for going away. All I have got to leave until the last minute is that, and my actual wedding dress and the bridesmaids' dresses. There is no point in getting a 'going away' outfit, for a summer wedding, and then it comes off in the winter, is there?

In your last letter you asked if we ever wore ankle socks, well we do for tennis and cycling, but in the summer, if it is very hot, we go without anything at all on our legs, and in the winter, it is much too cold to go without stockings. During the recent cold spell, I have been wearing ankle socks over my silk stockings, then my shoes, and then rain boots over the top of that for outdoors. I bought these little ankle boots at the beginning of the winter, and it proved to be a very good investment, because when we had all the snow, it was impossible to get them in the shops, there had been such a run on them that they couldn't get them from the manufacturers quick enough.

I must tell you about these last few weeks, they have been the hardest in living memory. The snow was inches deep for days, and there was only one house in our road that hadn't got all the water pipes frozen. It was a muck up, we had to keep on going into this one house to get all our drinking water, but we used the water out of the air raid shelter for washing in. This no doubt sounds funny, but you see our block of houses are in a dip, and as the dug-outs are about eight feet under ground, it doesn't matter whether it rains or not, there is always a certain amount of water that comes up. Times out of number it has been filled, almost to the entrance, and we have had to spend hours pumping it dry. Anyway, the funny thing about it was, there wasn't very much water in there, when the great freeze came, because for weeks Mum had gone out and given the pump a couple of pushes every day, and kept it reasonably dry. We thought of all the gallons we had pumped down the drain, and we almost wished it would rain so that we could get some more in it. It was terribly dangerous going to work in the mornings, the pavements were like glass, and the trams just crawled along. It is all over now, and we were lucky, we thawed out without any burst pipes, but there were many who did not fare so well. Through all this, I never once heard anyone grumble, you know apart from general remarks about the inconvenience of running across the street with buckets of water. We all used to say 'Well, now you know what it must be like in Finland', and with that in mind one cannot grumble.

Tuesday 13th February 1940

Don and I went to see the show 'Lord Haw Haw' at the Holborn Empire, London, last night. We have now seen all three of George Black's West End shows: 'The Little Dog Laughed', 'Black Velvet', and now 'Lord Haw Haw'. They were all very good and I cannot say which I enjoyed most. 'Lord Haw Haw' by the way had Bebe Daniels and Ben Lyon in the cast. They have been over here so long now that they have lost all trace of their American accents. In one scene, Ben said something about 'I haven't gotten it', and another member of the cast said 'A foreigner aye'. You see, we say, 'I haven't got it'. It is only a very slight difference, but it sounds funny to hear anyone with an English voice say it. When you write it in your letters, it doesn't make any effect upon me, because it fits in with the rest of your writing. That sounds a bit of a mess, but I hope you see what I am getting at.

I expect you have heard about the real Lord Haw Haw, that broadcasts in English every evening from Hamburg. We used to listen to him quite a lot. Mum would never listen to it. She used to lose her patience and say 'Switch it off, it's all lies', but I suppose us kids have a greater sense of humour. Anyway I used to find him very amusing but after a while he started to bore me, the same old thing, People of Great Britain, ask your government where is the 'Ark Royal', they cannot tell you, no of course they can't, the 'Ark Royal' was sunk by Germany. That sort of junk gets wearying when you hear it over and over again, it sounds funny at first. In addition to the fact that it has publicly been denied by the Government that the 'Ark Royal' has been sunk, I also have it direct from a sailor, who has been on another ship that has been with the 'Ark Royal' ever since the beginning of the war. According to Lord Haw Haw we are without food, without fuel, and apparently, as he seems to think we believe all he says, we are without brains. Never mind, he has done some good, he has earned the comedians a lot of money. This sort of thing reduces their audiences to even heartier laughs than the great bore himself. 'People of Great Britain, ask your Government, where is the 'Isle of Wight', the 'Isle of Wight' was sunk this morning.' Or 'Winston Churchill, you know you sunk the Noah's Ark'. His real name was published, but the public have christened him 'Lord Haw Haw' and it has stuck.

Wednesday 14 February 1940

Your letter arrived last night, for which I tender my thanks.

I hope you passed your exams, and that you did not catch another cold, and thoroughly enjoyed yourself sledge riding.

Your jokes about Hitler caused much amusement all round. We heard so many at the beginning of the war, over the air, and on the stage, that the novelty has rather worn off. There have been many song parodies for 'his' benefit, and these go down much better now. Have you heard the song 'Run Rabbit Run', well, there is a parody which goes 'Run Adolf, run Adolf, run, run, run, look what you've been and gone and done, done, done. We're going to knock the stuffing out of you, old fat-guts Goering and Gobbels too. You'll lose your place in the sun, sun, sun, so run Adolf, run Adolf, run, run, run.'

I am looking forward to the warmer weather so that we can get out on the bike once again. I have missed it so much these last four months, but it has been so cold, and the black-out started at about four, so you couldn't go very far, unless you wanted to ride home in the dark. The days are gradually drawing out though, and the black-out doesn't start until nearly six, and even then it is not properly dark outside, but just time for the lights to be screened. Summer time starts in a couple of weeks' time, so that will make another hour's difference.

I do wish you could see 'our baby'. He is getting very chubby, and talks fluently in baby language, once you get him going. He will be five months old on the 6 March. It doesn't seem that long ago to us that he was born. He weighs fourteen and a half pounds, and we think he will soon have a couple of teeth. Here I am, telling you all this, you would think he were mine, instead of just my nephew.

Grandad has been in hospital recently, his left hand is withering and his leg is going the same. They say it is something on a nerve all the way down that side. He is out now, and feeling very much better in himself, although his leg and hand are much the same. I think they were too far gone, when we finally nagged him into going to see a doctor. He is so stubborn. Despite his seventy eight years, he still goes to work, although he hasn't been for the last few weeks. He says that as soon as he feels better he is going to start again. He says he is happier working, so I suppose we shouldn't stop him.

Thursday 15th February 1940

I received two valentines yesterday, both from Don. He usually sends me one, but I suppose he took a fancy to both of them, because they were both in the same envelope. Anyway, I shall see him tonight, and ask him why I have had my rations doubled.

Well, that seems to be about all for now, I think I will post this before it gets too long, as per usual.

Cheerio, be good,
tons of love,
from,
    Win.

P.S. Thank you for your congratulations, and I did like your latest portrait.

23rd March 1940

My Dear Donna

Well here I am again with a bit of the 'After the Holiday' feeling, but other than that my usual cheery self, ha.

Putting the cart before the horse, I will start right in and tell you about how I spent Easter, and then go back to before that later.

On Good Friday, the boys (Sook, Don, my brother George, and another of the gang, John) went to a football match in the afternoon, and as neither Doris or I (you remember Doris, she was the one that got married at Christmas to Sook) wanted to go very much, we amused ourselves together all the afternoon, and met them in town for tea. While we were waiting at the station we whiled away the time spotting the regiments of all the uniforms that passed by. It was the first time I had been in London, in daylight, since the war, and I was amazed at the swarms and swarms of soldiers and airmen. There weren't many sailors, as they are stationed on the coast naturally. We thought we had made a great discovery when we saw a couple of Canadian soldiers pass by, but by the time we had seen a few more, the novelty wore off, London seems to be full of Canadians. The greatest thrill of all came later, when we were having supper. Two quite ordinary R.A.F. boys walked in. They wore ordinary uniform, and although they were very handsome in a tall dark sort of way, they might easily have been taken for Englishmen, had not the Polish Eagle on their caps told us that they were members of the Polish Air Force, now attached to the R.A.F. They seemed quite happy even though they were far from home. Still, home isn't what it used to be for them, so I don't suppose they care much about returning yet.

Anyway, the boys turned up half an hour late and we went and had tea in a Corner House. It was packed with the usual holiday crowds, and we had to wait quite a while to be served. It was getting fairly late when we came out, and we had quite a job getting into the pictures. Right in the heart of London, the West End, they always have the pick of the latest pictures, but everyone seemed to have the same idea, i.e. splash out and pay three times as much for your seat because it was holiday time. We tried to get in and see 'Another Thin Man', which has only just come to London, but the 'House full' notices were up at seven o'clock. After chasing all round the West End, on and off buses, we at last finished up seeing 'Mr. Smith goes to Washington'. We came out about half past eleven and went into the 'SPO' to have supper. The 'SPO' restaurant, I might explain, stands for sausages, potatoes and onions, and although it isn't a place people usually go when they are out all poshed up and celebrating, we don't stand on ceremony when our tummies say we need a good feed.

On Saturday Sook and Doris went by train to Hastings (we have forsaken our bikes this holiday) and arrived about six o'clock. Unfortunately, as Don has to open the shop on Saturday we could not go until later. It is difficult to hire a car these days because not many of them are taxed, and most people want to use their own at Easter, so nothing daunted we piled into Don's shop van for the journey. Don drove and I sat in the front with him, while George, John (who works with Don by the way) and another of the boys, Eric, sat in the back. Eric is an Air Raid Warden, and was supposed to be on duty until twelve Saturday night, but his father offered to do the last couple of hours for him, so we left at ten, and arrived at Hastings about twelve. There is a speed limit which says you mustn't do more than 25 miles per hour in the black-out, but it was a clear moonlight night, so we took a chance. I hope the censor doesn't read this and decide to give us away.

I don't know whether I have told you before, but the place we stay at Hastings, is a boarding house, run by a fellow who used to be in the club, so it's home from home, he lets us do just what we like. We did not get up until about nine on Sunday, and then went for a walk along the front. Sid (that's the fellow that owns the place where we stay) told us that they had had quite a bit of wreckage washed up, and some bodies of merchantmen off a sunken trawler. He told us that when a Dutch ship struck a mine a couple of weeks ago out in the Channel, the explosion blew the door off his shed in the garden, and he lives quite a good way up from the front. We saw none of this however, and except for a few buildings that have been taken over for military purposes, it still looked the same old sea-side holiday resort.

Another couple Ernie and Nellie (they got married just before the war) arrived at dinner time to complete our little party. Don and I are the only couple that aren't married, but George, John and Eric are looked upon as the three bachelors of the club. John and Eric are confirmed women haters, and although George makes a date now and again, he thinks too much of his freedom and having a good time with the boys, to ever get serious. Still, he'll fall like the rest one day. John and Eric are good pals with Doris, Nellie and me of course, but we aren't exactly girls to them, we're Don or Sook or Ernie's property and just part of the gang to them.

In the afternoon we started out to climb over the rocks on the beach and up the cliff on the easiest side, but it didn't happen quite like that. Firstly, we hadn't gone very far when we heard a terrible crying noise, and looking up, saw a tiny little puppy trapped on the rocks right up high. After being urged on by Doris and me, the boys were soon all scrambling up the cliff at various points, bent on the rescue of the little thing. When they had nearly reached it, it gave one look at them, as if it were calling them all the fools under the sun, and then ran along the edge and down the side on to the path again as easily as can be. Doris and I were helpless with laughter at the bottom, and the look of dismay on those boys' faces was comical. It had been quite easy going up, but when they started to come down again it wasn't such fun. I thought any minute one of them would fall, but it soon became just a joke again as soon as they had safely reached the ground.

We carried on again, scrambling over the rocks, until we came to the place you can usually climb up, only to find there had been a recent fall (England is getting smaller every minute, by the way, parts of the cliff are always being washed into the sea), and it was impossible to get up. We stood contemplating it for a few minutes, trying to make up our minds whether to try it or not, but decided in the negative. George went off to investigate whether there was a better place further along, and while he was gone the boys started testing who could throw stones the farthest. George, returning from his investigations, started the same thing from the opposite direction, and there soon started a glorious stone battle. George bobbed down behind a huge boulder and just came up now and again to throw his stone, while the others were pinging all around him. John is a marvellous shot, and he was throwing them so that they just hit the boulder, bounced off, and then missed George by a couple of inches. A dangerous sort of game, still they thought it was fun. It was while this was going on that I became the only casualty. I was standing there, minding my own business, when a stone came winging through the air slightly out of direction. I ducked to avoid it and slipped off the rock I was standing on. I bruised and grazed my leg, but what hurt most was my brand new pair of stockings ruined. I know they are not the sort of things to go scrambling over rocks with, but you never know what you are going to finish up doing when you go out with the gang. After about twenty minutes furious fighting, a white handkerchief appeared from above the boulder, and George came out to see what damage he had done. He laughed like the devil when told I was the only casualty, and that I wasn't playing. He said I ought to know that neutrals always cop out the worse.

Anyway, this little episode over there was nothing to do but go back the way we came as the tide was rising, and we hadn't got time to waste. When we arrived back in the town, it was too early for tea (we have tea about half past seven on holiday, instead of the usual five o'clock, as it makes a nice long afternoon) so we went for a ride on the bumper cars. When all the gang got on, we practically had the monopoly of the whole lot, and quite a bit of fouling went on, bumping and boring. John made a headlong drive at my car, and sent it such a bump up the side that my knee came up and hit the steering wheel. I tell you, I went home quite a mess after the holiday, what with my bruised leg and knee, and another bruise on my arm from the same fall. Still it was good fun, and you can bet we had an appetite when tea-time came. We spent the evening throwing all our money away on the slot machines, and then went home to play cards. Doris and I retired about one o'clock into the sitting room, and when the boys still hadn't put in an appearance at two o'clock, we decided to go to bed. We poked our heads round the door, and the sight that met our gaze told us it was no use expecting them to finish for quite a while. They all had their coats off and their shirt sleeves rolled up. Their ties were pulled loose, and the air was blue with smoke. They each had a pile of money by their side, and looked as though they were in the highest bliss of all. We left them to their game, and we heard next morning that they went to bed about 4 o'clock and then continued their game on the counterpane.

Monday, we spent much the same way, mucking about on the beach, playing golf, and generally having a good time. Sook and Doris caught a train home at half past eight, and as the moon was due to rise at ten o'clock, we decided to wait for this before driving home. Ten o'clock came, but no moon, it was pouring with rain, and the low hanging clouds would have hid it, even if it had risen. It was pitch dark, and it would have been madness to attempt the long journey home, so we waited for a bit. I fell asleep in the armchair and woke up about half past twelve to find that the boys had decided that it was light enough to go now, and had gone to get the van. It was still very dark when we set out at one o'clock, but it was just about light enough to drive. It was a terrible journey, it rained all the way. I fell asleep part of the way, and woke up with a stiff neck, but when we finally arrived home at 4 o'clock, I just took off all my things and rolled into bed – I must have been asleep by about five past.

I felt terrible all day at the office on Tuesday, but I had the grand feeling that despite everything I had enjoyed myself. It was the first holiday weekend we had been out without our bikes for ages, and I felt much more tired than when I had ridden 80 miles or so there and back. It will probably be the last holiday all the gang will be together, because most of the boys will be gone before Whitsun.

Thursday, 28 March 1940

As yet, this calling up business hasn't affected our immediate circle very much. A few of the very young members of the club joined up early in the war, but most of the boys are around the 24–30 class. Don, incidentally, is the youngest of the gang. He signed on for military service about a month ago, and expects to get his calling up papers any time now. There is a slight chance he may get an extension because he has a business, but there isn't any chance of total exemption. George and Sook sign on next month, and John and Eric in a couple of months' time. The calling ups have been speeded up, and I expect all the '30's' will be gone before the end of the year. Apart from the fact that you notice fellows suddenly disappearing, and say to yourself 'I expect he's joined up', there is nothing very startling to show that there is a war on. Life goes on much the same, and we have adopted the attitude 'Make hay while the sun shines'. It is funny how little things strike you. Last week I met the mother of a boy I used to know ages ago when I was about twelve. We used to swing on the gate together and snowball one another, and all the other daft things that kids do. He joined the R.A.F. some years ago, and she told me that he is now a leading aircraftman, and has been up over the North Sea several times, chasing the swine that come to bomb light ships and fishing trawlers. I don't know why it seemed to stick in my mind that David who used to swing on the gate with me is one and the same person who is now risking his neck in this mad upheaval.

There are one or two things that have happened that I am sure you won't think I am being gory to harp on. Firstly, the marvellous victory of the River Plate was brought back to our memories when the crews of H.M.S. *Ajax* and *Exeter* arrived home. What a welcome they got in London, beside the joyful tidings received from their home towns. The *Exeter* is a Plymouth boat, and it is singular that most of our greatest sailors of bygone days, Drake Raleigh and Frobisher, should have hailed from this same port. The *Achilles* was also given a grand reception when she reached her native land of New Zealand, but we in England would have liked to have personally welcomed this representative of the Empire, as we did our own boys. Then of course the crowning glory of all came when the thirty British sailors leapt on board the *Altmark* and rescued over three hundred prisoners that had spent many months in the hold of the 'hell ship'. I couldn't help feeling proud when I read one reporter's account of the scenes at the funeral of the German seamen that were killed in the fight. This is what he said,

'The rest of the crew followed after. Most of them had swollen noses or black eyes, proving that the damage was not done by guns and bombs, but by British fists'. What must those men have felt like when almost in the lion's den they suddenly heard the words 'The Navy is here', and within a short space of time were back with their families again? No, the spirit of Drake, Raleigh and Frobisher is not dead, England still knows how to breed seamen.

I see you've got our *Queen Elizabeth* to look after now. The news of her safe arrival across the Atlantic made us all chuckle with sheer delight. Keep her safe for us until she can take her place on the sea as one of the world's greatest liners.

Don's brother came home on leave about a fortnight ago, and were we all pleased to see him! He had been in France since September. He has changed a lot, looks more grown up, and is much taller and broader. He seemed very happy, and although he naturally didn't tell us what he has been doing all this time, he certainly looked none the worse. He was a bit fed up when the time came to go back, but he had enjoyed himself and really had 'Ten Days of Heaven' as the song says.

At the beginning of the war all the popular songs were about partings and saying goodbye, then they switched to such numbers as 'I'll pray for you while you're away', and now we have 'There's a boy coming home on leave'. By the way, if you want to know the song, all the boys are marching to, and all the girls are singing, it's 'The Beer Barrel Polka'. There isn't a camp concert goes by over the wireless without some time or another you hear the lusty strains of 'Roll out the Barrel'.

My nephew is now nearly six months old, and is just beginning to sit up and take notice. He gives you a smile when you call his name, and his photo proves him to be a spitting image of my brother at the same age.

My sister has started to write to an unknown soldier in India, and he tells her he comes from California. She has just written back to him, and asked how he comes to be in the British Army, but it seems rather a coincidence doesn't it?

Don has gone billiards mad, and says we must find a flat or a house big enough to have a billiard room. If he gets an extension, we will get married and I'll sling up my job, and we'll make the

Alfie aged 5 months, March 1940

most of what little time we have got. I can always get another job after he goes, although he says it isn't necessary. Still, I would soon get fed up not doing anything. It is very funny to see the girls in uniform here, but I couldn't help agreeing with Don's brother when he said that in France the women don't have any uniforms, they just get on with the job, while our girls have to have a smart uniform before they'll do anything. He's right, of course, I don't think it is necessary. Uniforms should be kept for the heroes that fight, and even though it is considered just as essential to carry on with your job if it is of national importance, there isn't any need for a uniform. There is none of the sort of thing that went on in the last war though, i.e. scenes when every man who didn't wear a uniform was immediately labelled a coward. Compulsory conscription has done away with all that. Everyone has to sign on, and if a man isn't in uniform everyone knows that he has been granted exemption because he is doing an essential job, and is therefore doing his bit equally well. There are a few Conscientious Objectors though, and I am not in a position to judge these; if the law says they genuinely don't wish to fight because of their conscience then there isn't much you can say. I still think though that if your country is worth living in, it's worth fighting for. I've no patience with those people who brag and are continually flag waving and consider themselves superior simply because they have the good fortune to be born British. I judge my country by what it does, and if I do seem a bit over patriotic please don't confuse me with the sort of person I have mentioned above.

Well, there doesn't seem to be much else to say. I just can't keep the war out of my letters, can I? Still when it is your whole life, day after day, everything you do gets mixed up in it somewhere.

Don came over last night, and apparently the gang want another evening in town next week. What a war, we are doing and spending our money ten times as much as we used to! Yes, it's not such a bad old world after all.

Cheerio for the present, remember me to all the family and the latest boy friend, whatever his name is; be good.

Tons of love,
  Win

24th April, 1940

My Dear Donna,

Many thanks for your letter. It was good to hear from you.

Don is still here thank goodness, but he has already signed on, and is expecting to be called up for his Medical any day. There is a slender chance that he may get an extension, but this he will not know until he has had his medical. I want to know, one way or the other, yet at the same time, I don't want him to be called for his medical too soon in case he doesn't get any extension. Everything is still fixed for June, circumstances permitting, though of course it is hopeless to make any arrangements yet awhile. It is going to be a lovely rush when we do find out one way or another.

I have still been adding to the b.d. a little bit, but mostly I am saving, because there are so many things that I cannot buy until the last minute. I expect you will laugh at this bit. Don has promised that the very moment he hears that he has got his extension (he is so confident that he will) he is going to take me out and buy me the most smashing nightie we can lay our hands on. This extension business is very important you see because it is the deciding factor as to whether we get 'hitched' this year or not. Personally, I hate nightdresses and have bought all pyjamas to put away, but I guess I'll have to humour him, and have at least one.

We have been out with the gang for a celebration two weekends since Easter. These celebrations consist of having tea somewhere, going on to the pictures, and then finishing up with supper at an 'S.P.O.' or a Hamburger joint. This may not sound very thrilling on the face of it, but when six really good friends get together, even tea in a restaurant becomes exciting. Of course, we always go up to town for these occasions, so we always see the pick of the pictures. We saw 'Another Thin Man' which has since been generally released locally, and 'Hitler, Beast of Berlin' which is still running in town. Although we enjoyed the first picture very much, we were disappointed in the other one. Doris and I didn't want to see it in the first place, because we knew it would be grim, but the boys wanted to see it because they thought it was going to be real rich meat. Well, it was quite horrible enough for Doris and me to dislike it, but not bad enough for the boys to think it was worth seeing, so when we came out we were all fed up. While we were standing on the pavement wondering what to do next, we espied a tiny little cinema, and for sixpence we had a whole hour of Mickey Mouse, Popeye, and the Three Stooges. We thoroughly enjoyed this, and it quite made up for the three and sixpence we had wasted on the other tripe. We want to see 'Gone with the Wind' which has just arrived in London, but despite the fact that it is showing at three London cinemas, it is very hard to book seats. I expect we will go, sooner or later though.

We have recently had a sudden burst of energy, and we are now soaring ahead with our rug, which was bought, incidentally, to pass away the long winter evenings. There have been no long winter evenings this year though, in spite of the black-out, which is now behind us thank goodness, because we have been out more than we ever used to be.

I have made myself a striped jumper, the most daring thing I have ever attempted. It contains five colours, white, pink, blue, mauve and green. I know it sounds hideous, but although I had the usual rude remarks from the fellows at the office, I think on the whole, it met with everyone's approval. I have not got it on today, and when one of the boys remarked on the fact, I told him I was keeping it for a special occasion. 'I know' he said 'Keep it for Peace Day, I can just imagine you with that jumper on, a flag in your hand, and a look in your eye'. In reply to my query as to whether he thought I would 'get off', he did not say anything, but his eyes spoke volumes.

A couple of Sundays ago, we got the old 'Bone-shaker' out, and had the time of our lives getting our 'bike legs' again. We kept asking ourselves why we had left it so long without going out, but we paid for it the next morning. You can't go six months without cycling and then expect to ride just as usual without getting a few aches and pains. Still, now the good weather is coming (at least that's what we hope) we will have the chance to get going again.

I have written and booked up for Whitsun. Sook and Doris, George, John and we two, are going to the Isle of Wight. The lazy way we went at Easter, by car, has got to be a habit, for now we do not fancy riding all that way on the bikes. It does make a little more time though, for the journey is halved, if you go by rail or road.

I was surprised when you said you had been for your first train and first taxi ride. Although I do not frequent taxis, travelling by train is just as common as buses and trams over here. There are more cars in America though, aren't there? Only the fairly well to do own them here, although we do sometimes hire them for occasions.

I bet you stunned them all when you arrived at the 'Easter Parade' in the outfit you described, I wish I could have seen you.

As you know, we are now fighting the war in Norway. It makes you wonder which country you are going to be fighting for next. One of our girls has a boy friend who is a marine on 'H.M.S. Renown', and she read us his account of the battle of Narvic 'straight from the horse's mouth'. At one time the mention of names of places, ships etc. was taboo, but as it was broadcast at the time, I see no reason why I shouldn't tell you the name of his ship.

Despite his doings in other countries 'Ole Nasty's' threats have not as yet materialised for ourselves. My Gas Mask is at home and it hasn't seen daylight for weeks. I long ago got fed up with carrying it backwards and forwards. I know this is not a sensible thing to do, it is only bravado, and I shall get caught one day. Because we have got away with it for so long, we are not kidding ourselves we are going to get off Scot free. The only point is of course, that the moment he bombs us, we'll just go right back and bomb him tenfold.

By the way did you hear about the gentleman that went into a German restaurant and asked for herrings? Upon being asked, what sort of herrings he would like, Dutch herrings or Hitler herrings, he replied that he would like Hitler herrings. In due course the herrings arrived and the man said, 'Hi, these look just like Dutch herrings. What's the difference?' Whereupon the waiter replied, 'There is no difference, for Hitler herrings we just take the backbone out and open the mouth wider.'

Thursday 25th April, 1940

Last week one of the girls from the office and myself, went swimming for the first time since last summer. We rushed out of the office at half past twelve, were undressed and in the water by twenty to one, out of the water again by one o'clock, dressed and ready by quarter past, back at the office by twenty past, and back at work by half past, having eaten our lunch in the last ten minutes.

The weather has taken a turn for the better (I am knocking hard on wood as I write this), and it has brought out a swarm of spring costumes and light blouses. What a difference a bit of sun makes! You get to thinking it's not such a bad thing to be alive after all.

The slogan today is 'Dig for Victory', and that is just what everyone is doing with a vengeance. Most people had already dug up their gardens to grow food, and many parks have been turned into allotments, of which anyone can become the owner for a small sum. Both Dad and my brother have got one of these in the local park, and every evening and weekends you can see them digging and sowing. Our garden is fairly long, but what with the dug-out, the greenhouse, and what we call the lawn, it does not leave enough ground to grow vegetables enough to last us very long. We are a large family, and we are all fond of our tummies. The allotment is a good size though, and it will enable us to grow enough to carry us through until the next crop. As you look out of a railway carriage window along any line in England on a Sunday morning, you will see everyone out in their garden digging.

Have you ever heard one of Churchill's speeches? If so, don't you love the way he says 'Nazi', as if pouring all the loathing of the entire nation in the word. A speech from him is as eagerly looked forward to as a message from the King.

The boss has just told me that he hasn't any work ready for me, so here I am for the first time writing this letter with a clear conscience, and I've dried up for news. It has been in and out of the machine all day, hence the crooked margin. By the way, I won't be able to post this until Saturday, because I have forgotten to bring the stamps with me, and I am going to stay at Don's house tonight.

Well, I think I'll get going for the present, maybe I will have more news after Whitsun.

Cheerio,
tons of love,
  Win xxxxx

11th May 1940

Dear Donna,

The sun is shining, the sky is blue, and the trees look lovelier this Spring than I can ever remember them looking before, yet we are working on this Whit Saturday with no excitement about the long Whitsun week-end that should lie before us, for the holidays have been cancelled, and we are at war. Yes, really at war this time, none of the waiting, waiting, waiting that has been so tiring for the past 8 months, and has made us get so discontented. By the time you read this, terrible things may have happened, terrible things that we were all steeled up to take on the chin last September, and things that, if they do come, which please God they won't, we are as ready to take after our breather as we ever were. Up till now we have played a clean game, but the days of honour and decency are temporarily gone, for to smash this monster, and smash him we must, we have got to be as unscrupulous as he.

Up till yesterday things were very unsettled. The Government had come in for a lot of criticism, and while I do not see what moral right anyone outside the country, has to criticise what we do, when we are at least doing something, it is the privilege of us at home, and we have been rewarded by a new Premier, who has the confidence of everyone.

This morning, things are different, we are full of confidence, we've got a job to do, and although everyone is most disappointed about the Whitsun holidays, for nearly everyone was going away somewhere, we are not really minding so very much, for we realise that something has certainly got to be done. It was just like the old September days this morning, to see everyone with their Gas Mask slung over their shoulder, and already my ears seem to pick up little noises again, and for a fraction of a second I wonder 'Can it be a siren?' I am glad though that I live in London, for just to look up and see the balloons in the sky, seems to give me confidence. They say the thing aeroplanes dread most, is the Balloon Barrage. I have never mentioned these before, I guess it's all right though. Everyone knows London has a Balloon Barrage, and very pretty they look too, glittering in the sunlight.

That's enough about the war. Oh, one other thing, I still do not know what is going to happen about Don. He has had his medical and passed A.1. or to quote himself 'sound in wind and limb'. He is now awaiting news as to whether he will get an extension of service or not, and failing this, it is a matter of weeks or perhaps even days, before he gets his 'Calling-Up' papers, and that will mean he will be gone within a few days. My younger brother has registered for service, and he is also awaiting his medical.

About three weeks ago we went to see 'Gone with the Wind', and I haven't finished raving about it yet. I think it is the most marvellous film I have ever seen, although there is a bit of a rumpus about the very high prices of admission they are charging. The strangest thing that struck me was the interval. Everyone got up and walked about, some went to the bar and had a drink, while nearly everyone took some form of exercise, even if it was only standing up in their seat, because you often sit for longer than half the length of 'Gone with the Wind' for just an ordinary cinema programme. Still, it may or may not have been imagination, but I certainly did feel stiff. I have never been an especial admirer of Clark Gable, but I thought he was very, very good in this.

As I mentioned before, we were all booked up to go to the Isle of Wight for Whitsun, Sook and Doris, George and John and Don and I. We were going to drive down tonight, and catch the last boat over, so that we had two clear days, but that is now all off now, of course. A Royal Proclamation yesterday said the Bank Holiday was cancelled, and as the banks are going to be open that means everyone else will have to go to work, and shops will be open on Monday as usual. Still, we are making the best of it, and the boys who have always wanted to play on a full size golf course, are going to make up for the game they will lose at Sandown, by going to a fairly local course on Sunday morning for a game. I am not going — I can manage the semi sized course at Sandown, but I do not think I would be any good on a full size course. We are going up to town on one of our jaunts on Sunday evening, so we have made up our minds to forget that it should have been a holiday, and look upon this as just an ordinary weekend.

By the way, 'our' baby has got a tooth. The first one to find this, is supposed to buy him a present, and while we have always said that if we were the first we would keep quiet about it, I got so excited when I saw it, that I completely forgot all about keeping it to myself. I rushed out and told Mum and Dot, and while they led me into believing for a while that I had been the first, they admitted afterwards that Dot had found it, and Mum already knew. So, his own mother has got to buy him something, despite my brother's oft repeated assurance that he would be in our house when it was found. You see, having them living next door, he is as used to being in with us, as he is in his own home. He is getting very chubby, and I will try and send you a snapshot of him soon.

You will notice that the stamp on my letter is different. This is because the postage rate has gone up recently from $1\frac{1}{2}$d to $2\frac{1}{2}$d. Although big business firms that write a lot of letters notice the difference, people like me that only write a few letters every week, never notice the extra penny. There is another new stamp just come out, with our King and the late Queen Victoria's head on it.

This is to commemorate the centenary of the penny post. I will try and send you one of these on my next letter.

I bought a new hat last week, and while this in itself is nothing exceptional, it has the privilege of being the first hat I have ever bought that Don has fallen for. It is just an ordinary pill box hat, that goes up higher in the front than most. It is half navy and half pale blue, and is adorned by a veil in the front and a couple of ribbons down the back. It only cost half of what I paid for the new one I bought for my winter coat, but it managed to bring forth from Don such remarks as 'Now, I like that', and 'Boy, what a smasher!' Take it from me, my girl, if you live to be a hundred you will never fully appreciate the workings of a man's likes and dislikes. At least, I don't think I'll ever understand mine, bless him.

Well, I think I had better end this epistle, for the morning has nearly gone, and I have a couple of scraps of work to clear up, before I go away for the weekend.

Cheerio for the present,
let's hear from you soon,
loads of love,
from,
    Win xxxx

THE END OF THE PHONEY WAR

Suddenly the partying had to stop. Events in Europe occurred with such rapidity that we were scarcely able to comprehend all that was going on.

Soon, with the tragic/heroic events of Dunkirk, it began to sink in that we were fighting for our life. The only thing standing between us and the same fate as the rest of Europe was that little strip of water called 'The English Channel'. We knew we were now alone and that the full force of Hitler's might was soon to be turned on us, but we had a new leader – Churchill. He was our hero, we would follow him anywhere.

Of course all personal plans went out of the window at this time, and I was resigned to the fact that there was not going to be a June 1940 wedding for me. I remember on my 20th birthday on 18th June 1940, a few of my friends from the office returned one lunch-time with a variety of white items as a gift. I remember clearly with a sob in my voice and a tear in my eye, saying 'It all looks so bridal'. They were full of consternation; they hadn't meant to upset me. How unimportant was the dashing of just one young girl's dreams at that tremendous moment.

8th June 1940

My dear Donna,

To attempt to describe the ever changing situation to you, or to give you any sort of outline as to what has already passed, would be like trying to grasp the moon. My poor muddled brain has given up trying to piece things together, and so if the following appears a bit disjointed or hazy, I hope you will forgive me.

Out of the darkness and tragedy of the loss of Flanders, following the capitulation of the King of the Belgians, has come an example of courage and daring which the pages of history can never rival. 335,000 men have been saved from what at one time seemed certain annihilation and the happy smiling faces of the boys that have come home have given us all added hope and vigour to carry on.

I will give you an account of our own personal little worry at this time. As I have mentioned before Don's young brother is one of the B.E.F. and as both of my brothers are on Government work, and Don has yet to go, he is the nearest person I knew that came out of that Hell. At first, we didn't worry very much, because we weren't certain whether he was in Belgium or France, but when the news came through that some of his regiment were home, we all brightened up and looked forward to receiving a telegram. Two days went by, and although all his pals' parents had received telegrams that their sons were safe, nothing came through from Eric. For two days the telephone rang incessantly like an exchange and the door bell was forever being answered to callers anxious to know whether any news had come through. Then, when we had nearly given up looking on the bright side, a trunk call came through, and Don's mother nearly fainted when a familiar voice said 'Hallo, is that you, Mother?' After a few questions, it turned out that he had been in England two days, and had actually posted off a telegram five minutes after he landed. For two days he had rested in the almost unbelievable quietness that is England, totally unaware that his whole family were worrying about him. He had only rung up quite casually to ask them to send him some money, and if he had not done that, goodness knows how long it would have been before we heard. I felt so relieved and happy about it when I heard, that it might almost have been my own brother. Well, that is the tale of one of the 335,000. He did not say anything about what he had been through, and if I know Eric, he never will, but tales of courage and bravery are for ever leaking out, and one thing remains certain, we have the men, no-one on this earth could ever dispute that, and now it is up to every one of us to work as hard as we can, and arm them efficiently, so that next time they go forth to risk their necks for us, they shall not lack anything that it is in our power to give them.

9th June 1940

Today is Sunday, it has just started to rain and I am glad. These last four or five days have been a glorious heat-wave, but it was getting almost unbearable this afternoon. My hands have been hot and sticky, and was I glad when the boss said, 'You've done enough for one day.'

I have no quarrel with the seven-day-week, in fact I am glad to do it, as everyone is, glad to feel I am doing something. Already I am planning what I am going to do when I get a day off. Gosh, it seems ages since I did. I am going to get up early and go swimming, that is if it is as hot as it is today, and then I am going to lie out in the sun all day and just relax. Working all day and every day isn't so bad really, it is just the heat that has made it uncomfortable recently. There is one thing though, it makes letter writing such a strain. There is nothing much to write about. Life is just work, sleep and the war, and as no-one could talk about sleep, and no-one does want to talk about work, there is nothing left but the war.

A letter came from Eric last night. Though he is in England, he is many miles from home, and he hasn't had any leave yet. He sounds very happy and glad to be home. His sister wrote to him and asked him whether he arrived home with any of his kit and whether he had a beard. He said the only kit he came home with was his tin helmet, which he guarded with his life, and that when they got to Dunkirk they spent the time whilst waiting for the ship, washing their faces, shaving, and polishing their boots. Don says that is something to remember when ever I am fed up: Eric and all the other boys, waiting patiently on the beach at Dunkirk to be brought back to safety, being bombed incessantly all the time, and yet polishing their boots and cleaning themselves up, ready to come home. That's the spirit of our boys, and that's the spirit that is going to win the war, provided everyone does their bit to help them. He came over on the 'Golden Eagle', a pleasure cruiser that has many times taken Eric and thousands of other Londoners down the river to the seaside in the summer time. The 'Crested Eagle' another of these pleasure cruisers, engaged on the same job, was sunk. I bet the crews of these harmless paddle boats never thought they would be engaged in the strangest and greatest Armada of all time.

There is one thing that struck all the Tommies while they were out there, and that was the ruthless way helpless refugees were mown down by the Germans. Hundreds and hundreds of them have sought safety in England, and the very sight of them tears at your heartstrings. Many have nothing save the clothes they stand up in, and a few belongings in a sheet. Nearly all of them I saw wore only slippers. We have no room at home, but my brother put his name down to take a couple in. As yet he has heard nothing, for I think all those so far have been found homes, but there is bound to be more of them. These Belgians are as furious as we are at their traitor King. It hardly seems possible that a short while ago we were a peace loving nation, but the terrible treachery of the past few weeks, has made all our boys fighting mad to get back and pay for the harm done to those helpless refugees, the terrible position the B.E.F. were left in by King Leopold and all the other filthy doings of the Nazis.

It is really teeming down now, and the thunder is terrific. It looks as though we are in for a right royal storm, and little me has only got a cotton dress to go home in. Still, why worry, what's a drop of rain anyway?

There will be no wedding for some time now of course. There is a job to be done, and all personal matters must take a back place for a bit. Don only got a few extra weeks' extension owing to the situation, instead of the six months we all expected he would get. Although I was terribly cut up about it at first, in my heart of hearts I was glad. Don was only anxious to get his extension because of me, and I know how he would have felt if he wasn't in it. The worst thing is of course the shop. Goodness knows what is going to happen to it when he goes, that was the actual reason that extension of service was given to shop owners. Still, I have made up my mind that I am going to work hard when he goes, and save all I can, so that after the war, if the shop and all his money is gone, he will at least have something to start again on. Don says 'After the war we won't worry about houses or jobs or anything, we'll just get married, and work hard and get on our feet again, and at least we'll have some sort of future to look forward to'. We've saved and planned to have so much, but really the only thing that matters is that we can be together. I wanted to make the most of these last few weeks, and at first I was sorry that I had to work seven days a week, which meant we didn't have any weekends. I thought I would be only too pleased to do it when Don went away, but I realised Hitler won't hold the war up to settle my affairs, so we are just making the most of what time we have got. Usually, you get about four or five days' notice after you receive your calling-up papers, and so if the boss is willing, we are going to snatch a few days' holiday. All official holidays are cancelled for this year, which isn't such a tragedy really because all the seaside places are far from being inviting at the moment.

10th June 1940

Did we have a storm last night or did we have a storm? Today is very dull and heavy, and all the lovely June sunshine has gone, but it is much cooler. According to the papers this morning the London children are going away again on Thursday. Young Phylly will be among them. She came home from her last evacuation at Christmas, so we have had her at home for six months. There is some talk about evacuating children to the dominions, Canada and Australia, for though we may send them out of the big cities to little villages in the country, nowhere can actually be considered safe. Those murderers would as soon bomb a tiny village full of children as they would any Airport.

The baby is going to miss her, they are such pals. I wish you could see him, he is quite a picture these days, with his cheeky smile and his sun burnt little face.

I received your Commencement Card a couple of days ago, and although I have heard a little about it before, I don't really understand exactly what it means. Still, it is very lovely and you may be sure I will be keeping it safe.

By the way, many happy returns for your birthday. I haven't forgotten and when I get the time for a spot of shopping I will let you have something.

Well I must away. I have stacks of work, and I really feel like it this morning, so I had better get on with it, in case we have a return of that heat-wave.

The war will soon be over, and then I can write you something cheerful again.

Cheerio for the present,
be good,
tons of love,
      Win xxxx

25th June 1940

My Dear Donna,

Well, here I am again, still alive and kicking, feeling in the very best of spirits, despite the fact that my eyes need a couple of match sticks to prop them open, as a result of spending half the night in an Air Raid Shelter.

To begin at the beginning, last night we had the first Air Raid Warning over London. At least, we did have a couple far back in last September, but they turned out to be false alarms, and the 'All Clear' was sounded not many minutes after. When we heard them last night though we knew there was no false alarm about it. They have started their air attack on England in real earnest now, and every night for the past week or so, there have been raids up and down the coast. Last night as it happens, I was staying over at

Don's, and at about a quarter to one his sister woke me up with 'Win, sirens, sirens'. I listened and I heard them in the distance, gradually getting nearer and nearer, as each district picked it up and sounded theirs. We were halfway through getting dressed when the local siren started. It is an awful noise. It rises and falls continually, and your tummy rises and falls at the same time. We all got safely established in the dug-out, when there was a scuffling at the gate, and the couple from next door and their baby came down with us. I worried a bit about them over at Eltham, but I realised that if anything was happening there, I would hear the noise pretty loudly from where I was, but all I heard was very distant gunfire.

At first it was pitch black and we were all very sleepy, but gradually it began to get lighter. I never knew before how much lighter it gets between two and three in the morning. The time dragged on and the gunfire did not get any nearer. An occasional aeroplane went over, but we recognised them as our own by the sound of the engine. We began to get a bit fed up, thinking about all the time we could have had in bed, but as Don's Mother remarked we ought to feel glad we weren't getting it, as somebody evidently was getting it badly, because it was taking so long. Don went up above and stretched his legs, and then went into the house and made some tea. He came back after a bit to find out who took sugar, and that struck us all as being funny. Imagine enquiring as to who took sugar when there was an Air Raid on. We had just finished our tea when we heard the 'All Clear'. Clear and loud it sounded like music to our ears, and we were glad to get up on top again. Somebody said 'I wonder how many poor devils lost their lives tonight' and Don said 'There must have been a terrific battle somewhere', and with that we went back to bed. I heard the church clock strike four as I snuggled under the sheets again, and that rotten heaving and falling noise kept singing in my ears.

That endeth that. We had the warning, we had the waiting, and we had the 'All Clear', and we thanked our lucky stars that as yet we haven't had the bombs also. The early morning news said that there had been raids along the coast, but fortunately the loss of life wasn't as great as usual. I don't know whether all London had the warning, or just South East London, but anyway it was confirmed this morning that no bombs fell anywhere on London. Everyone at the office is talking about the raid this morning, and although those that live further out in the country, heard the guns and bombs very close, no-one actually had them overhead.

Talking about Air Raid sirens, life is one long listening process these days. There is, as I said, the rising and falling of the Warning, and the loud shrill note of the 'All Clear'. In addition to this, the sound of a hand rattle, you know the sort used by enthusiastic spectators at ball games and things, means 'Gas', and the sound of a hand bell means 'Gas Cleared Away'. Church bells are no longer rung for service or for weddings. In future, the ringing of a church bell will mean that there are parachute troops in the district. We haven't heard any of these last three peculiar noises to date.

Eric has been home on leave since his home coming from Dunkirk, and after some of his tales, we realise how lucky we are. We have at least got a well built dug-out to go down to, and plenty of warning, and time to take with us what ever we want, but the soldiers have a terrible hard time of it. He found it very hard to talk about anything to do with the war, without using some of his newly acquired army language, and he can't wait to get at them again.

A friend of my brother's came to see us last week, he is in the Royal Naval Medical Corps. He was wounded whilst himself attending the wounded on the way over from Dunkirk, and this is what rankles. He is a non combatant, engaged only upon saving life, so therefore in accordance with the rules of war, he is unarmed, but that didn't stop the Jerries coming down and machine gunning the deck while he was caring for the wounded. He was very bright and cheerful, despite the fact that he has only just come out of hospital. He also is anxious to have another go, but he says this time he's going to have a gun in his hand and give as good as he gets.

Young Phylly is very happily settled in the country, and although I say she ought to go abroad, I know that Mum will never let her go. Mothers are funny aren't they? If you tell them that they are being selfish because they consider their own feelings before their children's safety, they feel very hurt, and just say 'Oh, you'll understand one day how I feel'. All I can say is I'd feel darn sight happier if both of them, Mum and Phyll, were safely tucked away in Australia or Canada, but I suppose that is as far as it will get.

Don's extension ends next week, and after that he is liable to get his papers at any time. My brothers have joined the 'Parashots', but I think they will not have to go in the army for the time being, as they are doing war work.

I had the day off last Sunday, the first one for five weeks, and did I look forward to it. Of course it rained in the morning, and this put paid to all my hopes of a day out on the bike, but I was glad of the rest. Don and I sat curled up on the settee all the morning, reading together, and watching the rain. It cleared up a bit in the afternoon, and so after a couple of games of Monopoly, we got out our glad rags, and went up to town. The West End of London is like a League of Nations these days, for in addition to the now familiar Canadians, we have the ANZACS, those tough looking boys from Australia and New Zealand. There are also quite a number of French soldiers, and a handful of Poles, Dutch and all the rest, you know the list as well as I do. We had a shilling's worth of news and 'Mickey Mouse' the "Three Stooges' and 'Popeye', and then we went to see 'Virginia City' which has only just come to the West End. We just managed to catch the last train home, after having had quite a good evening. Every time the gang meets on one of these occasions, we know it won't be long before one of them goes, and that will be the end of our outings for the time being.

Don bought me a gold bracelet for my birthday, and I had a white outfit from four of my pals at the office. A white blouse, gloves, turban and spray of flowers for my lapel. I had several things for the good old b.d. which still continues to grow despite everything.

If you were to meet my eldest brother any day now, you would see his chest sticking out a mile. The reason, his son has just learned to say 'Dada'. The fact that he uses this word for everything doesn't matter to him in the least, he is as proud as punch.

I must away, I have spent far too long already, and I am sure everyone is wondering what is making me type so furiously this morning. Work is so important, and even a common or garden shorthand typist like me is necessary to the great scheme of things in this blue pencil war.

★

Don't worry about us, we are standing alone now, fighting by ourselves, for ourselves, and we'll come out on top, never fear. You've heard haven't you about that Empire upon which the sun never sets, and this little Island is its heart, so we cannot fail.

Cheerio, for now,
tons of love,
  Win xxxx

I have just thought of a song we used to sing at school on Empire Day. I can't remember the beginning, but it ended like this:-
 This happy breed of men, this other Eden,
 This precious stone set in a silver sea,
 This blessed plot, this earth, this realm, this England,
 We highly dedicate oh Lord to thee.
We know that ultimately right must prevail. We are trusting in God, but we are also going to fight as hard as we can.

12th July 1940

My Dear Donna,
I really must write straight away and let you know how very, very welcome was your letter that arrived by this morning's post. You cannot realise how refreshing it is to hear from you.

You sounded worried because you had heard that there had been an Air Attack on London, but do not I beg you, pay too much attention to these items of news. I wrote and told you in my last letter what actually happened – the Warning went, and after four hours in the dugout, without hearing so much as a plane or a bomb, the 'All Clear' sounded and we went back to bed feeling none the worse.

I am not kidding myself that it will always be like this though. We have got to be prepared for anything, and we are, and you can take it from me it takes more than German Air Raids to intimidate us. Nothing actually happened that night, we had the Warning I know, but it was likely to happen any minute, and I remember sitting there in the shelter and saying to myself, 'Jerry ole man, you think you've got me scared, but I've got the laugh on you, because

I'm not, so come on and do your worst, I can take it' and that I feel is what everyone else was thinking.

The fate of poor France along with all the rest makes me feel sad every time I think about it, so I don't think about it, because there is no time or room for depression. When I look at the map and see little us at the top, and our vast enemy before us, I think 'We've got a nerve', but it does not make me afraid, for I know, as assuredly as I know that the sun will rise in the east tomorrow, that the end of all this will be victory for us and our cause. We English are funny you know, we enter into wars to help others, and put all we've got into it, but when someone comes along and threatens our little castle, well then sparks really do begin to fly. Perhaps it is hard for you to understand, and it must be even harder for the Germans what it is that makes Englishmen so crazy for England, so determined that whatever happens to anything else, she will never fall as long as there is one of them left to defend her. If you knew, and if the Germans knew England as we do, you would find it perfectly easy to understand. If you had lived all your life, taking for granted your freedom, your free speech, the lovely fields and hedges, and the beautiful old buildings which have stood for centuries, you would know that to be robbed of these is to be robbed of life itself. Victory will ultimately be ours, and we will try not to postpone it longer than we can help. We have a notice on all the walls in our office. This is how it goes 'PLEASE UNDERSTAND there is no one depressed in this house, neither are we interested in the possibilities of defeat, THEY DO NOT EXIST'. That is the spirit of England today, so do not worry about us.

You said you were surprised to learn that I had moved to London, but I think you must have misunderstood something I wrote. I am living where I have always lived, and this is London, or at least a suburb of London, and I am not going to move either, I am staying here where my work is. I stay over at Don's house a couple of nights a week, and maybe that is what gave you the impression I had moved.

I count myself one of the luckiest for Don is still with me. His extension ended on the 1st July, and he doesn't know whether they are going to give him any longer though. If they don't, and he doesn't expect it, he is likely to get his papers almost any day. If it hadn't been for this extension because of his business he would have had to go months ago, for all those that signed on when he did have been in the services quite a time. Both my brothers have signed on. One of them I think will be exempt because he is on Government work, the other one may be, but we are not quite sure. All the rest of the gang have now signed on and are awaiting their papers, but as yet we have been very fortunate in that our immediate circle has not been broken up.

You have heard me mention my girl friend Win. She is evacuated with her work 'Somewhere in England', and she is very unhappy because her brother is missing. He came home on leave just before Hitler invaded Holland and Belgium, and they have heard nothing from him since he went back. She is being very brave, and says knowing that he is not actually dead is one consolation. It is possible that many things may have prevented him from writing, and he may of course be a prisoner. I tell her this to comfort her, but personally I feel I would rather know some-one I loved was dead, than hear that they were a prisoner of war. I should worry all the time about how they were being treated, and whether or not they were getting enough food. I sincerely hope though that when I write to you again, I may be able to tell you he is safe. With the fighting over here it does mean that we won't have to be parted for quite so many miles, and may be Don will be stationed near enough for me to see him once in a while.

Last Sunday we went out on the bike, and it was just like old times. (Anything that is 'like old times', is the seventh heaven of delight, these days). We did not ride very far, but it was good to get some fresh air, and forget all about the war. We were riding along blissfully, the sun was shining and I was thinking to myself that it just couldn't be possible for all this to stop, when Don suddenly said 'See the Machine Gun post, hidden over there'. Back to earth with a bump, it just isn't possible to get away from it anyhow. One thing amused us though, and that was the aeroplanes. You see, an aeroplane over London these days is as rare as the truth is from Hamburg, but out in the country you see very many. We saw a whole lot going in one direction at one time, and immediately realised that there must be something in that direction which they were going to put right. Three cheers for the R.A.F. What great lads!

★

We are continuing our jaunts up to town on Sunday evenings, and the week before last we saw 'Virginia City'. It is going to be awful when the boys go, and these outings are over. I don't think us girls will have the heart to go alone.

You said in your letter that a newspaper man wanted me to write an account of my life day by day. Well, upon thinking this over, I really don't think I could make a go of it that way. You see there are some days when nothing out of the ordinary happens, and it is no good repeating news that I heard over the radio or in the newspapers, because you can read that yourself. I feel also that if I knew I was writing something definitely for the papers, it would cramp me a bit, and I would not write as freely as I do to you. This is my idea however, and perhaps you will see what he thinks of it. Suppose I write to you very often, as often that is, as there is something interesting to write about, and then he (with your permission of course) can quote any such extracts as he feels would interest people other than yourself. If he agrees with this, and would like me to send them by Air Mail so that they reach you quicker, then just let me know, and I will see what can be done.

Mum and Dad are going away this weekend to see my little sister in the country. She went away at the beginning of the war you will remember, and then came home again at Christmas. As soon as things began to get a bit hot though, we sent her away again, and she is now spending her life in the loveliest part of England. Dad has been working terribly hard and needs a holiday, so it will be killing two birds with one stone. Probably, the whole family, because I am going to cook for them while Mum is away.

My nephew now nine-months-old is just the darlingest little fellow you ever saw. He has four teeth and can walk all round the room holding on first the table then a chair and so on. It will not be long before he is able to walk without holding on.

I don't think I ever really described the inside of our dugout to you, did I? Well, we have the walls painted cream and green. There is a rug on the floor (excuse my French, I mean an old mat that used to grace the kitchen), two forms along each side, an electric fire and electric light, first aid equipment, a pack of cards, books, cushions and a table. There is a black curtain over the entrance, and outside of this a dark blanket, which has been treated to keep out gas. The dug-out itself has been built up solidly all round with sand bags, and a sort of porch about three feet away from the door. This is to take the blast.

My brother next door has done his much the same, but as there are only two of them and the baby, they have fitted up hammocks, so that they can lie down and continue their sleep. If there is a raid in the daytime, Mother and Doris will go into one or the other of them, so we don't have to worry about them being alone. Over the door of ours we have 'Peace Haven', and my brother has put 'Duck or Else'. Every night Mother puts the tea cups ready on a tray, with some biscuits, in case we have a long session. Edna and I have put all the things we value most, some money, and at night I put my bracelet and ring, in a box, and we have this ready to grab. I have my knitting handy too, I couldn't bear to sit for any length of time without it. Tea has just been rationed, this is because so much has been drunk, during and after Air Raids. The first thought is 'Let's have a cup of tea'. Still, it is worthwhile economising on tea at

Alf and Doris

other times, so that we have some handy if you want it when things are bad, because there is nothing like it for keeping your pecker up.

I was very interested to read about all your doings, and so glad to know that somewhere people are still doing the simple, harmless little things that make life worth while. Don't waste a minute, enjoy your life as much as you can, for I know how I regret every single minute I wasted grumbling or quarrelling with people. When all this is over, I swear I'll never grumble again, and never, never will I take my happiness for granted.

I am very happy to hear about your sister's engagement, but sorry to hear that she has had to give up her nursing. Does this mean you will not be taking it up after all? My one blot on the skyline is that I can't be a nurse, Don is absolutely and positively against it. He won't even hear of me joining as a part time nurse for evening work. I have tried to make him see my point of view, tried to make him understand that if anything happened to him, I should like to know that there was someone who would take care of him, but although he says he understands all this, he just won't entertain the idea of my being one.

Well, I can't think of anything else to say at the moment, but I'll leave this letter open in case I think of anything tomorrow. By the way, please excuse the very cramped way I have set out the heading of this letter. That is the fruits of being crafty, you see I put the address in afterwards, and then if anyone sees me typing it doesn't look so obvious that I am writing a private letter.

Saturday 13th July 1940

Mum and Dad went off this morning just before I came out, and the thought of the house all untidy to go back to makes me shudder. Still, Edna and I will slog into it this afternoon, so as to leave only the dinner and the bare necessities to do tomorrow. It isn't a very nice morning, the sun is struggling to come out, but as yet the rain clouds have got the better of it.

I must give you a couple of extracts from my little sister's letters. 'Dear Mum, Are you happy? I am. I have had a barf and an Exlax.' This reduced the whole family to a spell of laughter which I feared was going to turn into apoplexy. Here is another: 'Please send me some stamps if you want me to write to you, as I only have 1/10½ d. left in my purse'.

Monday, 14th July 1940

Well, here I am feeling tired out after my weekend. Honestly, I would rather have worked Saturday and Sunday overtime than look after our family. Still, most of the work is done now, and if they can manage to keep the place reasonably tidy, there won't be an awful lot to do for the rest of the week. The dinner turned out very well, in fact, I even surprised myself.

Sook, Doris and John came to tea and with Edna, George, Don and me this made quite a nice little card party for afterwards. I lost, and so did Don, but we enjoyed our game, so what matter? Anyway, I have the house-keeping money, and I warned them that it would mean cold suppers all the week if I lost.

I had a letter from Win on Saturday, and although she couldn't give me any definite news about her brother, she did say that her Mother had been to the Record Office, and they told her that as she had not heard from the War Office to the contrary, she must assume that he is alive and well. Where of course is another matter. Still, she says it has relieved them a bit and given them hope.

I don't know much about it, but the Record Office is where you can get information about any member of the forces. Don's Mother went along to enquire about Eric when they were not sure whether he had returned safely from Flanders.

I have stacks of work, as I did not work over the weekend, and so I must away,

Cheerio for the present,
tons of love,
    from Win XXXXX

2nd August 1940

My Dear Donna,
I received your letter this morning, and you cannot imagine how pleased I am to hear from you so often.

Well, nothing very startling has happened since I last wrote to you, except that we are still doing Oky Doky in this war, and bringing down the enemy planes with amazing rapidity. Invasion or attempted invasion, so often promised us, has yet to materialise and life is going on much the same.

Last Sunday, Sook was away working, and George was on the night shift, so Don and I had a lazy day, and did not go up to town in the evening. The week before that we had an evening out though, and saw Bing Crosby's latest 'If I Had my Way', and another good film that I enjoyed very much called 'Florian'. We had the time of our lives spotting all the nationalities and regiments. There are Canadian soldiers and airmen, any number of Anzacs (the Australian and New Zealand army corps), Polish airmen, and we also saw some Polish sailors, Frenchmen by the score, and of course plenty of Irish and Scotsmen, and dozens of A.T.S. and W.A.A.F. girls. Not forgetting our own English Tommies, Jack Tars and R.A.F. – God Bless 'em.

The variety of uniforms is a pageant in itself, and we are getting quite good at knowing what they are as soon as we see them. The Polish sailors look very much like English sailors except for the writing on their hats, and they give us flashing smiles. The French officers are very short and stocky, but look very smart as they stride along. The Canadians with their typical drawl and their funny pronunciations win everyone's heart and are by now as used to London, as London is to them. The Aussies in their turned up hats, are for the most part very tall and bronzed, and the New Zealanders in their round hats, looking for all the world like very tough Boy Scouts, look as if they could knock the stuffing out of twenty Hitlers.

When we came out of the pictures it was such a nice evening that we decided to walk part of the way home. We walked past Westminster Abbey, and somehow or other, the sight of this stately building standing before us, made us all stop for a moment and look. I have not been inside the Abbey for years but from the outside, apart from the many barricades and the soldiers on guard, it looks very much the same. Westminster Abbey was built in the reign of the last man to invade this island, William I in 1066. It has stood all these hundreds of years, and been through quite a bit too, for she was knocked about quite a bit by Cromwell during the Civil War, but she has never seen another conqueror since that one that built her, and as we stood and gazed up, it seemed as though the Abbey was as certain as we, that she never would.

When I last wrote to you I told you how lucky I considered myself, because my brothers and my own immediate circle of friends had not been seriously upset through the war. Well, things have moved a bit since then, and I will endeavour to explain the position now. Firstly, Don, he is still here, much to my joy, and everyone else's amazement. I am keeping my fingers crossed tightly as I type this though. My elder brother passed his medical A.1. and is going to be a Flight Mechanic in the R.A.F. He expects to get his papers quite soon. George, my younger brother, has heard nothing because his work will keep him reserved for a bit. You have heard me mention Eric (not Don's brother Eric, but the Eric of our gang), well, he has been called up, and is by now quite an old soldier. Ernie (you know, Ernie of Nellie and Ernie who have had a baby daughter) has had his medical, and is awaiting his papers for the Navy. Sid, who had a boarding house at Hastings, and who we stayed with at Easter, has given up his boarding house, and has joined up. John went for his medical yesterday, but neither Sook nor George (not my brother, but another member of the gang) has heard anything yet, but both of these are in reserved occupations.

There is going to be no Bank Holiday this August as usual. Of course, we don't expect it because of the war, but we can't help remembering all the past happy times we had on these occasions. If you refer back to the first letter I sent you after the war started, I think I told you then how we spent last August Bank Holiday. I remember it as clearly as if it were yesterday. Don had a poisoned hand, and this became very useful for all the crowds refrained from hustling our little party when they saw his arm in a sling. What fun we had that day, the boat ride up the river, and the high jinks on the roundabouts and swings when we got there. Then there are all the other Bank Holidays when we have ridden on the bikes to Hastings and the Isle of Wight, what grand days those were!

Never mind, when we have all worked hard and got this war won and finished with, we will have those days back again. They won't be quite the same, nothing will ever go back to being quite as it was before, but it will be peace – what heaven!

You certainly seem to be having some better weather than us. This last week or two has been quite chilly. Still, I think it is breaking now, and I expect Monday will be a lovely day, because we have to work. We will not be having our annual two weeks' holiday this year either, but we are being paid two weeks' salary in lieu, and although the National slogan is 'Save for Victory', I am going to invest part of this little windfall in some stockings. These are getting an awful price, and apart from that they are being made shorter in the leg, and if you have long legs like me, you must know that there is nothing worse. Still, I have quite a few pairs in hand, and if they do get such a price that I can't afford them, well then I shall have to wear thick ones and like it – it's all part of the war effort. The boss has promised me some time off when Don gets his papers, so I must save some of this money for then.

Talking about 'Save for Victory', you remember I told you about the slogan 'Dig for Victory'. Well, we actually have. Everything we eat now in the way of vegetables comes from our allotment. Potatoes, cabbages, sprouts, lettuces, carrots, parsnips, turnips, marrows and peas are growing in plenty, and of course Dad is still crazy on his tomatoes that he grows in the greenhouse. If THAT MAN has any ideas about starving us out, I could tell him here and now that he is wasting his time. Some people are even turning an 'eye sore' into a blessing, by growing marrows on their Air Raid shelters. Sook is growing tomatoes on his even.

We had an evening in town on Monday, and tried to get in to see a show, but all the seats were gone for the one we wanted to see, so we went and saw 'The Grapes of Wrath', 'The Men of the Lightship' and 'Conga Dances', and I thoroughly enjoyed the programme. I hear that 'The Men of the Lightship' is going to America, so you must be sure not to miss it. It is all about the sinking of the East Dudgeon lightship last January, by two German planes. This is a very sad story, but it does not upset you, it just makes you furious, at least it did me, and I am sure it will you, and every other decent-thinking person. I dare not put on paper for fear of shocking the censor, all the names I was calling those filthy swine under my breath.

By the way, I have been receiving all your letters I think. The last two have come within three weeks or so, but before that there was a long gap. None of them have been censored, but I am glad mine have been though, because it is difficult for me to decide for myself just what is all right for me to say and what isn't.

Well, all the while I have been writing this, a whole lot of 'war effort' has been piling itself up on my desk, so I must away.

For the present then,
Cheerio and tons of love,
Win XXXXX

3rd August 1940

I must tell you this: the Nazis have taken a page out of our book, and started to shower us with leaflets. One woman collected hundreds from a field near her home, and sold them for a penny each, the proceeds going to the Red Cross. Another man sold them to his workmates for a shilling each, the proceeds going to the same place. Contrast this with the fact that in Germany there were severe Punishments for even reading the leaflets we dropped, so heaven knows what would have happened to anyone who sold them. Come on Hitler, let's have some more leaflets. They make amusing reading, and the Red Cross could do with some more money.

16th August, 1940

My Dear Donna,
Well here she again, that girl I mean, the one who keeps worrying you with her presence.

I have been going gay since I last wrote to you, so I will start right in and tell you of my goings on. Last Monday we had an evening in town. Don had booked some seats for a show earlier in the day, so, as we had a couple of hours to kill before it commenced, we decided to walk around for a bit. We remembered that we hadn't been down to the Palace for ages, so we walked in that direction, and arrived there just in time to see the changing of the guard. Although the soldiers have exchanged their peace time garb of scarlet and black for the more ordinary khaki, it still manages to impress me a great deal. We walked through St. James' Park which leads down to the Palace, and I caught my breath at the scene that met my gaze as I entered the gates. All the seats were full, and many were sitting on the grass, reading, knitting or just drinking in the wonderment of it, as I did. The ducks were swimming on the lake, and the birds walked along the pathway beside you. In fact, everything was so normal and peaceful, that it just had to be seen to be believed. A Canadian soldier who sat on the same bench as us, contentedly smoking away at his pipe, turned to us and said 'Did I hear something about there being a war on, buddy?' Just as some things serve to bring home to you just what is going on at the moment, so that half hour in the park made me realise how very little things have changed since a year ago. Outside the Palace is a huge statue of Queen Victoria, and around this are some flower beds, full of glorious crimson geraniums edged with cool green grass. These seemed as though they were at their best last Monday, and although the square was very nearly deserted except for us two, I suddenly remembered Coronation Day. It had been packed then, and you couldn't have got a pin between the people. In my mind's eye I could clearly see that tall Irishman that led us all in community singing, while we shouted ourselves hoarse and finally brought the King and Queen out on the balcony. We mooched around for a bit, playing our favourite game of spotting the nationalities and regiments and finally left it so late that we only had time for a cup of coffee and a sandwich before the show started. I can't describe the show very much to you, except that it had Leslie Henson and Binnie Hale in it, and was screamingly funny. We came out just in time to catch the last bus home, where we tucked into a darn good feed before turning in.

The Monday before last we went up to town also, and this time we saw a very funny play called 'High Temperature'. The critics had given this a bad reputation, and although it was a bit naughty, it wasn't half so bad as they had painted it. Anyway, it kept me doubled up with laughter from start to finish, so it must have been good. We came out fairly early from here, as the show started at half past six, so after having had something to sustain us, we went and had an hour of Mickey Mouse, Donald Duck, Popeye and The Three Stooges. Talk about laugh and grow fat, I ought to be enormous, but I think I can safely say I am not. When we came out of the pictures it was dark, but it was such a lovely evening we went and sat in Trafalgar Square for half an hour. It was dark, and all I could see were the stars, and there seemed to be millions of them, and the dark tall silhouette of Nelson's Column looming up in front of me. We sat here until Don nearly fell asleep, and I got a stiff neck from gazing at the stars, when we stumbled along to the nearest Milk Bar where I rounded off my evening with the largest strawberry ice they made.

It was funny last night. You know I usually sleep over at Don's on Mondays because we always get home late, and it saves two journeys in the dark, and I also sleep over there on Thursdays when his Mother and I endeavour to beat Don and his sister at Cribbage. Well, last night, we had just finished tea, Con (Don's sister) was pottering about in the garden, Don had gone upstairs to wash, his Mother was making jam, and I was mucking about with the wireless, when Con called me into the garden, and told me to listen. Well, I did, and it didn't take me long to recognise that what I was listening to was gunfire. It didn't sound very close, so we all resumed our occupations and Con came in and started to count out the shop takings for the day and do her books. Less than ten minutes later, off they went, those wailing sirens. That gunfire had been closer than we thought. I ran and got my coat, my handbag, my knitting and my gas mask, the only things I had with me. I also dashed to the sideboard and grabbed the crib board, a pack of cards and the sweets. When we were all safely in the dug-out, save Don, who insisted upon staying outside to finish his cigarette, we stopped and took stock of all the junk we had brought with us, and doubled up with laughter. The whole of one corner of the dug-out was packed with gas masks and coats, in addition to which Con had brought her knitting and her books with her. Don's mother had brought a tin of biscuits, and the woman from next door, who had been in the middle of bathing her baby, had brought a pile of napkins but no safety pins. This caused another guffaw of laughter, and yet another when her husband offered to go and get them off the dresser. Well, Con had just finished her books, and we had got the cards dealt out for a game, when the 'All Clear' rang out. We were still helpless with laughter and it took quite ten minutes to remove all the junk out again. Anyway, it put us on good form for Don's Mother and I won every game we played afterwards, which is very unusual. We heard later that they had bombed an airport not very far from us, but apart from the distant A.A. guns we heard very little of this. Several people at the office who live nearer actually saw the falling bombs, but I am sure we were much too busy laughing over the baby's lost safety pins and our preparations for a 'long sitting'. Air Raid Warnings are still quite a novelty to us in London, but people that live on the coast, and get them two or three times a day, are quite used to them by now and think them quite a bore.

Our good old Spitfires have been bringing down the enemy planes so quickly lately that the daily scores are as equally awaited as were the cricket scores of a year ago. Don put on the news early this morning, and when he brought up my tea this morning said 'Guess what, yesterday's score was? 144 to 27, 8 not out', which interpreted means, 144 Germans down, 27 British down, 8 British pilots safe from machines brought down. Not so bad, eh? And this is typical of every day's score.

The position of all the club boys is just the same as when I last wrote, although we haven't seen Sook and Doris for a fortnight or so, as they have been on holiday.

Well, I must get on with my work, although it is so hot, I don't feel the least bit like it. Still 'Go to it' that's the slogan,

so I must away,
Cheerio for a while,
tons of love,
Win XXXXX

P.S. Whilst I was writing this a fellow at the office came up behind me, and I told him what I was doing. He has spent nearly all his life in America and only returned to England a couple of years ago. He said, 'You tell her from me, that although I admire the calm courage of my own people I shall always have a soft spot for the gay Americans, there's nobody like them.'

So now you know.

After lunch, same day

Such excitement! I had just finished writing this letter, it was past twelve, and I had just picked up my towel to have a wash before lunch, when woooooooooooo off they went again, those sirens. All the men in the Works disappeared down in their dug-outs and all the girls went down into the cellar of the local pub. It only lasted an hour, and we were making such a row, we didn't hear the guns, although they were going right enough. When it was all over, we came back to earth again and went out to lunch as usual. We got back at half past two instead of half past one, so I shall have to get my back into it this afternoon. I just thought I'd let you have it hot off the press. Boy, it is hot this time.

20th August 1940

Dear Donna,
Just a short little note to let you know that we have all come up smiling, after our first taste of Air Raids.

When I wrote to you last week, ironically enough I said that Air Raids were still a novelty to us in London, well since then we have had four. I told you in my P.S. how we had been disturbed at lunch time, but that wasn't enough, they had to come again at teatime on the same day. I did think of unsealing my letter and telling you about this latest addition, but I thought that if they go on at this rate, it will be impossible to tell you about every one.

Saturday we had a quiet day, but on Sunday I had a very thrilling experience. The boys were playing golf some miles from our home on the outskirts of London, and near that airport they bombed last week. Doris and I had gone with them, and were sitting in the adjoining park knitting, when we saw a formation of bombers fly over, very slowly. We looked at them for a few seconds, unable to tell from such a height whether they were enemy bombers or not, when suddenly the sirens started up and removed any doubts we might have had on that score. There we were in the middle of the park with planes actually over our heads, perfect targets for would be machine gunners. The nearest shelter was only a couple of minutes away, but we ran in the direction of the club house where the boys were. We had nearly reached the club house and shelter, when one broke away and dived right down, I did a bit of hurried thinking I can tell you. Had I been a good girl? etc. etc. but just as he had almost touched the ground, or so it seemed to us, he flattened out and went up again. I have heard since two or three tales about people who actually were machine gunned by a dive bomber in Sunday's raids, but he must have thought twice about it in our case, and I am still here to tell the tale. The noise overhead was terrific, although most of it was coming from anti-aircraft guns. We saw them swoop down in the distance and drop their bombs on those poor people who live near that airport, but the only noise from them was a dull thud. The most heartening noise of all was the screaming of the Spitfires as they chased the blighters. One extra loud burst near us sent everyone scurrying down in the shelter, but when the noise had calmed down, we laughed and came up again. Mum nearly had a fit afterwards when I told her how close they had been and I had been watching them. I know it was foolish, because although I wasn't scared, being bombed and machine-gunned isn't exactly my idea of a picnic, but the boys would watch, and we couldn't go down into the shelter without them.

We got home to a very late dinner about half past three, and I was just wakening from a quiet doze about six o'clock when the sirens went again. This time, nothing much happened. I was at home then, and not only was I obliged to stop in the dug-out but we are further in London, and they haven't penetrated as far as us yet. Says she, knocking on wood. We brought down at least another 141 on Sunday, but yesterday they had a day off to lick their wounds and we weren't disturbed at all.

I am getting to be quite heartless though. I cheer like Hell when a Jerry is brought down, and don't for one minute stop to think that probably a crew of dead men are coming down with it. Still, these are the same men that bomb lightships and machine-gun helpless people, refugees and sailors in open boats. Yes, and they even machine-gunned a handful of our sailors who were trying to rescue a fellow pilot of theirs that had been shot down. Can you wonder there is hate in my heart? We have no illusions about these

Nazis, they are all alike, every one of them, heartless, ruthless and unnecessarily cruel. At the beginning of the war we didn't hate them all, we said that the ordinary folk didn't want war any more than we did, it was all Hitler's fault. But it has been those ordinary folk who have committed these awful crimes, and even if they were obeying orders, they are just as bad for being weak enough to obey them.

Here, I'd better stop. Get me started on this subject and I'll rant and rave nearly as much as Hitler, I get so mad. Still my main object in writing this is to let you know just how we feel about this: we are not scared, but we are mad, real mad. I will quote you a paragraph from a newspaper article last week, written by a woman. 'We're mad because we have to take the vegetables down to the shelter to prepare them for dinner, we're mad because the noise of the bombs hinders our letter writing, and we're mad when we take navy blue socks down to darn, and find we only have grey wool.'

My eldest brother fell down a man hole on Friday and cracked his skull, had to have a couple of stitches in his chin, fractured a rib, and generally covered himself all over in bruises. Poor Mum was a bit scared when Dad came home with the news, she thought he had been hurt in an Air Raid, but he is much better now. He looks like a Dunkirk refugee with his head all bound up, and a plaster on his chin, and he said himself that if he had been a soldier those wounds would have been something to be proud of. Poor fellow, it is awful to see him try and sit in a chair, he has so many bruises in uncomfortable places. Still, he had a lucky escape, he might easily have broken his leg or even his neck.

I had better try and find a cheerful note to end this epistle on or I will give you the Willies, and be accused of spreading depression.

We saw a darned good programme at the pictures last night – 'Little Old New York' and 'Big Guy'. I enjoyed both of them very much, Richard Greene's voice is so English.

Win is coming home for the weekend this week, and her father has got the weekend off also, so there looks like being quite a reunion at her old home, where her married sister is living now. It is six weeks since she last came up.

Well I guess I had better hurry up and get my work done before the crooners start up.

Cheerio and keep smiling,
tons of love from,
your old pal, Win xxxxx

27th August 1940

Dear Donna,

I have just returned from a darned good lunch which has put so much energy into me that I have decided to start a letter you, while the boss is getting some work ready for me.

Well, there is not an awful lot of news. We are by now quite used to Air Raids, we get them all hours of the day and night, we get raids when we hear nothing save the drone of an aeroplane or two all the time, and we get raids when the bombs are very close, but if there is one in the Storeroom with my name on it, it hasn't yet been passed out.

Last night we had the longest raid to date, and as this makes it unique, I will tell you about this one, and skip the rest.

We (Don and I) were in the pictures, nicely thrilling to the dancing of Fred Astaire and Elinor Powell in 'Broadway Melody of 1940', when the screen faded and the manager came on to the stage and said the fateful words 'Air Raid'. A few people who lived near, or who wanted the security of a dug-out left, and within a couple of minutes the picture re-started. We stayed until we had seen the programme round, and then went out. It was completely black out, for even the minimum of light allowed to trams and buses ordinarily is put right out when a raid is in progress. We rode part of the way by tram until we had to change. The sky was a mass of searchlights, but the clouds were very low, and though you could hear the blighter, you couldn't see him. We waited at our tram stop for about half an hour, and as the particular tram we needed didn't seem to be in the offing, we decided to walk. We walked for about half an hour and still no tram came along. Things began to get a bit sticky and we heard the bombs in the distance, so we took shelter. We had been in the shelter for half an hour or so when a tram came along, so we came out and got on it, and it wasn't long before we were home (Don's home). We found the rest of the family in the dug-out, so we went in and got undressed ready for bed and made some tea. It struck me as being very funny, because here I was two hours after the start of the raid, upstairs, calmly getting undressed and into my 'Siren Suit', when in the ordinary way, as soon as you hear the warning, you fly out of bed, and get down into the dug-out. Don laughed too, because while we had been dodging about walking and riding home, the others had been sitting in the shelter all the time. I didn't seem to be hurrying and Don had to remind me 'There is a raid on, you know'.

Just as we were ready to take the tea out to the others, things really did begin to get sticky, and Don gave me strict instructions to stay in the house until there was a clear patch and then run down into the dug-out and stay there. He made me laugh because he said as we were padding up the garden path in our slippers 'If anything starts coming down, drop the tea'. Well, nothing did just then and we all drank our tea and settled down, quite convincing ourselves as we heard the clock strike one, that the 'All Clear' must go soon. Actually, it didn't go until four o'clock this morning. They caught one Jerry right in the centre of the searchlights. The others stood up and saw it, but I had just got the baby of the girl next door asleep in my arms and dare not move for fear of waking her, so I missed it.

Everyone looked a little dull about the eyes this morning after being awake best part of the night, but after looking around the office just a minute or two ago, everybody looks perfectly normal. It is wonderful what a difference a mid-day meal makes. When I get home tonight I am going to do something about the seating accommodation in our dug-out, so that if we get a repetition tonight, I might be able to get a little shuteye. I haven't been home yet for a night raid, I am always over at Don's – they used to call me the Air Raid sign because I always brought them with me, but we have so many now during the day as well, that they can't put the blame on me. It was very exciting being out in it last night, although I must admit it gave me a funny feeling inside to hear the planes above, because up until then my only experience of night raids had been from the security of my dug-out.

By the way, I will describe my 'Siren Suit' as they are called. This is merely a one piece suit with trousers and top with a zip right up the front. It is a wonderful thing to get into when you are called up at night, for it is on, and over your pyjamas in no time. Topped by a dressing gown this should keep the cold out on the darkest winter night. There is always a pullover ready in my dressing gown pocket, and I have a pair of socks and my torch in my suit pocket. You can't afford to be caught 'napping' these days.

Air Raids at night are a blank blank nuisance, but during the day they are not so bad. If I have not got any work that urgently has to go the same night, I don't mind an hour or two down in the cellar playing darts and knitting, during the day, but when I have to work late because an Air Raid holds up important work, then I curse. At home during the day, it's not so bad, you can take what ever you are doing and continue it in the shelter, but to be perfectly frank they are a bore, these blankety blank Air Raids.

Wednesday 28th August 1940

Evidently I wasn't the only one that had ideas about sleeping in the dug-out, for Dad came home with news that he had ordered the wood, and intends to make some bunks, so that we can resume our sleep when called up at night. Many people have had beds in theirs for a long while, but we had never bothered before because we hadn't had enough raids to make loss of sleep uncomfortable. Not that we have now, but we intend to nip it in the bud and 'Be Prepared'. Last night we made some temporary arrangements with planks and old coats etc., for padding. My brother next door has the same sized dug-out for only two of them, so we divide ourselves up evenly over the two.

I called in at the library on my way home, intending to have my supper and go to bed with my book about eight so that I could get some sleep. I know that I soon drop off if I start to read. Things didn't turn out quite like that though, for it took quite a while to fix the beds up, and I was just washing my stockings when the Warning went. I ran up and changed my best skirt in case it turned into another all night session, collected the pillows from my sister's and my own bed and together with my Gas Mask and book I ran down the garden. We sat up for a bit, reading, knitting and playing cards, for it was only a quarter past nine when the warning went.

About eleven we got the beds down and settled down for sleep. The 'All Clear' went about five to twelve, so we all trooped back to the comfort of our real beds. I lay there for a bit when suddenly I heard a plane. I called out to my sister 'There's a plane up', and she said 'Yes, I know, I've been listening to it'. Suddenly the sirens screamed their Warning and once again we got out of bed. Nothing daunted we resumed our sleep again in the dug-out and I vaguely remember hearing Grandad saying he was going back to bed because the 'All Clear' had gone, but the rest of us stayed there, we were so comfortable About three o'clock Mum woke up with a stiff neck, and her restlessness woke us all, so we got up and went back to the house. Actually, the 'All Clear' had gone about two I think, but if it hadn't been for Mum, we would have stayed there all night and not risked being called out again. As it turned out however, the rest of the night was uneventful, so what with my couple of hours in the dug-out and the rest in bed, I didn't do so badly last night. I will hold this letter over until Dad gets the bunks made, and let you know the result. I shall go down there and sleep every night and all the 'Warnings' and 'All Clears' in the world can sound, but I shall get my sleep. When I think of the times I used to stay up all night at Christmas and 'New Year' and other parties, I think I must have been crazy. Still, when this is all over, I expect I shall do those crazy things again.

Lying beside me on the desk is the book I got from the library last night, it is called 'The Citadel'. I know I am a long way behind the times, but I just managed to come across it, and remembered that I had not read it, when it was 'All the go'. I have just remarked to my friend sitting next to me, that if we have an air raid, I shall want to read my book, but I expect I shall have to keep the dart team up. It is as much as I can do to keep from opening it and reading it now, but with quite a bit of 'War Effort' waiting to be done, I have thrust it away, and I will also resume this letter as soon as anything of importance happens, or I get some slack time.

3rd September 1940

Owing to the fact that one of the girls is at present on holiday, and already with Air Raids butting in every five minutes we have our work cut out to get our own jobs done, I have not been able to resume this letter until now. Dad got the bunks finished over the weekend, but I haven't sampled them yet for we had no night raid on Sunday, and last night I was over at Don's house. He has made a very good job of them, four in our house and four next door, and they conveniently hook up on the wall during the day and leave room for seats. You can't prevent Air Raids, but you can do the next best thing, and make yourself comfortable, so that they don't bother you more than necessary. We really are seasoned veterans now, as far as Air Raids are concerned, and instead of the excited 'Sirens, sirens' that everyone used to cry, all we now say is 'There they go again' or just nothing at all.

Today is the first anniversary of the war. Yes it really is a year since war was declared, although at times it hardly seems possible.

Tuesday 10th September 1940

Sorry for the break, but last week was pretty hectic with all the extra work, and on Saturday the Air Raids started in earnest. We have an all night session, every night now, and as soon as the Warning goes, we each take our pillows and blankets and tuck down for the night. I usually sleep through it all, and only a very near bomb, or a plane coming down very near, wakes me. This weekend has been like Hell let loose though, and I never would have thought it possible to have seen so much heartbreak, and been in so much danger, and come out of it still fairly normal. I say 'Fairly normal' for a spirit of fighting mad is the right spirit for these times, but it can hardly be termed normal. When you see the damage wrought by this indiscriminate bombing your first feeling is one of sympathy for those on whom the blow has fallen, your second is a feeling of gratitude as you thank your lucky stars it wasn't you, but your third feeling which quickly overcomes the other two is a terrible feeling of anger, of a longing to do something to avenge the wrong you see staring you in the face.

As I watched with horror the news reels during the fighting in Poland and France, and prayed that it might never happen here, I never could really believe that I would see those self-same sights here in my own beloved London. There is no pretence at all of bombing military objectives. Hospitals, houses, schools and even Air Raid shelters suffered direct hits. I went on a 'Cooks tour' with Don in the shop van yesterday, and although some of the things I saw made my heart ache, I couldn't help feeling so proud of those brave people who have lost everything and still manage to come up smiling. Many shops with their windows blown out, carry such signs as 'Bombed, but not Beaten' and 'He may get us up, but he'll never get us down'. You can't floor people with spirit like that. Hitler will learn that sooner or later, but you in your country must know it already. Don't worry about us, London may be laid in ruins, but Great Britain will never fall.

I really must close now as there is so much work to do. We couldn't get into the office yesterday because we had a couple of 'Time bombs', but they have gone off now, and the only signs that the place has been hit are the fact that everyone is working at fever heat, and the sickening sound of falling glass every couple of minutes.

Cheerio for the time being,
tons of love
    from Win XXXXX

19th September, 1940

My Dear Donna,
I received your letter complete with photograph, last week, which came as a very welcome surprise. Many of the fellows at the office are seriously thinking about catching the first boat to America after seeing your picture, and even Don went 'Uhmm', which if you knew him you would take as a very big compliment.

I was so very sorry to hear the sad news of your sister, and kicked myself for always filling my letters with such tales of trouble. It seems so long ago that things were normal, and the days of peace seem so far away, that I had forgotten that tragedies can happen even in that blessed state of existence.

Well, I expect you have been hearing on the radio, much of what has been going on here lately. South East London is copping it the worst of the lot, and although I could fill this letter with tales and tales of bravery, heartache and fortitude, I fear that many of these tales must remain close secrets until after the war. One thing I can tell you though, and that is that the morale of our people is even higher than it ever was before, and if you were to hear some of the things said by the homeless refugees, victims of Goering's valiant airmen, you would know, as we know, that the idea of us ever giving in is absolutely out of the question.

Our dug-out is our second, or I might say, our first home these days. Every evening at about 8 o'clock, the Warning screams, and we all tumble down below. I have described our shelter before, and now that it is complete with beds, it is even more comfortable than ever. We usually knit, read, play cards or write letters until eleven or so, and then we pack down for the night. The new gun barrage continues unceasingly all night, but this never worries me. Now and again the shelter rocks with the blast of a bomb, and there are a couple of anxious seconds as a 'Screamer' whizzes through the air, and you hold your breath and wait for the explosion. The explosion comes as music to your ears for you know by then that it hasn't fallen on you. That is enough of Air Raids and bombs, I am not going to blight your life with such things.

You asked me to give you some details of my work, well, I am afraid that this, along with those many other things, must remain a secret for the time being. All I can tell you is that I do shorthand and typing, and the nature of my work is such, that it is helping to beat 'Ol' Hitler'.

We got so fed up with staying in every single evening, that we decided to dodge the bombs and go to the pictures last week. We saw 'North West Passage' which we enjoyed very much. It was quite a game getting home, door-hopping in the quiet periods. Of course everyone at home, and at the office when I told them next morning, thought me completely mad, but it was worth it.

I have just finished reading 'Gone with the Wind', but most books bore me to tears these days, they seem so uninteresting. Life seems so uneventful always in those pre-war novels. Life around you is as good as any thriller or romance you can read.

Throughout the letters I refer to my place of work as 'The Office'. I wasn't able to explain at the time exactly what this meant, so it might make understanding the letters easier if I go into a few details at this point.

I left school in the summer of 1934, just a month after my fourteenth birthday. In fact, actually on my fourteenth birthday I went for a job interview at the local High School. This job was that of a laboratory assistant, a bit of a dead end job, as it entailed just setting out equipment needed for each lesson, in the Science, Physics or Biology labs, and clearing it all away at the end of the lesson. Because the local council were only prepared to pay 'peanuts' for this job, I was told at the beginning that it would only last for three years. However, during that time they were prepared to send me to a commercial college to learn shorthand and typing for two afternoons per week. I thoroughly enjoyed my three years there, especially as my school friend, another Win, got a similar job at the local Teacher Training College. We both had the advantage during this time of the long summer holidays as though we were still at school and this is how our friendship developed, and still exists until this day, for whilst all our contemporaries were at work, we went out together enjoying these long holidays in a variety of ways.

Thus it was that aged seventeen, I got my first proper job as a junior shorthand typist in the office of an engineering works about ten miles from home. This engineering works was situated in a rather grim, very old building. The ground floor was The Foundry, where they used all the moulds for the various components they made. The middle floor was The Machine Shop – self explanatory, and on the top floor was 'The Office'. This consisted of various winding staircases with little glass-fronted enclosures, and two main offices. The first housed the typists and clerks. The clerks sat at long, high, bench-like sloping desks, very Victorian, and the typists at similar long benches that were flat. Back-ache was an occupational hazard. The second office was the Drawing Office, and beyond this a large room known as The Kitchen. The walls of this room were lined with filing boxes going back many, many years, all covered in many layers of dust. Into this room which boasted a sink, a cooker and a table, a lady arrived each lunch-time and cooked 'fry-ups' for the young, single men among the employees. Most of us shuddered at this unhealthy food, cooked in such unhygienic conditions, and chose to go out for our lunch.

One morning, after a particularly bad night of bombing, we arrived for work to find just a smouldering open space where the building had stood. As well as high explosives, the building had been devastated by incendiaries. Absolutely everything went up in flames. There was nothing left, not a machine, not a typewriter and none of those rows and rows of dirty filing boxes.

Just before the outbreak of war a new factory was in the process of being built adjacent to the old one, but although it was three-quarters finished, they were not allowed to complete the work. Mercifully, this new building was unscathed from the bombing, and permission was given under the circumstances for it to be finished as economically as possible. I am sorry to say I have no memory of what happened to the factory during this transition period, but we in the office were housed in the cellars of the local pub. Somehow typewriters were acquired, still second-hand, but heaps better than the antiquated machines we had had prior to the bombing, and for some three months we went to work each day down in the pub cellars, surrounded by barrels.

At last came the time when we moved into the new offices, again on the top floor. No kitchen this time, although we had a tea lady with a trolley who came round morning and afternoon. I have no memory of where she was able to make the tea, or how she got the trolley up the winding stair case – no lift as I remember.

Here at least everything was shiny new. We sat at normal, individual office desks, typists at one end, and clerks at the other, and the whole atmosphere was entirely less grim.

Most importantly, during the war all production was turned over to wartime needs, mainly aircraft components, so although I was only doing the same work as I had been doing before, subject to my several promotions, it was deemed work of national importance, and I had to stick with it, like it or not, for the duration. As a lot of senior staff moved away for various reasons, I got more rapid promotion than I would have done in peacetime, and ended up as secretary to one of the directors, which was unheard of in those days, at the age of 21.

I used to type my letters to Donna during my lunch time, or whilst waiting for the boss to return to the office to give me dictation. This often meant working late into the evening, but I filled in the waiting time with my letter writing.

I used to make the journey to work by train and tram, provided both were running, but you just got to work every morning in whichever way you could. It didn't matter if you had been up all night with bombs falling around you, there was never any question, you got up and went to work. I remember arriving one morning on the tail board of a dust cart. Army lorries were always a good bet for stopping to pick you up.

None of this of course I was ever able to write about.

A literary footnote:

About three weeks before the old office and factory were destroyed by bombs and fire, my name finally came to the top of the list to borrow 'Gone with the Wind' from Eltham library, its only copy. I used to take it into the air raid shelter every night and I remember so well reading of the burning of Atlanta, the image of which was fresh in my mind from having seen the film, and then going outside to look at the sky line, yellow, orange and red as the dock area of London burned a few miles away.

I used to take it to and from work every day, reading a little whenever I could either on the journey, or during the lunch half hour. I had actually finished it on the day before the bombs fell on the factory, and as I had a lot of shopping to take home that night and knew I wouldn't need the book in the shelter that night, I left it in the cupboard under my desk.

Of course, it perished along with everything else, and I had the unenviable task of reporting its loss to the library. Of course, there was nothing they could do as it had been lost due to 'enemy action', but I often thought about all those other people whose names were on the list below mine, and wondered how long it was before the library was able to obtain another copy.

24th September 1940

We went to the pictures again last night and thoroughly enjoyed the break. We dodged home with an arch of searchlights over our heads and shrapnel falling all round. I had a tin hat but refused to put it on because Don had nothing, and he refused to wear it because then I would have nothing, so we walked home and carried it. We thought we heard a bomb falling as we got to the front door, and flattened up against the porch, but it turned out to be an A.A. shell going up, so we went indoors and got ready for the night. Don's mother was very relieved to see us when we finally put in an appearance at the dug-out, but we soon laughed her fears away. If any one had ever told me a year ago, that I would go through so much, just to spend a few hours in the pictures, I would have thought them crazy, but now it seems that I'm the crazy one.

I must tell you this, our office cleaner came in today. Her house has been bombed, she has no windows, and only one room has the ceiling still above it, and that is the kitchen. When we asked her if she was going to move out, she said 'Oh no, there are plenty of people with no homes at all, I have got one room, and we sleep in the dug-out at night'. We asked her if it had made a terrific crash, and she answered 'Yes, but my husband said 'Don't worry, when you don't hear it you know you're dead". This is typical of the way people all over London are taking their misfortune, and I wish you could see the number of houses, without a pane of glass or a roof on, but a Union Jack proudly flying from what was once the window frame. You can't beat people like this, they just won't accept defeat, that is why I never worry.

It makes my blood boil when I see all our lovely buildings that have stood for centuries, and always been our pride and joy, so wantonly destroyed. I don't know whether I have ever told you about the old Palace we have, or I should say, had, at Eltham. This was the country home of many Kings and Queens years ago, when Eltham was out in the country. It is the reason we bear the name Royal Eltham. Well, this became a 'military objective' and they ruined the beautiful place. There was no loss of life, and of course its destruction will not make the slightest difference to the winning or losing of the war, but the fact that some tuppenny-ha'penny gangster should come along and muck our country about, just makes our blood boil. This man is going to have so much to answer for when the day of reckoning comes.

We heard yesterday of the sinking of one of our sea-evacuation ships, and the loss of many helpless children, who were being taken away from all this. This made us all feel sick, and although I feel like screaming with many others for reprisals, I know in my heart of hearts that this could do no good. I am firmly convinced that that is what the Germans want, for they must have learned from the effect on us, that bombing non-military objectives, only makes people stronger and more determined to carry on, and they know that we are doing more towards victory by sticking to Aerodromes etc., than they are.

You know, somehow, I like being here in the thick of it all. I should worry incessantly about those I had left behind, if I moved to safer quarters, and anyway it was always so easy to talk about our brave, soldiers, sailors and airmen, it is quite another thing to be in the soup with them. It gives you a feeling of equality, and when I scramble to work on lorries and vans, and hitch hike my way home in the same way, I feel that I am sharing in a small way, their trials and tribulations.

27th September 1940

The boss is out for a few minutes, hence this slackness.

Well, the order of the day is Aeroplane buying. Every borough of London, every town, big business firms, and all sorts of organisations are buying an aeroplane that will bear their name. There has been a dearth of Spitfires, everyone wanted to buy one of these. One local borough thought they would be different and buy a bomber, and at work we are buying a Hurricane. The boss has promised a model of the plane to everyone who collects £5 or over, and I only have a few more shillings to go. It will take months to raise all the money of course, but we are making it, slowly but surely. Eltham is buying a Spitfire, so I divide my money between the Hurricane and the Eltham Spitfire. Motorists have been very good these past few weeks, offering lifts etc., when transport has been a bit tight, and while you can offer a commercial driver, a tip, or the price of a packet of cigarettes, you cannot do this to a private driver, and many have solved the problem by having Spitfire boxes in the back. Of course when you have had a lift to work, you are only too pleased to put your fare towards an aeroplane. Talking of aeroplanes, it is lovely to watch our machines returning from a raid over Germany. You can always tell whether they have been successful or not, for if they have, they do a victory roll. The first time I saw them diving thus I wondered what on earth they were doing, but now, we always run out into the garden when we hear them coming, and invariably they do their victory roll.

Mum thought she was being very brave yesterday, when she went and had a perm during an Air Raid, but we laugh at her because we are continually travelling and caught in the street, so much so that we lose count of the time. You don't know whether the period you are living through is between a 'Warning' and an 'All Clear', or an 'All Clear' and a 'Warning'.

Don expects to go any time now. His last period of exemption ended on the 20th of this month, and the silly idiot purposely sent his appeal for an extension in too late. He wasn't going to send it in at all, but I nagged him so much, he finally promised to, but he knew all along he had sent it in too late for consideration. I don't know what will happen to his shop when he goes, for now that John has been called up, he is managing the shop almost single handed.

Great news, the baby can walk, yes really, right across the kitchen – boy, is he proud. I have just finished knitting him a suit for his birthday next Saturday. It hardly seems possible that he is nearly a year old, although we cannot imagine ever being without him now. What a year his first one has been! Let us pray he will live to see many better ones. Talking about living, at the beginning of the war I didn't care two hoots whether I lived through it or not, but now I feel that having seen so far, I would like to live and see the end of it all. I want to live and see the new London rise up, the London that will be free from slums, which Hitler is so keen on knocking down.

I am sending a piece of shrapnel from our garden and a 'photo – what a combination! About half a dozen of us went out one lunchtime and had our pictures taken, and as they only cost $6\frac{1}{2}$d for three, which is about 11 cents or so I think, you will know why they are nothing terribly special.

Now I have a request. Have you any odd scraps of knitting wool for I am making a striped bedspread in the dug-out at night, and while I started off with plenty of wool, this is rapidly disappearing. Of course I don't expect much, it would cost too much for postage, but a few odd scraps would certainly help. This may sound a funny request, but I hope you will have some.

Please excuse the many typing errors, but I have just whisked this last bit off in no time, for there is heaps of work be done.

Cheerio for the time being,
tons of love,
from,
    Win xxxxx

15th October 1940

Dear Donna,

Here I am again, still alive and kicking, despite a certain person's endeavours to make me otherwise.

Things are certainly getting rough round here, although when things are quiet you would hardly think there were such things as Air Raids, everything and everybody is so normal. It amazes me, and I'm in the midst of it. One of the girls in the office had a letter from a relative in the country who said 'Everyone here is talking about the bravery of the Londoners'. That surprises us, for we don't think we are being brave, in fact we just don't think about it at all, and it is only when we read things like that, that we even mention it. Another girl had a letter that sent us all into hysterics. Her aunt wrote, 'Things are getting bad here, we had a bomb TWO MILES AWAY.' My God if the nearest bomb to me had been two miles away, I wouldn't know there is a war on, which only goes to show that people just don't realise exactly what things are like here. I wish they did in one way, because it would save many fears as to our mental attitude, which I have explained enough times to you, to leave no doubt on that score.

There is one thing I am glad of though, and Mum has repeated it times out of number since the 'Blitz' started, and that is 'I'm glad Phyll is away from it all.' Whatever happens, she must never experience what we are experiencing. At first we just left all mention of the war out of our letters to her, but she must have heard the news bulletins, for now, whenever she writes to us, she enquires as to our safety. The first time she wrote thus, I answered indignantly 'Of course we are all right. Why on earth should you imagine we are not?' but you can't fool even a kid for long.

As I write this I can see the afternoon tea putting in an appearance, and as I usually get my work when this is over, I will have to break off here. By the way, the secretary of one of the directors left suddenly for a healthier spot, and yours truly got the job. Boy, do I feel good. You can dodge bombs any day, but it isn't often you go out in the morning, and come home a secretary.

16th October 1940

What a night, the worst I think so far, but I am still here, so that doesn't mean much. I will begin at the beginning. First thing yesterday morning I was travelling to work during a raid, when suddenly, swish, swish, swish, rent the air. We all ducked and waited what seemed like eternity for the explosions to come, but they finally did, and everyone on the bus looked at each other and laughed. The conductor crowned it all by calmly saying, 'Them, ladies and gentlemen, was bombs' which sent us all into hysterics. It wasn't until I got to the office and heard the many questions that were going round 'Where were you?' 'What did you do?' etc., that I fully realised just how near a thing it had been. We had raids on and off all day but they don't make much difference to us, for we work through them now, and only go down under when things get really sticky.

The 'Allnighter' started noisily last night, and instead of calming down for a while later on, continued unceasingly for hours. We counted 19 bombs in our own immediate locality, and one was so near that it sent Dad and my brothers scurrying out of the dug-out, to see what had happened. Everyone that can possibly help is needed when a bomb falls closely, because there are usually people to be dug out and fires to be extinguished. This particular bomb however, turned out to be an oil bomb, and luckily it had not done much damage. They came back not long afterwards, reeking of oil, but none the worse for their adventure. So ended a perfect day.

Last Saturday night, we were sitting in the dug-out, with Jerry monotonously droning overhead – 'The uneven beat of a Dornier' my sister calls it – when suddenly the droning gave way to a definite chug, chug. As if with one voice, six people all well equipped with well trained 'aeroplane ears' said 'There's something wrong with that engine'. Almost at the same time, Don and my brother, who had been on guard outside, came hurrying down. Swish, swish, swish, Jerry was running true to form. They always drop their lot and scurry away, once they get in trouble, although I don't think this particular buddy did much scurrying, not with a knock like that in his engine. Anyway, I wouldn't mind betting my whole week's money, and that's courageous seeing that I expect to get a rise, that that was one more Jerry who won't trouble us again.

Sook and Doris came over on Sunday, they are now living further out of London, and it was quite a treat to dress up in my best coat with high heeled shoes and fine silk stockings, topped by a silly hat with a veil, instead of my now everyday attire of thick warm coat, flat heels and scarf-cum-turban.

All my treasures, together with my best dresses and dainty shoes, are packed away in the most bomb-resistant place in the house, until such time as it will be possible to wear them again. This is time for action, times for pleasure and nonsense will follow when our job is done. Although as I said before, it was quite a tonic to stop being practical just for a couple of hours.

Sook and Doris have properly let the side down. They have bought a motor bike, a thing that all of us in our cycling days vowed we would never do. Still, they promise to go back to 'pushing' after the war, and say that they have only bought the bike for travelling. It certainly is handy, for it enabled them to come and see us, and leave in time to get home before the night raid, without having to worry about catching trains and buses.

By the way, there was an awfully funny picture in the paper one day last week. It showed a captured Nazi airman on his way to an internment camp, and for some reason known only to himself maybe, he was carrying a large case with 'Lifebuoy Toilet soap' on the outside. Well, you know the old advertisement about 'What even your best friend wouldn't tell you' etc. Bearing this in mind, under the picture were these words: 'Maybe he doesn't want to be a wallflower in the prison camp he is going to, or maybe he hasn't got any friends, anyway we predict a great social future for this lad'. This struck me as being very funny.

The boss has just returned from lunch so I must away, back tomorrow maybe.

17th October 1940

It rained cats and dogs all night, but things were much quieter than the previous night. Today is bright and sunny and we have already had two raids this morning, the time is now half past ten. Still why worry?

Human nature is a funny thing you know. I don't suppose there is a single person these days, who upon waking in the morning and realising that they have lived the night, doesn't say 'Thank God'. But what do we say 'Thank you' for? The right to live another day of uncertainty, followed by yet another night of Hell? Funny isn't it, that despite everything, we still hold life dear. No one really has any desire to leave the world no matter how wicked it may be. I think the secret of it all lies in the future, hopes for the future, plans for the future, faith in the future. Yes, that is why we say 'Thank God' for being alive.

Oh, by the way, I don't know what to do about sending newspapers as you request. You see I don't know anything about the censor regulations, and whether or not they will pass, but I will post them to you, and if they do not arrive, you will know regulations will not permit.

There is much newspaper talk these days about your new conscription bill, and many seem to think you will be in the war before long. Whether this is a good thing or not, I will leave to those better qualified to pass an opinion, but there is one good thing, even if you do, you won't have air raids to contend with, so you won't even know anything about it. We didn't until we had it right on our front doorstep. Battles, soldiers, sailors, airmen and aeroplanes were just names that meant war, we now realise more than that.

Did you hear the princess's speech last Sunday? It was relayed to America – I thought it was very good.

I hear Charlie Chaplin's new film has made a great hit in New York, I am dying to see it.

On Monday we went to see 'The Private Lives of Elizabeth and Essex', which was very good, taking it as fiction, but I could no more imagine Elizabeth calling anyone a 'Snake in the Grass' or a 'Slimy Toad', than I could imagine Hitler laughing at 'The Dictator'. Still, it was good entertainment. Things were a bit rough when we came out, and the night raid was already a couple of hours old, but door-hopping, and shelter-hopping, we made it. It is surprising the confidence a tin hat gives you. Don has one now, so we both wear them when we are out in the street and muck is falling. It is amazing what you can get used to, isn't it? I can now wear trousers, flat heeled shoes and a tin hat, with as much ease and a great deal more comfort than I used to get from my peace-time clothes.

I am glad more than ever now that we are not married. Imagine having spent all our savings buying a lovely home, only to have it ruined in a split second. We may have to have inferior furniture after the war, and we will probably have to pay more for it, but that will be better than having nothing at all. Well that seems to be about the end of my news for the time being. I will hold it up until the morning, and if nothing exciting happens I will post this to you.

18th October 1940

I spent last night over at Don's home, and it was the most terrible night I have ever experienced. Bombs fell like rain, and one fell so close that Don's mother was sure the house had gone. Somehow, I knew it hadn't been quite as close as that, but the sound of falling glass was sickening. Don went rushing out straight away to see what had happened, and my heart was in my mouth all the while he was away, for the bombs were still falling. He came back about twenty minutes later, much to my relief, reporting that that particular one had hit a house, and there were two people trapped in the basement, but they were getting them out, unhurt. (Here, let me take off my hat and salute the rescue squads, who have done marvellous work, under great stress and in terrible danger.)

It is worse for people like Don's mother. She is not hard like us young ones. We have seen so much of it on our journeys to and from work, that it no longer has any power to hurt us. If we hear a bomb come down, we just say 'Thank God it wasn't me' and promptly forget it, but to the women like Don's mother and my mother, who just go short journeys back and forth to shops, and then only when there is not an air raid on, every single bomb seems so bad to them, and they always think about others. They say 'It isn't me, but some poor soul has got it'. This attitude is right of course, I have no need to say, but hardness is a great help these days, it saves you loads of suffering. Many people at the office are out this morning, and although we have heard bad news of one of them, we can only hope that all is well with the others.

I won't write any more now for my head aches. That near bomb last night did something to my ears, and they are still hurting this morning, and what is more, I am in a depressing mood, which is very rare for me, but it is fatal to try and write cheerfully when you feel like this, so I will be back later.

Same day 2.30

I feel better now. My tummy was a bit upset after last night, and it made me feel a bit grouchy this morning, but all is right with my world again.

My new boss is in the habit of taking several hours for lunch, so that means I hang about, and then have to rush my work at the last minute.

Talking of angels, here he comes, and he wants me,
Cheerio for the time being,
tons of love,
from,
    Win xxxxx

Saturday morning, 19th October 1940

P.S. I got the rise I expected, and a promise of another one in the near future, if I come up to expectations, so I am going out to have a good spend this afternoon.

22nd October 1940

Dear Donna,

Herewith three newspapers which I have picked at random from our pile. I don't know whether censorship regulations allow these through, but I hope you receive them, and that they will show you something of the spirit of the people today. They will show you pictures of the ruthless destruction we have to contend with, but there is not a single person who doesn't believe that these acts will be avenged and what is more, after we have won the war, the buildings and houses will rise again, and this time they will be more beautiful, and the slums that Hitler is so intent on destroying will be replaced with healthy dwellings.

I must not stop to write any more now, for the nightly siren has already wailed its warning, and 'that man' is chugging around overhead. Already though, the guns of our barrage have made themselves heard, so I will bid you goodnight and get down under.

Cheerio,
I hope the censor lets the papers through,
tons of love,
  Win XXXXX

1st November 1940

Dear Donna,
The inevitable has happened: Don has received his 'Calling Up' papers, and officially becomes a member of His Majesty's Army on the 14th November. Although I get a funny feeling in the pit of my tummy when I let my mind wander to what it will be like without him around, the thing that really keeps me going is the fact that we have been so lucky. He expected his papers long ago, but received an extension because of his business, and although that extension ended on the 20th September, he has only just heard. In addition to this he has been given a fortnight's notice before reporting, instead of the usual six days. This too, is an extra extension because of his business, I believe. We had intended to go away for a holiday before he went, but he has so much to clear up at the shop, that I don't suppose we will have time. Anyway, he suggests that when he gets settled, I go and visit him for a week. He is stationed not too far away, but far enough to be out of the 'Blitz'. That is one thing I am glad of, no more Air Raids for him. We were going home the other evening when he broke it to me, and our conversation ran something like this:-

Me: What are you smiling for?
He: I know something you don't know.
Me: What's that?
He: I've got my four bob.

Me: Aw
He: I said, 'I've got my four bob'.
Me: Oooh
He: I thought that would do it.
A short silence
Me: What?
He: Royal Artillery.
Me: Where?
He: ———
Me: How far away is that?
He: ———
Me: That's not too bad. (an afterthought) When?
He: A fortnight's time.
Me: Gosh, fancy, a fortnight.
Another silence
What happened next is nobody's business.

In a way I don't feel too badly about it, because I know how much Don wants to go. He has felt so out of it these last few months, despite the fact that he stood to lose all his savings and his business had he joined up before.

The 'Blitz' has not been so bad this last couple of weeks, due no doubt to the fact that the weather has been absolutely lousy, freezing cold, and dark windy nights. Of course, if it keeps the blighters away, we don't mind how cold or dark it is, we can stand all that.

Don's Mother has gone away for a couple of weeks to get a rest, and last night I stayed over at Don's with himself and his sister. We had an 'All Clear' about 9 o'clock which was very unusual since the air raids usually last all night. We went in and got out all Don's collection of Crosby records. He is a supreme favourite of both of us, and what a host of memories they all hold.

I snuggled down in the armchair, still in my 'Siren suit' and dressing gown, and Don settled at my feet, with his head on my knees. It seems like eternity since we last enjoyed such an evening. One by one the records rolled off, and we neither of us said a word, but I would bet anything you like that we both had the same thoughts.

First 'June in January'. My mind flies back to the January of 1936 when I first met Don, that tune was very popular then, and he has since confessed to me, that he used to play it often those first few months. 'I think of you with every breath I take', another favourite from that first grand year, when we were both kids, with no responsibilities, or thoughts of the future, save perhaps a hazy vision of 'Someday'. That 'Someday' still hasn't come, and is not likely to come now, this side of peace, but it is still the day round which all our schemes are woven. 'Shoe Shine Boy' and 'My Little Buckeroo' were Christmas presents one year. 'Sweet Lallani' sent us back to one summer holiday at Bognor, where we first heard it. How I remember that year. I had just got over an attack of mumps of all things, and we were not quite so hectic as usual. Stretches and stretches of sand, blue sea, and lazy, lazy days on the beach. 'The One Rose', this is Don's favourite, and how apt are those words now:

> You're as sweet as the red rose in June dear.
> I love you, adore you I do.
> Each night through love lanes we'd wander, sweetheart,
> Telling love stories anew.
> Out of a blue sky a dark cloud came creeping,
> Breaking my heart in two.
> Don't leave me alone, I love only you.
> You're the one rose that's left in my heart'.

How am I going to get on without him? Letters, no matter how often written and received, are a poor substitute. How do other girls manage, who have never given another fellow so much as a passing thought? They carry on I suppose, the same as I will. He has made all the horrors of these past months easier to endure, he has been my sheet anchor, my one link with sanity in a world gone mad. Enough of this. What is the matter with me? He will still be in England, and for a while, while he is training, he will not be in any danger. Why, millions of women have been separated from their husbands and boy friends since last September, and have seen them for only a few brief periods of leave. They have had to carry on knowing that they were fighting in France, Norway and Dunkirk, so surely I can be lonely for a bit, without letting it get me down.

To get back to last night. We heard all the records, and a few other favourites – Nat Gonella singing 'Georgia', 'Basin Street' and

'Limehouse Blues', and then had our supper in front of the fire — what heaven. We sat up until twelve listening to dance music on the radio, another pleasant reminiscence of peace days, and were undecided whether to go to bed, or retire down under. We finally decided to go to bed as usual in the dug-out, for by that time the moon had come up, and another attack was inevitable, and it is no fun getting out of one bed, running down the garden, and getting into another, in the middle of the night. The 'Alarm' did go again, about three, and Don said things got pretty noisy, but I didn't hear anything at all, I slept all night. I did enjoy my evening, I hope we get more evenings like it. I can't bear to think of spending all this precious fortnight in the dug-out every evening.

We went to the pictures last Monday, and saw 'The Doctor takes a Wife', which I thoroughly enjoyed. It is a long while since I saw one of those gay light-hearted films. I don't know whether you have seen this or not, but in the story, the young man is terribly stubborn, which he attributes to his short stubby thumbs, and every time the girl went against his will, he just showed her his thumbs, and she gave in, knowing full well it was no good arguing. This has given Don ideas, and already he has stopped two arguments that way.

By the way, it was very funny yesterday, he wanted a drink, and I said 'Get it Yourself' or words to that effect, to which he retorted 'All right you'll be sorry, you'll say soon, I wish he was still here for me to do things for'. I laughed, and got him his drink without a murmur, and he whispered to his sister 'I ought to do all right this next fortnight, if I use my head'. Of course I told him it cut both ways, he was only going in the army I said, we were still staying in the front line. That made us all laugh, and Don wanted to know 'Who's fighting this war anyway?'

We have just returned upstairs after ten minutes or so in the dug-out. We have a system of spotters now. This is how it works. Every day there are two spotters on the roof, complete with whistles and field glasses. When the official 'Warning' sounds we carry on working, and a green light is shown in the office. When there is immediate danger overhead, the spotters blow their whistles like mad, and the green light changes to red, whereupon we all tumble down stairs as quickly as possible. When the danger has passed the red light in the dug-out changes to green, and we return upstairs. This procedure may occur several times during one official 'Alert', but it does save wasting time down under, when there is nothing actually overhead.

4th November 1940

I have just spent my first full night in a bed, in a bedroom, with only pyjamas, for weeks, and boy, does it feel good. It has rained unceasingly all over the weekend, in fact I can't remember a worse weekend for weather, but that didn't worry us. Saturday night we got the 'All Clear' about half past eleven, but we were already tucked into our dug-out beds, and so we stayed there for the night. Sunday dawned, with the rain pouring down worse than ever. We spent all day pumping out the dug-out at intervals of an hour or so. It was so wet that we decided, raid or no raid, we would stay in the house all night and sleep downstairs. Well the time for the usual 'Allnighter' arrived, and no sirens, no guns, no bombs. The prospect of an evening in the house made me feel like a kid on a school treat. We played cards until about 1 o'clock, and as no 'Warning' had gone by that time, we all went to bed as usual. How lovely does your bed feel when you haven't slept in it for weeks, and how easily you can get back to normal. As I undressed and got into bed, it seemed as if I had never stopped doing this. All those nights I have packed down, dressed up in umpteen pullovers and a dressing gown, seemed to fade away. For one brief evening, life was normal again. Well, we slept all night, but even so, I had given the others strict instructions not to wake me, even if something did happen. I wasn't going to have my night spoilt. For the first time since the 'Blitz' started London had no night raid, but it looks very much as if we will pay for it today, for the sun is shining now, and the sky is beautifully clear. Still, our boys can get them when the sky is clear, so we need have no fears.

5th November 1940

Despite the good start made by the weather yesterday, it rained again, so we decided to sleep indoors, as the water was coming in to Don's shelter. (I stay at his house, Mondays, Wednesdays and Thursdays). Well, we went to the pictures in the evening and saw Mickey Rooney in 'Andy Hardy meets Debutante' and 'The House of the Arrow'. This was a very good programme, the first picture being very funny, and the second very creepy. We came out about half past eight, and was it dark or was it dark? You couldn't see a hand before you, and the only indication you had that there were swarms of others coming out of the pictures with you, was the fact that every now and then you heard 'Sorry' and 'That's all right' as persons collided. Suddenly there was a terrific whistle and a scream. Someone yelled 'Keep low everybody'. Don and I crouched against the wall, and there about half a dozen others on top of us. When the excitement concluded, we got up and groped our way home. It was worse than the blackest November fog. We got in, and found Don's sister sitting in front of the fire (his Mother and Father have gone away for a while, and there are only his sister and himself at home). She was a little nervous and wondered whether or not she should go into the shelter, wet or not wet, but I think our presence gave her confidence, for she stayed with us while we toasted in front of the fire and ate our supper. After supper we sat listening to the wireless, and I mended three of Don's pullovers that were fraying, a job I had been meaning to do for a long while. About half past eleven, we went upstairs and brought down a big double mattress, which we put under the large dining room table. We then piled all the chairs on top of the table, and all tumbled underneath. It was quite a feat I can tell you, doing this without banging your head. This morning I lay in bed listening to Bing Crosby on the radio – even peace does not offer opportunities like this.

Talking about opportunities peace does not offer, it is funny the number of things that are quite the thing now, but which were unheard of before. When I used to snub, and treat with a withering look, kerb crawlers in the old days, I never thought I would stand on the kerb and thumb my way to work, and ditto home again. Sometimes I travel in as many as three strange cars a day, and I have yet to find one who needed one of those famous looks of mine. They have all been splendid, and many bear a label 'Help your Neighbour', and you know that you are certain of a lift from one of these. Another thing is the friendliness of everyone. You can now talk to perfect strangers without fear of being considered a bore, and many a strange girl has poured out to me the story of her bombed home, or husband in the Air Force, on a journey home together on the back of a lorry. Another thing is the communal sleeping necessitated by sleeping in Air Raid Shelters. Women sleep with other women's husbands, and visa versa, brothers sleep with sisters, fiancés with fiancées, and it is all quite above reproach. The other evening, Don's father wanted to borrow my spoon while we were having tea. He said 'Do you mind if I spoon with you? I sleep with you, so you shouldn't mind.' This wasn't so bad as it sounds, but I have spent with him, many nights in their dug-out. I never thought that I would sleep under the table with Don and his sister, without her so much as raising an eye-brow, but it only goes to show. Out of many evil things has come good, so let us hope that after the war we will not go back to being so stiff and starchy as we were before. The last war helped to bring equality for women, this one should complete the job, and it should also do away with silly class distinctions. Many a top hat has been glad to ride home on a coal cart, I can tell you. Enough of this, I am getting too serious.

6th November 1940

Well, there doesn't seem to be much more news to tell you today. It rained like Hell again last night, and this morning, it was still teeming down. We have been down under for about a couple of minutes, once today, but nothing exciting has happened.

It is nearly four o'clock and my boss hasn't returned from lunch yet, and here I am with no work to do, an opportunity to write to you, and nothing to say.

By the way, I don't think I ever told you how my home is faring, sort of not wanting to tempt fate, but up to the time of writing, we still have it safely over our heads. We have had one window broken, as did nearly everyone in the road, when a bomb fell just round the corner, and there are a couple of holes in the roof, caused through shrapnel, but this is nothing at all. Don has not been quite so lucky, although, even their little bit is nothing compared with some. A Landmine came down very near, and as a result, the front door was blown off, turned completely round, and stood up again in the doorway. Many of their windows are broken, there is a hole in the garage roof, and they did have many holes in the roof, but these have been mended of course.

I meant to explain yesterday, the idea of getting under a table is to save your head and chest from debris. Our legs were sticking out, but these are not so important, should they get injured. Of course you would not be safe under a table if the house got a direct hit, but then you wouldn't be safe in a shelter that got a direct hit. It is blast that causes a lot of the damage, and falling debris.

Another thing I had better explain, when Don said he had 'Got his four bob', I knew what this meant, because every man receives with his 'papers' this sum of money (a little under a dollar) which is supposed to be an advance of pay. Actually, it is just tradition I suppose, although Dad says all he got during the last war, was one bob, not four. (Another explanation – a bob is a slang expression for a shilling).

Well, I think I will dry up now (I wish the weather would too) and get this posted to you.

By the way, it seems like years since I heard from you. How's about it?

Cheerio for now,
tons of love,
from,
    Win xxxxx

P.S. I have just heard that Roosevelt got in. I don't know what your political tendencies are, but I don't think anyone over here cared who won. They had both promised us all the help they could, and as it would be contrary to the benefit of their own country if they did not, we know we can rely on this. I think though I am glad about Roosevelt, we know him and he is one of the best.

21st November 1940

Dear Donna,

After having been up to my ears in work for the last couple of weeks, I am at last taking this opportunity of writing to you again. Well, Don has gone, and I am now one of those girls who watch for the postman every five minutes of the day, and plan and scheme to visit him when ever possible.

He is very happy, and thinks the Army a grand life, although he is now in the throes of all the tiresome preliminaries, inoculations, vaccination and teeth, but to quote his own words 'As soon as we are through with this, we can get down to a nice quiet time of route marching, rifle drill, brass cleaning etc.' If possible, I am going down to see him this weekend. It is funny isn't it, that it takes a separation to make you really realise just how much someone means to you, though of course I always knew how much I loved him.

The day before he went I had the day off from the office, and we went up to town, the first time since the 'Blitz' started. We spent the morning shopping. By the way, I am a lucky girl – he took me to one of the biggest shopping streets in the West End, and said 'You can have anything you want, anything you see and like is yours'. Well, I ask you, what a state to be in. Believe it or not, I didn't know what I wanted. Anyway, I finished up with a marvellous multi-coloured tweed swagger, and afterwards I bought a lovely little fur pill box hat, brown suede shoes, brown handbag and brown gloves. It was lovely to be so extravagant. I hadn't bought a new hat for ages, as I went hatless last summer, and since it has turned cold, I have been wearing a woolly turban. Also, I had not thought of buying any such unpractical sort of shoes as high-heeled suede ones for many a long day, but it is nice to forget you're 'a soldier in the front line' and a 'Londoner' once in a while, although I was never so proud of being a 'Londoner' in my life, as I am now.

To get back to where we started – we finished our shopping, or I should say – we finished my shopping, and had a marvellous lunch of chicken salad, and fresh fruit salad and icecream. Boy, did I enjoy this. After lunch, we went to see a show called 'Diversion', which is one of the few theatres still open, for naturally, no-one stays in town during the night 'Blitz'. It was quite a good show as shows go, and we arrived home about six o'clock quite satisfied with our day. Of course, had we known that the 'All Clear' was going to go [censored] o'clock that night of all nights, we would have stayed in town all the evening like we used to.

It has struck me that my letters of late have been too much like news reels, and not enough about my own family and life.

Well first, we are all alive and kicking, none the worse for our experiences, which will give us many a laugh in years to come. My little sister is still miles away in the country of course, where she is having the time of her life, becoming a proper country bumpkin. Mum and Dad are going to try and go down to see her in a week or two, to take her Christmas presents. My elder brother is wondering what he can have done to be forgotten, for he had his 'Medical' months ago, and is still waiting to be called. I think his work has a lot to do with it though. My other brother is definitely exempt because of his work, but he has been growing gradually more and more impatient, as one by one his friends have joined up. Now that the last one left, Don, has gone also, I don't think it will take him long to throw up his work, if they will let him, which I doubt, and join also. I think that if his work is important enough for the powers that be to consider it necessary to keep him at it, he should do so, but I know it is hard, for they all long for a real opportunity to hit back.

Sook and Doris will not have to be separated, as Sook also is in a reserved occupation. They now have a little bungalow in the country. Ernie and Nellie, complete with family, who incidentally is a spitting image of her father, came to see us last Sunday. Ernie is still, like my brother, wondering why he hasn't been called, but thinks that maybe his work has something to do with it too. All the rest of the club boys are now soldiers, sailors or airmen, and we only see them occasionally.

My friend Win who has been evacuated since the beginning of the war, now has her family spread all over the globe, more or less. Her mother and father have moved out of London, because of his work, her sister has been moved also, but to an entirely different quarter of these islands from either Win or her parents. Her married sister and her baby have now joined her mother and father, her brother-in-law is the only one still in London, and her brother is a prisoner of war in Germany. Incidentally, she is very worried about him, because apparently they are not being clothed and fed as they should be, but what else can you expect of the B———— Germans? It makes my blood boil when I think how good we are to our prisoners. She wants me to go and stay with her for a weekend, but I don't suppose I will be able to go before Christmas. What with presents to buy, and all my other money being spent on fares to see Don as often as I can, it doesn't leave much for other trips. Still, I would like to see her again, and she doesn't come home now like she used to, because her people are not here.

Many of my other friends have had their houses bombed and damaged, but '23' is still pretty whole, being only minus a couple of windows.

We now take not the slightest notice of the 'Blitz'. We sleep in the house, because, personally, I would rather be killed by a bomb, than die of pneumonia.

They say English people find it easy to adapt themselves, well I am thinking that this must be true, because life now seems quite normal, despite all the fireworks. We laugh now when we think of how we used to listen for the siren to start and dash for shelter immediately it did. Now the siren still sounds, but it goes right through us. Often if I am busy, I just don't hear it. As for taking shelter, well the only time you do this, is when you actually hear a bomb coming down, and then the only shelter you can give yourself, is to lie flat on your face, against a wall, if possible. I used to think this awfully degrading, and used to fume at the thought that someone had me in a position where I had to do this, and not be able to fight and stand up for myself. Still, now I just content myself with sticking at my job, and trying to make it easier for those who really do get a chance to hit back. Maybe when that time comes, someone will be good enough to strike my blow for me.

I expect you have heard about Coventry. Well this made us all furious. I felt dog-in-the-manger about it somehow. I can't say I liked having old London knocked about, but I just couldn't bear to think of anyone else getting it too. I kept saying 'How awful it must have been, how the people must have felt etc.' and although someone did say that it probably wasn't any worse than some of the bad raids we have had, it seemed different somehow. I think it must have been worse when you are not used to it, it is always worse. Still, he won't get away with it, he'll pay, to the very last man, woman and child that he murders, he will pay.

Imagine how our airmen feel, when they come home and find their houses and treasures bombed, and their friends gone, imagine too how they feel the next time they fly over Germany, yes, he'll pay all right.

Here is an amusing true story you might like to hear. A German airman was brought down, and rescued from the wreckage of his plane, very badly injured. He was a tough guy however, and despite his injuries kept up a long stream of abuse, cursing the doctors and the nurses, and all the other folk that danced attendance on him (so would I). Anyway, he finally lost consciousness, and they gave him a blood transfusion. When he came to, the doctor said 'Young man, you now have two pints of good Jewish blood in you, I hope it will teach you better manners.'

We had some excitement the other day. Many soldiers are working in London, clearing up the damage, and a party of them arrived near our office to pull down some unsafe walls that were still standing after a building had been hit. At first we didn't notice the soldiers. It was so exciting to watch these great chunks of wall come hurtling down. We stood with open mouths as they tugged and tugged at particularly obstinate pieces, and let a cheer rip when it finally came tumbling down. We noticed one particularly good looking fellow, that had rather a foreign sort of look, and then decided that they all looked rather that way. Tall, dark, rather a sleek sort of appearance, to us who prefer the fair open good looks of an Englishman, but very nice none the less. We found out afterwards that they were Poles, Czechs etc. who had escaped from their own countries into France, where they had joined the French army, and later escaped again from France and joined up here. The particularly good looking one that we all liked had been an officer in the Polish Army, and was now only a private. We gave them cigarettes and this made them our friends for life. They used to stand 'neath our window, and really amuse us at their quaint attempts at English, and their slow charming accents. I am afraid we were rather disillusioned when we saw them face to face, and not with the height of the building between us, for they had rather a frightening look, but they were nice fellows none the less, and I hope it will not be long before they can return to their own countries, and be free to live their lives as they wish.

They say that anything that is worth having is worth fighting for. Who should know that better than we, who have taken our stand, and will remain firm until that which we want is ours. What is this thing we want? Is it power or wealth, or revenge? No, it is merely the right to live our own lives, and for the rest of the world to be able to do likewise, with no fear of anything or anyone that has other ideas, taking this right from you. In one of Don's letters to me, he started a sentence 'When this rotten mess is over – '. It is a rotten mess, but one day it will be over, and is it not conceivable that the God in whom we put our trust and faith today, will in some way make it up to us, even if it is only in the security of knowing that our children will never have to go through all this again? They said 'Never again' after the last war, but another generation has grown up since then, a generation that knows that the only way to keep what you treasure, is to keep both your feet firmly on the ground, stick your chin out, and fight, and while that generation still lives, no-one is going to dare to take on such a foe. It must be very aggravating to have an enemy that just refuses to crumble up and give way. I can tell you this definitely, straight from the horse's mouth, there is not so much as a slightest crack in the determination of the people. WE WILL NOT GIVE IN – WE WILL WIN.

It is lovely, the sun is shining brightly, and it is more like a spring day than November. The 'All Clear' has just sounded, and so ends the first raid of the day. It is nearly lunchtime and I am feeling starved. Don says he is going to try and get through on the 'phone tonight, I hope he can. Usually though, only important Government calls are put through to London. Still, I have a feeling he will be lucky. I feel so pleased with myself this morning. Who could feel otherwise with this lovely sunshine, after the bleak wet dark days, we have come to call 'lovely days' because of the safety they offer. I even feel it is worthwhile to have a nice day and be unsafe, just for once. ———The 'Warning' has just sounded again. Looks as though I am getting my wish. Still, as long as the sun keeps shining, everything will be all right.

Well, I must be off, my inner man calls, and so does that work that has accumulated whilst I have been writing this.

Cheerio for now, and in case this reaches you round about the right date 'A very Merry Christmas, and a Joyous New Year.'

tons of love,
     Win xxxxx

4th December 1940

My Dear Donna,

I have just arrived home and found your marvellous-looking parcel waiting for me, and the whole family on their toes, anxious to know what was in it. Imagine my delight when I viewed the contents. My dear Donna, how can I thank you enough? I did not for one moment realise that just one casual remark from me, could bring forth such a hearty response from you. The slip too is lovely, and more acceptable than ever now that these things are termed as luxuries, and are therefore terribly expensive.

I knit every evening. It is all you can do with the 'Blitz' outside, but even so, I have always heaps to do. Don needs knitted comforts of course, and I cannot pass a soldier, sailor or airman in the street, who looks cold, without saying to myself, 'I must knit you some new gloves' or whatever it is he needs. I promise though that just as soon as I get through with this huge programme, I will make something for you.

By the way, there was no letter enclosed with your parcel. Perhaps one will follow in a post or so. I hope the customs did not lose it.

I will not make this letter a long one, as writing is not only a penance to me, but also a strain for whoever has to read it. Also, I have my usual daily epistle to write to Don. If I keep him waiting more than a day, I get a frantic letter asking if I am all right.

Nevertheless one of my usual typewritten letters to you will follow in a day or so.

I am going down to see Don this weekend. I live like an angel all the week, and save all my money for my fortnightly weekends with him. I will go into more detail about the grand times we have when I write next. I never thought I would settle down to being a sit-at-home soldier's gal, but it only goes to show what a difference a little bit of a war can make.

I should dearly love to send you a Christmas present, but it is so difficult these days. If we are really patriotic we do not buy unnecessary things, for this makes the burden that our Navy has to bear, even more hard. I will keep my eye open though, and if I see something very nice that is definitely 'Made in England', and will not take too much space on board coming over to you, I will get it directly. Never mind, after the war, I will really repay you for your friendship, which is so appreciated by me in these hard days. Meanwhile, please let me have news from you in plenty, for next to Don's, I look forward to your letters more than anything.

For now then, I will say,
Cheerio,
tons of love,
from,
    Win xxxxx

P.S. If this writing is even worse than I usually do, it is because I am writing this on my knee.

9th December 1940

Dear Donna,

It is nearly time to go home, but I will start this letter tonight and maybe I will have time to finish it tomorrow.

Well my dear I am feeling particularly happy today, for I have just returned from spending the weekend with Don. This is the second time I have been to see him since he went away, but the first time I stayed the whole weekend, and boy, have we had a good time. We are only having one day for Christmas this year, and so he won't be able to get any leave, but he is hoping to get a pass for this weekend, and then I can go down to see him the following weekend. That way will mean that we will see each other nearly every week, and I feel that whatever the cost, or inconvenience, for travelling is enough to try the patience of a saint these days, I must see him as much as I can, while he is still in England, for who knows when he may be shifted abroad, out of my reach for perhaps months. I have had many strange new feelings since the war, but I think the most strange of them all, was when I first saw Don in uniform. He was like a stranger, someone totally different from my usual Don, but somehow twice as dear. When I saw him again this weekend, I was quite used to him, as if I had always known him as a soldier. Every soldier I see now, I have a soft spot for, for they all look so much alike, that they all remind me of Don.

Last Saturday night was the first night I had spent out of London since the 'Blitz', and would you believe it, London did not have a raid that night. I was glad about that of course, but what added insult to injury was the fact that Sunday night when I came home, we had the worst raid for many weeks. In fact all the newspapers called it 'A Coventry on London'. To make matters worse, I was alone in the house, as all the rest of the family had gone away for the weekend also, to see my sister, and were not returning until Monday night. I had quite a lively journey home, dodging shrapnel and bombs, and when I did get in the house I didn't feel any safer, for it was so quiet that I could hear every sound so plainly, and the French doors kept banging in, with the blast of one 'Brandy Ball' after another. The dog was not much comfort, for the poor thing was scared stiff, and had missed everyone over the weekend, so I waited for a lull, and then with Peggy tucked under my arm I dashed next door to my brother's house, and spent the evening there. Every time a bomb came down, he kept saying it was a gun only, which convinced my sister-in-law, but I knew differently. I went back indoors about twelve, and made up a bed in front of the fire. I was so tired that I went right off, and did not hear another sound until morning, although I understand the 'fireworks' kept up all night.

Tuesday morning

I have just learned that I had a nearer escape on Sunday night than I realised, for a spot where I had stood for about three quarters of an hour, whilst travelling home, was bombed soon after I left. I have just received a lecture from the boss about being out in the raid. He said I should have come home earlier, and wagging his finger at me said, 'You'll get caught one of these days my girl.' You know, it is funny, but I don't feel like that. You see Don is convinced, I don't know how or why, but he says he feels, he knows, that both he and I are going to come through this business unharmed. At first I didn't share his convictions, I just didn't really care much, I used to think that if I had a packet coming to me, I'd get it all right, but now I feel like he does, somehow I know that all will be well, and that nothing will harm me.

Wednesday morning

I had a letter from Don last night saying that he heard about the bad raid on London, but adding, 'Of course I know you are all right though.'

Mum and Dad and the others enjoyed their weekend with Phyll. They say she has got terribly fat, and is talking with a broad country accent. She and the little boy at the house where she is staying are firm friends, and she is fast becoming a regular country lass. Despite the fact that we very rarely mention anything about the war in our letters to her, she seems to know all there is to know about 'planes, bombs, etc., although thank God she has not known an Air Raid yet.

We are all looking forward to Christmas, although it will not be such a gay affair, kept up for two or three days and nights, as usual, for we all have to resume work, the day after Christmas Day. We've got a job to do, and the quicker we get this business settled, the sooner we will be able to lead our own lives again. Still, I expect we will manage to enjoy ourselves, we usually do, and although I am sorry that Don won't be home, I am sure that all the boys will have a good time in their various camps etc.

I wish you could have seen me last weekend, at the Garrison

town where I stayed. I had never seen so many soldiers, and the amazing thing is they all look alike, despite their different caps and badges. What a place for a lonely girl! Believe it or not whilst Don was getting the tickets for the pictures, I had quite three or four give me the 'How's about it?' look. This comes as a surprise to me, for I have for so long been a 'one man girl', that I hadn't noticed anyone else. They are grand fellows all these soldiers, many of them having come miles across the sea, just to help us out in our task. I hope that after the war, they will never be forgotten. Their cheerful faces and outlook must live for ever, for they are certainly giving life some of its few bright spots these days.

I have made Don some gloves, and have nearly finished a pullover. After this, I have only to make a scarf and some mittens, and he will have a full set of hand knitted things as well as his official ones. His sister has made him a balaclava helmet, and his mother is making him socks, so he will not get cold. I had an evening off from my khaki knitting last night, and did some of my blanket, the temptation of all your lovely wool before me, being too much to resist. By the way, although I got your parcel quite safely, as I told you in my previous letter, I still have not received a letter for months. I expect you have written and something happened to the ship.

I don't know, I never seem to have anything interesting to write about these days. You see, I don't go out as much as I used to, and the only time I really have a good time is when I go and see Don, and I can't very well tell you about that can I now?

Well, how is life these days in your part of the globe? Still very much the same I hope, and for your sake I also hope it is a little warmer than it is here. It has been absolutely freezing these last couple of weeks. I feel the cold terribly, for I am essentially a fair weather bird, and although no amount of heat can get me down, I don't like the cold. Still, it keeps the Jerries away, so I mustn't grumble about it.

I will try and send you a photo of Don in uniform, if I ever manage to get one myself. He just will not go and have one done, says he will feel a silly ass, but perhaps he will, if a couple of the other fellows go too.

Well Donna I think I will hold this letter up for a day or two, and then if nothing exciting happens, I will post it. Maybe the day will soon come when I shall really have something to write about again.

16th December 1940

Monday morning again, and I have had quite a good weekend.

I had the morning off on Saturday which was officially for 'Christmas shopping'. We have always had this on previous years, and so the boss let us have it as usual this year. I say 'officially for Christmas shopping', because actually I had done most of mine already, but I had a nice lie-in.

On Saturday evening, John came over. He is home on seven days' leave, and it was lovely to see him again. George was as pleased as punch to have one of his pals home again, and we had a good evening, playing cards and yarning. On Sunday morning, George and John went to have a game of billiards, as John has been pining for a game ever since he went away. About twelve o'clock there was a knock at the door, and in walked Don. I was terribly excited, and rushed about and got ready quickly, so that we could catch George and John before they left the Billiard Hall. We managed to see them all right, and while I went back to Don's house for the rest of the day, the other two arranged to come on after dinner. Don's mother was naturally pleased to see him, as this is the first time he has been home, though it isn't so bad for me, for I do go down and see him.

There was quite a jolly crowd on Sunday afternoon, and the talk was shop, shop and more shop. Don and John were comparing notes on their own particular part of the Army, and George and the husband of one of Don's sisters, who are both Home Guards, were discussing their jobs. We played cards until it was time for Don to catch his train back, and then I went to the station with him. The guns were banging away, as his train drew out, but the 'All Clear' went later, whilst George and I were on our way home. We hadn't done anything special at all, all day, just talked and played cards, but somehow I thoroughly enjoyed myself. I think it was just the fact that some of the boys were home and part of the gang were together again. It is so lonely without them all, although I don't mind it so much during the week, it is mostly at the weekend, that I remember all the marvellous times we used to have.

Still, this is the beginning of another week, and it won't be long before we have the weekend with us again, and then I can go down to Don. Isn't it awful to wish your life away like this? I get a bit peeved sometimes, when I think to myself that these years should be the happiest of my life. I have spent my nineteenth and my twentieth years during war time, and no matter how hard we try to make things up, after the war, you can never put the clock back. It is really like taking those years right out of your life. Enough of this, I mustn't start getting morbid, not today for I feel too happy, so I'll close this epistle for now, and wishing you all the very best for the New Year, will sign off.

  Win xxxxx

P.S. I finished Don's pull-over which looked very smart, and I am now firing away with his scarf. I shan't rest until I know he has got all he wants, and then perhaps I can keep my promise to you.

1941

3rd March 1941

My Dear Donna,

How very lovely to get a letter from you at long last. It arrived last Thursday, and the rest of the family could hardly contain themselves until I got home on Friday evening. You see they are as excited as I am, when a letter comes from you. I thought it sounded from your letter though, as if you had written since the last one I got in September, and I suppose it must have got lost. I am glad mine are coming through slowly but surely. I have been writing about once a fortnight since September, so it won't matter if a few get lost.

Well Donna, at the moment I am on my toes with excitement, for my darling is due for seven days' leave very soon, and boy will we get weaving. I am going to get the boss in a good mood, and try and get a bit of time off so that we can go places during the day, but whatever happens we will always have the evenings to make merry in. We have already planned to get together as many of the old gang as we can muster, and try and re-capture the old spirit in a visit to town. There will be a lot of gaps though, for the boys are now spread all over the globe. We miss John more than anybody, for until he went away he used to spend quite a bit of time at our house. He is now on active service somewhere abroad, and when ever we hear of any action anywhere, we always think 'I wonder if old John is in that'. Don has been home for the past three weekends, which is almost too good to be true, but he manages to wangle it somehow. He is very much an old soldier now, and I wish I had a 'photo of him I could send you. He did have half a dozen taken, much to his disgust, for he compares this with having a tooth drawn, but they were soon snapped up by his Mother and sisters and me. Still, when he is home on leave we will take some snapshots in the garden, and I will send you some.

Whilst on the subject of 'photos, what a surprise to see that some misguided person thought my picture worth printing, it was a very nice surprise all the same. Of course I don't mind how much they print of what I write. It is entirely up to you to let them know what to do, and what not to do. After all they become your property when I write them to you. I did say I never wanted to keep any souvenirs of the war, but if you wouldn't mind I would like to have some cuttings from your paper. They will be interesting to keep, and might even make good reading when all this is over, and the happenings they speak of, are just memories.

It is a lovely day, the sun is shining, and the sky is a beautiful blue – spring is definitely in the air, and it makes one feel 'good all over'. Old Nasty keeps reminding us that 'Spring is coming' with his invasion threats, but they don't mean a thing to us. The coming of spring still means sunny days and shooting buds, and nothing he can say or do will ever take precedence over these things.

In your last letter you asked after Irene Ford. She went to the same school as I did, and started to write from school the same day we did, but she is three years younger than I am, and was there when my sister was at school. I think we are the only two of our batch that kept it up, aren't we? How we have both changed in the years that have passed! I was thirteen I think when I first wrote to you, and I am twenty-one this year. (Since you are not easily put off, and to save you any further time in asking, I guess I had better tell you here and now, the fateful day is 18th June).

I don't know whether it is the same with you, but over here your twenty first birthday is the most important one of all, and you always have a smashing party, but it looks as though I shall have to go without mine, or at least postpone it for the duration. We started saving in the New Year for our Peace Party. We each put sixpence a week in a money box, and boy, will we have a flare-up when the lights go up.

I am glad you got the newspapers quite safely. They were hopelessly out of date when they arrived, weren't they? What did you think of them? I will send some more as soon as I can get round to doing up a parcel.

We all fell for Mr. Wilkie when he came over here, in fact we feel quite flattered to have so many distinguished visitors. The 'Aussies' have been doing great things in Libya, haven't they, and the Greeks too, although as I write this events in Bulgaria don't make things look very healthy for these plucky people. Still it is useless to say what turn events will take, we shall have to just wait and see. In the end it will all come right, but it is going to be a tough job, still never fear, we shall make it.

I don't think I have told you before, but I go fire-spotting now. Everyone is definitely fire conscious, every house has buckets of sand and water outside. Many have stirrup pumps, and clearly indicate this with a large P on the pavement outside or a card in the window. Another useful piece of fire-fighting equipment is an old dustbin lid, which acts as a fine shield for your face, whilst you tackle an incendiary bomb. We have a system working in our road, and all the other roads have similar systems, varying in hours with the amount of people available, whereby everyone takes their turn at spotting. We are fortunate, in that we have quite a number of men still left in our road, most of them being men like my father, who went through the last war, and are still young enough to do active work, although they are above military age. Many too are like my brothers, in reserved occupations. Our rota works like this: two or three times a week we go on in pairs for two hours at a time. As each pair finishes their duty, they knock up the next pair, and so on, all through the night. A fire spotter's job is to patrol up and down the road, and tackle any incendiaries that come down, although if too many come down at once, they blow their whistles, and the whole street wakes up. My sister and I are the only two girls in our party. As I said before, we have quite a number of men. Many of these men are Wardens, firemen, or Home Guards, and we are needed to take their turn when they are on duty at any of these things. So many of them come home from a hard day's war work, and nearly every evening spend their time on some sort of voluntary service like this, that I think an easy job like fire-spotting should be done by the girls. In fact I quite enjoy it. A couple of hours' fresh night air is good for you, and you get quite invigorated walking round and round the block, occasionally meeting people from other roads out on similar missions or a warden or policeman on his beat. If it is quiet, we take the dog with us, but when things get noisy we take her in, because the guns make her bark, and then she'd wake up all the neighbours and there would be a fine ado. I don't mind being out in the raids at all. Don certainly did me a good turn when he broke me in well, by taking me out in them so much when he was home, and I have done so much travelling backwards and forwards to see him, with guns booming and searchlights streaming over head, that they just don't have any effect on me. Actually we are only supposed to patrol our own road, but Edna and I walk round the block to take off the monotony.

I must tell you this. Don's pride and joy are his boots, he cleans them umpteen times a day, and in all fairness I must say they really look good, and he says himself they make him stand on the end at parades and inspections, because he shows the others up. We are always pulling his leg about them though, because as soon as he gets in he takes them off so that no-one shall stand on them, and if anyone should tread on his toes in a train or a bus, well the air is blue. There is so much rivalry between him and my brother in the Home Guard. Naturally the Home Guard being a part time 'army', although they wear the same uniform, you can always tell the difference because they do not get the rigid training that the real army get, which certainly leaves its mark. Don looks ever so much taller now that he is so absolutely upright, and he can out walk me too, which is saying something when I remember that since I met him I have never been on a really long hike, which I used to enjoy so, for the simple reason that he would have taken a bus across the road, if one would take him. George is trying hard to get his boots as good as Don's, but I am afraid it will take many hard days 'spit and polish' to do this.

Joy of joys, we now go upstairs to bed every night, and to Davy Jones's locker with the consequences. Mum doesn't like the noise very much, and it certainly sounds worse from upstairs, so if it gets very bad she goes downstairs for a while, but Edna and I both sleep dead as a doornail, and often don't hear a thing all night. We often have nights now with no raids at all though, and then it is hard to imagine those hectic days last Autumn when we used to dash home, and then just about have time to snatch a meal and change, before the siren sent us tumbling down below.

4th March 1941

Hallo again, we had rather a noisy night, but I slept through most of it. I was due to go on duty from 2 a.m. to 4 a.m. and about half past twelve Mum came into my room and said she was going downstairs because it was so noisy. A couple of seconds before she came in I had woken myself, so it must have been noisy to wake me. I was still half asleep when Mum came in, and was just conscious enough to wonder why she had bothered to come in and tell me she was going downstairs. I heard nothing more until I awoke this morning, so the 'All Clear' must have gone before two, but Mum said she woke me so that I should be on the 'Alert' since I might have to go out. I am afraid I didn't appreciate this, being much too fond of my bed.

I have joined a Book Club and mean to build up a good collection of books to grace our bookcase when we are married, and to be ready for Don to spend all those nice quiet evenings by the fire, that he keeps talking about. This month's book came last night, and it is 'Nanking Road', by Vicki Baum, and so far it seems very good. You pay half a crown a month, and they send you the best seller every month, which you keep. These books are published at two or three times the amount, but you get a special cheap edition. Over here half a crown is another way of saying 2s 6d. It is also known as half a dollar, but actually it is worth a little more than this I think.

The other evening we were having a good laugh, looking through the old snapshots, and I found some that you sent me in 1935. There was one of your little sister and brother, they looked at a rough guess about nine years old and six years respectively, so they must be getting very big now. How old are they both? The old holiday snaps brought back many memories of weekends by the sea with the old gang. The poor old tandem lies in the bike shed neglected and wondering if she will ever be used again. Whenever I am with Don on a nice fine Sunday, I say 'Wouldn't it be lovely to get out the bike and ride down to so and so' and he always breathes a deep sigh and agrees with me. So many of the old gang are married now that I wonder if we will ever go back to the same old care free days. We laughed heartily at old racing snaps of Don and my brother, and they both wonder how they ever had the energy to get up in the small hours and push a bike for a hundred miles just for the pleasure of perhaps getting a silver cup or a medal, but more often than not, umpteen punctures and aching limbs. Still, it was good fun, and didn't we used to tuck into a large size breakfast when it was all over? Photographs taken at the club dinners, when everyone forsook their shorts and socks for evening dress and dancing pumps. What memories this brings back of speeches and prize giving, my brother slightly tight, telling everyone that 'My Daddy is going to make a case to put my medals in'. The Palais Glide, the Lambeth Walk, and Knees up Mother Brown, what fun.

We came to a page of snaps that my brother took while he was in Paris in 1937. He was furious as he looked at them, and kept pointing to pictures of little cafes and the many ancient buildings, saying 'I bet they are all full of Jerries now' and he softly hummed to himself one of the latest songs. Have you heard it? 'The last time I saw Paris her heart was young and gay, I heard the laughter of her heart in every street cafe'.

5th March 1941

Well it was a quiet night last night, just one short raid, but it was all over before midnight. I had a nice lazy evening snuggled in the armchair, reading my book, and went to bed early. Well Donna, I seem to have exhausted my news for the moment. I hope to have some jolly tales to tell you after we have had those marvellous seven days we are looking forward to, meanwhile, please write to me often, won't you.

Cheerio for now,
tons and tons of love,
Win xxxxxx

24th March 1941

My Dear Donna,
As I write this, my eyes are droopy and I feel so desperately tired, I should like to go to bed for a week, and the reason, need you ask – Don has just finished his seven days' leave that we have been looking forward to for so long.

He is going back sometime this afternoon, and when I left him this morning he promised to 'phone me just before he catches his train. The week went much too quickly, but we had a marvellous time, and it was quite a treat to see him in 'civvies' again, even though the extra height and breadth he has gained from his Army life made him look rather like a prize-fighter.

Well, I think the best thing for me to do is start right at the beginning and work my way through the week. He didn't know exactly when he would be coming and I got a letter on Friday asking me to come down for the weekend. Of course I went, although everyone thought me crazy to waste my money, when he was expected home, still that is beside the point. We went to the pictures on Saturday afternoon and saw 'Waterloo Bridge' which was very good, and as I was wearing a pair of high-heeled shoes, which, after spending almost the entire winter in brogues, were almost killing me, and as there was the prospect of a nice cosy sit by the fire, we returned to the house where I stay fairly early in the evening. I don't know whether I have told you about this place. It is a private house, just an ordinary little one, in which live a middle-aged couple, whose living is made by taking in temporary boarders. This however is no ordinary boarding house, for all the people who stay there are soldiers' wives who come down to see their husbands for the weekend and girls like me who visit boy friends. It is a real home from home, and although some of the husbands manage to get a 'sleeping out' pass, even those who have to be back at camp for the night are welcome to stay for the evening. We always have quite a jolly time, and the boys generally spend the evenings playing darts etc. while the girls just yarn. It is about a mile up hill back to the camp, and it is always with a regretful sigh that Don buttons up his great coat, and gets going. The people are so nice and friendly, and the house is nearly always full to overflowing, so yours truly, being usually the only single girl there, usually has to pack down on the settee or a camp bed, but I'd far rather stay here, than at any other more expensive place.

Well, we seem to have gone off the course a bit. On this particular Saturday we got back and found a lovely fire, but the house empty, so after discarding my tight shoes, we settled down in a big armchair, and there we stayed until the others returned. Don thought perhaps he might be starting his leave on Monday, so I decided to travel back with him early Monday morning and go straight to the office, instead of travelling back on Sunday night, which, although I have done it very often, isn't exactly a pleasant journey with the addition of an Air Raid. I usually manage to have a nice lie-in on Sunday morning and then meet Don in the village after Church Parade. Anyway, this particular Sunday he came bursting in at half past eleven saying 'I'm going today, there's a bus going in half an hour, we'll be home for tea', and before I knew quite what was happening, he was off again to collect his kit. I met him at the bus stop at the appointed time, and you should have seen him, he was laden from top to bottom almost, with kit. Anyway, to

In the garden at 23 Dumbreck Road just after Don joined up

cut a long story short we did not stop for anything to eat until we got home, and then as we tucked into the remains of the Sunday joint, we tried to work out some sort of logical plan for the week. There were so many people who had asked for visits, and so much that he wanted to do, that I think he needed a couple of months instead of a week.

I think I have mentioned Don's cousin Bern, sometime or other, haven't I? Well, as it happened he was home on leave at the same time, but his was nearing the finish when Don's started, so we spent the first evening going to see him, and can those boys talk when they get together and start swapping Army stories. We rounded off the evening at my house, where Don had a few games of billiards with Dad and my brothers, and then we played cards until 1.30 or so. Don spent Monday visiting one of his married sisters, and his old friends where he used to work before he had the shop, and then met me from the office in the evening. He was a great topic of conversation amongst the other girls, who hadn't seen him since he went away, but they were disappointed because he had availed himself of the 'on leave' privilege, and gone into 'civvies'. Monday evening we went to see 'The Thief of Baghdad' which I thought was lovely. I spent the night at Don's house, and we played a few games of cards with his Mother and sister, before retiring. Tuesday, Don spent visiting once again, and also booking seats for the latest shows in town. We spent this evening with another married sister of his. On Wednesday, once again, Don went a-visiting, but he was disappointed when he called on Ernie, for he learnt that he had been called for the Navy, just a short while before, so that is yet another of the old gang gone.

On Wednesday evening, the sparks really flew. Don met me, and came home to my house. My brother's billiard table isn't a full size one, and so they decided to go up to the High Street and play a couple of games. Don said 'We'll be back at half past nine, and then I'll wipe you all up at Monopoly'. Well, it didn't work out quite like that, for a very heavy blitz started, which I first realised when I got up to get something, and the floor swayed beneath my feet. Both Dad and I said 'Gosh, I felt that one', and we dashed to the door. The sky was ablaze with fire and gun flashes. It was a painter's perfect conception of 'Hell let loose'. I couldn't help thinking of the boys being out in it, as I stood with my sister at the door, all ready in my coat and tin hat, in case any incendiary bombs should need putting out. One very near bomb sent us both sprawling in the hall, and when I got up I heard a dreadful stream of abuse coming from my sister, what she wasn't going to do to that Jerry if she got her hands on him – she had laddered her stocking. I breathed a sigh of relief when the boys came in, but they had hardly been in a couple of minutes when there was a terrific crash and a sickening sound of breaking glass. Before I knew what was happening, Don had grabbed my tin hat off my head, and with my brother close to heel, was gone into the blitz again, to investigate. Things got a little quieter later on and we were all sitting round the fire drinking a cup of Mum's sure recipe for frayed nerves, when down came another one. I had my eyes fixed on the wall, and it was incredible to see it swaying backwards and forwards. We got through the night quite safely though, but many of my colleagues at the office weren't so fortunate. They had it very badly up where your friend's friend Irene Ford lives, and before I close this letter, I will go up there and find out if she is all right.

On Thursday and Friday, as I had asked him so nicely, the boss gave me the time off, so I went to town both literally and figuratively. On Thursday we saw a show called 'New Faces' and on Friday another called 'Applesauce'. Both of these were a riot of fun, and it was heaven to go places once again. Except for the weekends, and my fire-watching duties, I haven't been out at night after about half past six, since Don went away. We had a marvellous time wandering around between shows, for the West End of London never fails to thrill me when we go up there. We were very extravagant and had a marvellous salad each for our lunch on Thursday, and all in all it was a wonderful two days. I went into the office on Saturday morning, so as not to let the work get into too much of a muddle, and on Saturday afternoon, George and Ida and my brother George came over to us at Don's house, and we had another grand little reunion. Yesterday Sook and Doris came to see us, as they were unable to come as arranged on Saturday, owing to Sook having to work all night. It seemed a lovely long day. We played cards over at Don's house in the morning, and then all came back again to my house for dinner. We had another gamble in the afternoon – Don had been looking forward to this ever since he went away, and I finished up half a crown in, which was quite good. I never mind if I lose though, for it is worth it for the fun we get out of it. Sook and Doris left at tea-time so as to be home before the black-out, and the rest of us rounded up the evening with yet more billiards and more Monopoly and more cards, and finally turned in about 2 o'clock in the morning.

Don came halfway to work with me this morning, and then went home to get his packing done. You can imagine, I am feeling very tired after my hectic week of late nights and blitz, and not a little sad that the time has come for yet one more 'Goodbye'. Life seems one long 'Hallo' and 'Goodbye' these days. Still, as Don always reminds me when I get sad and say, 'I wish you didn't have to go away again, I wish your leave was just starting', 'Every day is one day nearer the end of the war', so we mustn't wish to go back a day, or even a few minutes.

You are no doubt wondering how I have managed to type all this in office hours. Well, the truth of the matter is, I have heaps of work to do if I go and see the boss, but I didn't want to get stuck in his office in case Don rang through and I missed him.

I seem to have run short of news now that the happenings of this previous week have been told, and maybe you are already bored stiff. Maybe it doesn't seem terribly exciting to you but to us, just being together again, and having just a bit of a gay time, is certainly something to write home about, in these grave days. When I am an old, old woman, basing this on the assumption that only the good die young, I don't think I shall ever forget these last years. They have brought worry and sorrow, and not a few lines on my forehead that weren't there before, but they have also brought a deeper understanding of what really matters in life, and a sense of values that I never had before, but which I shall never be without again. So much that seemed important in the old days counts for nothing now, and daily bread, our friends, and even life itself which used to be taken so much for granted, are now the only important things, in fact, the only things that matter.

Mum and Dad are going to try and visit my little sister at Easter, but they are not going to make any plans, in case they go astray. It seems impossible to realise that I haven't seen her since last June. I bet she is getting to be grown up now, even though I still visualise her as the little tot she was, before the healthy country air had a chance to meet her.

25th March 1941

Well, I certainly feel a bit better this morning, after a nice quiet night of good sound sleep. Don rang me yesterday as promised, saying he was all packed up ready to push off. I expect the first couple of letters I get will be full of what all the other fellows did while they were away, though as he says himself, 'They couldn't have had a better time than me'. I don't seem to have much else to write about at the moment, so I will sign off, and write again soon. I haven't been up to Castlewood Drive yet, but I will let you know as soon as I do.

Cheerio for now, keep smiling,
tons of love,
  Win xxxxxx

10th April 1941

My dear Donna,
As I sit down to write this the day before Easter, I find myself strangely lacking in the true Easter spirit, and remembering with not a little note of regret all the happy Easters of bygone days.

Even last year we had a marvellous time, and most of the club boys were still here then, but now there are little more than a handful who are not wearing the King's uniform. Instead of our usual four days, we are having but one day off this year, and tomorrow, Good Friday, instead of seeing us cheering cyclists of all nationalities, yes Germans and Italians too, at the race-track, will see us all busily engaged in our job of getting on with the war.

Mum, dad and my sister are going away however. Edna has been working an extra hour and a half all this week to make up, and Dad will have to do the same, but it will be worth it for them to have a change. They are going to see my little sister, and you should see the pile of stuff they have ready to take down with them, you'd think they were going for a month instead of but four days. I am spending tomorrow night with one of my friends from the office, and unless he is lucky enough to get home, I shall be going down to see Don for the weekend. My friend Win is coming home for a brief visit to her married sister, the only member of her family still left in Eltham, the rest of them being spread all over the country and her brother in a German prison camp, so I expect I shall spend Monday with her, so I shall not be lonely while the folks are away.

By the way, whilst on the subject of Win's brother, I think I have mentioned before, she wrote to me last month and told me she had had three letters from him all at once and that he was quite well. He said an air of quiet confidence reigns over the camp and he is just as sure as always that the end of it all will be just as he always knew it would. One other thing pleased me, for it was good to know he hasn't lost his sense of humour; he said, 'I hope you had a good Christmas, I didn't go far myself as the weather was too bad.'

The most important item of news at the moment is that it is Easter and for the first time for as long as I can remember I haven't bought a new outfit. Still, I am being very Pollyannaish about it, and thinking of all the other Easters when I have put my new outfit on, and felt freezing cold all the time. This year I shall comfort myself with the warmth of my tweed swagger and little fur hat.

Wednesday, 16th April

Hello again. Sorry for the long break, but there was a rush of work waiting when we returned after having Monday off. Well, it wasn't such a bad Easter after all, the weather was good and in fact I quite enjoyed myself. Good Friday came and went, and we worked as usual, the only thing to remind us of same being our hot cross buns.

On Saturday I went to see Don, and he broke the good news to me that he had Monday off, so we were able to have a lovely weekend. We went for a long walk all day Sunday – it is beautiful country where he is stationed, and the air is so good after London. We passed one or two Canadians on our travels, on sentry go, and we were always greeted with such remarks as 'on a route march, buddy?' or 'you guys must like walking.' After I had told them that there was a certain something about one's own private route march, they heartily agreed with me that it was a fine thing, and were only sorry they couldn't join us. I got home about nine o'clock on Monday night, feeling very happy and contented that it hadn't been such a bad weekend after all, although I did have a yearning once or twice for the good old cycling days, or the roundabouts and swings.

The rest of my family thoroughly enjoyed themselves and says my sister is very well although she treats them almost like strangers which rather hurt Mum I think, but then it is quite feasible, for she is only young, and it is nearly a year now since she went away. I tell Mum that she will soon get used to us all again when she comes home, and anyway, anything is better than having her in London with us. They say they found it hard to understand what she was talking about, for she has lost all her London traits and talks terribly broad. During the school holidays the children help the farmers and think it great fun. It will be the making of a lot of those kiddies who had never left the big cities or seen a stretch of green field land before the war. The open air and hard life will make them strong and healthy as never before.

I have to register for National Service on Saturday, my age group being the first for women. I am glad they have decided to conscript women. At least it gives us some chance of equality with men. If it is good enough for the men to give up easy jobs and join up, it is good enough for us. If I have to join one of the women's forces or exchange my typewriter for a munition-making machine in a factory I shan't mind, but somehow I don't think I will have to change my job, because it is important enough for them to have to get someone else to do it, if they take me, so there wouldn't be much point in it, still we shall see. Personally I would welcome the change; even though someone has got to do office work there is something much more direct in actually making a shell or a part of a Spitfire or a tank.

17th April 1941

Phew, it is a lovely bright sunshiny Spring morning, but what a night, gosh the blighter was busy last night. The official news this morning said, 'A very heavy air raid on London and it is feared casualties are heavy', but we have yet to learn just how far this affects our own immediate circle.

All at '23' came through O.K. and I for one found my salvation in the age old recipe – work. I was on the go unceasingly until one this morning, when I said, 'Hang this for a lark' and went upstairs to bed. Most of the people at the office that are in this morning were up all night though and marvel that I could manage to sleep through it. I turned out drawers, mended stockings, cleaned shoes, did my nails, did my hair, wrote letters and a hundred and one other jobs that just kept me going. It is the finest thing out for forgetting the scream of bombs. The office is strangely empty this morning and although we have heard from a few that they are all right but are staying home to clear up the mess, there are a lot whom we haven't yet heard from. It is very funny, no matter how bad it is the night before, when the sun comes up there is always the steady stream of folks going their usual way trying to get to business even though transport is slightly out of order, and succeeding in the end too. As I walked up the street this morning I heard a pitter-patter behind me, and looking round saw one of the girls from the office; she was the first one I had seen and I was so relieved to see she was all right. We dashed up to one another, and I think I said very stupidly the first thing that came into my head, 'Are you all right?' and she gasped, 'Yes, are you?' One by one the people began to arrive, and although I won't bore you with all their tales of the night's activity, it gives you a marvellous feeling to see each face and think to yourself, 'Oh he's all right then' or 'Glad to see she's come through.' The boss said this morning to those of us who were here, 'I'm glad to see your smiling faces again, I'm glad you're here' and I made them laugh when I answered him, 'We're glad to be here too.' As I said before, nearly everyone had been up all night, so we did a most unheard of thing when everyone had said their piece and got it off their chest: we made some tea and now everyone is working again as if nothing had happened. Like every true Englishman, I always liked my cup of tea but since the war I swear by it; it is the surest way of putting yourself on your feet again and not half so expensive as brandy. By now we have heard from most of the absentees and they are unhurt, although some have had their homes bombed. There is only one girl we haven't heard from yet and it gives me a queer feeling every time I look at her desk and see the typewriter still covered. Still it is early yet and maybe we will hear soon. Mum and Dad brought some lovely flowers home with them from the country, and I brought some with me this morning, and you would be surprised what a difference they make to the office as they stand on the window sill.

Friday, 18th April

We heard with great sorrow of the very bad earthquake in Mexico last week, and I can't help wondering what kind of powers that be they are, to allow such things to happen to harmless people. A couple of healthy earthquakes in Germany wouldn't come amiss to my way of thinking. This may not be yours of course, but then your mind hasn't become warped with a mad desire to wipe out anything that is even slightly Hunnish like mine has, and I can hardly believe myself when I realise what a blood-thirsty, inhuman creature I have become.

Tuesday, 22nd April

Sorry for the long break again but this was due to yet more work and more excitement. Don came home for the weekend and on Saturday afternoon we went to see 'North West Mounted Police' which was a smashing film, quite the best I have seen for a long while. We got home about a quarter to nine and Don and my brother George had made up their minds to have a few games of snooker after we had something to eat. Whilst we were eating the siren wailed, but we didn't take any notice, until things started dropping, and we became aware that we were in for another 'Wednesday Nighter'. I was glad Don was with me, although this was a purely selfish thought for his mother needed him much more. My sister and my brother were at the front door, and Don was in the kitchen and myself in the bathroom, when he dropped a stick of four. I thought they were never going to stop, those four seemed like forty, and as each one got nearer and nearer, and I became more and more sure each time that the next one was for us. I got lower and lower on the floor. When the first one came down I just crouched behind the door, but when the second one came and was quickly followed by the others, I finished up flat on my face. After this I told my sister to take Mum down in the shelter and stay with her, but Don said the most sensible thing of all and suggested we all went down since he knew that I wouldn't go without him. There isn't anything you can do by standing at the door if an H.E. comes down; you are only endangering your life unnecessarily, and we could always hear the fire whistles if we were needed by incendiaries. Anyway despite his good intentions, neither George nor Don actually came in with us, but stood just outside the entrance to the dug-out, except for their quick skirmishes into the porch every time a bomb came down. My other brother who was out on Warden Duty came in to see us for a minute and made us laugh when he told us that he had been lying on the ground with his chin just above it when the blast of the bomb had sent the ground up and cracked him such a one under the chin. It eased up a little round about twelve and between twelve and two George and Don actually got their game of snooker in, although many a good shot was spoilt by an unpleasant visitor.

On Sunday we went over to Don's home and found that everyone there was O.K. and then went round to investigate the damage at the shop due to the Wednesday raid. It was a very bitter weekend but there was certainly a comfort in having Don beside me, for I knew that if anything happened to one of us, it would more than likely affect us both. (Poor consolation you might think but funny ideas do strike you in these times.)

Well Donna, it seems that if I don't close and post this letter now, I shall always be finding something else to say, and you will never get it. For the present then I'll say cheerio, don't worry about us, we will always be all right, and with the help your government is giving us (give Mr Roosevelt a personal thank you from me please) and our own fighting spirit, victory will soon be ours and mark the end of all this suffering. Please write soon for a letter from you is quite one of the most refreshing moments I get and I haven't heard for nearly three months.

Cheerio, Tons of love
from,
  Win

2nd May 1941

Dear Donna,

Here I am again but I should like to get a letter from you. It seems such ages since I heard. Still I must be patient; I expect one will come shortly.

We have had two good pieces of news. Firstly a cable from John telling us he has arrived safely and he is well and happy wherever he is, although naturally we don't know. The second piece of good news is that Don's sister received a letter from that French family that were so good to his brother Eric when he was in France. I think I told you about them at the time. They properly 'adopted' him and he made their house his home while he was over there. We had heard nothing from them since the collapse of France, although Don's sister, who had previously exchanged correspondence with one of the daughters of the house, wrote to them soon afterwards, telling them that if they can get away to England to come to them. A reply never came to this letter and I doubt if it ever reached them, so it was more than grand to hear from them. It was only 52 words, this being all they are allowed to write, but they said they were all well and hoped all were well here. You see, they never knew whether or not he arrived home safely from Dunkirk.

By the way I received a letter from a fellow in Illinois. Is he a friend of yours? He had my address so he must have got it from somewhere. He wanted me to find a pen pal for him. I answered his letter promising that more than likely a letter from someone over here would follow very shortly. I was pleased to hear from him. I am always pleased to get letters no matter who they be from and of course when the letter comes from another world almost, a world that doesn't know pain and suffering as this poor little island and even the whole of the other half of the world does, it comes as a tonic, refreshing as the spring sunshine.

One of the club boys, Eric, is home on leave this week and my brother is like a dog with two tails having one of his pals home again, although he does see quite a bit of Don. It will be a pity if Don isn't able to see Eric before he goes back because he missed him last time he was home and it is months since he saw him. His brother Eric (this must sound awfully confusing to you) also hopes to get home for a couple of days soon and you can bet your life we always make the most of these brief visits, for you never know how long it is going to be before the next.

I must tell you about something Mum did. You must know that the shortage of onions over here is now a standing joke. In fact, I am beginning to wonder how comedians got by, before they had the onion subject to crack jokes about. There is scarcely a Music Hall Artist who doesn't make some use of this humble friend at sometime or another. To procure an onion these days is like procuring a corner of Buckingham Palace, but personally I think it is only the fact that you can't get them that makes them so important. Who ever gave a second thought to an onion when they were two a penny? And I feel that if we never have to go short of anything more important than this before the war is over, well we shan't do so badly. Anyway, to get back to my story, in the shed at the bottom of the garden there are several bowls of old bulbs, that have been planted year after year and are now no good and only sprout leaves if planted. A few weeks ago Mother noticed that some of them were beginning to shoot in the bowl, so she planted them in the front garden but only green leaves came up, so the other evening when she was planting some fresh flowers she pulled these up again. Imagine her amazement when she found them smelling strongly of onions and found that they actually were onions. We all laughed about it but she can't imagine how they came to get there. They must have been picked up in mistake with the old bulbs ages ago because it is ages since a large quantity of onions were possessed by any one person. Anyway, now we have a few onions to eat with our summer salad but as I said before, if it hadn't been for this fluke we would have had to go without, and I don't suppose it would have cost us any sleep.

Jerry has been conspicuous by his absence for quite a while now at night (touch wood) although I expect it will come round to our turn for a tousling before very long. By the way we over here love your neutrality and are more than grateful for the way your navy is helping our poor hard-worked navy. Keep it up, and keep up the supplies of armaments and airplanes, for as Mr Churchill said, 'Give us the tools and we'll finish the job' and the sooner we finish it, the sooner the world can set about getting back to normal again. How lovely to be able to stop hating people and look for friends. D'you know, I think if every one in every other country wrote to at least one other person in every country, like we do, there would never be any wars, for everyone would have the chance to see the other fellow's point of view.

Things haven't been going so well lately and our gallant ally Greece has fallen yet another victim to the 'stab in the back' policy, but we are not down-hearted. Nothing can weaken our resolve to work and work to make the machines necessary to beat such an evil monster and we know that ultimate victory relies on our ability to 'hold on' no matter how grim things get, and you need have no fear, we'd stick like glue to our guns, and you'd see every Britisher die fighting before you'd see any Nazi conquer England.

The clocks go on another hour on Sunday and that will mean black-out time will not start till about ten o'clock and in June it will be eleven before it begins to get dark. It will be cold in the early morning for we will be two hours in front of the sun, but it will be worth it to be able to enjoy the long hours of sunshine in the summer. We will need all we can get to carry us through the winter again, and this idea of putting the clocks on is a fine way of securing it.

Did you get the book 'The Battle of Britain' I sent you quite safely? There is an illustrated edition out now and if you are interested I will get you one of these. I read in the paper recently that mails to and from America posted on certain dates had been lost from enemy action, but as I very inefficiently never make a note of the posting dates I was unable to remember whether this referred to any of mine or not so I am going to number this letter and all my subsequent letters and then you will be able to see if any are lost. You get the idea: say for instance you get this letter numbered one and the next one you get is numbered three or four, then you will know that No 2 has gone down. It is one of the many methods we use to check the safe arrival of our business letters and I am sorry I didn't think of the idea before.

5th May 1941

Monday again, but it was a smashing weekend and I am feeling thoroughly pleased with life at the moment. I went to see Don for the weekend. He has moved by the way but nothing can stop me getting to see him, and we had our usual good time. He had been feeling rotten all the week with a lousy cold but when I left him last night he admitted he felt much better. Saturday afternoon was rather cold so we went to the pictures and saw 'Arizona'. It turned out to be a lovely evening however and we went for a long walk. Sunday was a glorious day, the hottest we have had so far. So with a picnic lunch we set out for the country and spent the entire day lazy in the sun. It was even warm enough for me to take my coat off and the first time in the year you are able to do this is always an event.

Today, needless to say, is very dull and bitterly cold, but that's the English climate, and they say it's the best in the world – I wonder.

I took some snaps of Don yesterday and I will send some copies to you as soon as they are developed. I am keeping a couple of prints until next weekend, so that I can take some of him with his brother; so it may be a week or so, before they are ready.

Well Donna, this seems to be all the news for the moment. Cheerio, and if possible be good.

Tons of love,
Win

13th May 1941

My Dear Donna,
I have managed to snatch a few minutes whilst waiting for my boss

to let you know that once again we came through a very bad raid quite safely.

I think I told you in my last letter that Don's brother was coming home for the weekend (none of his family have seen him since Christmas), so Don managed to get home as well, and we had quite a family party on Sunday, with all his married sisters and their respective husbands and children. Of course the two boys talked soldiers all Saturday evening and then when my brother and all the brothers-in-law, all of them Home Guards, arrived on Sunday afternoon the conversation was still Army and it was a really funny sight to see them all drilling and mucking about out in the garden. It was the first time all the family had been together for years and Don hadn't seen his brother since some time last year when he was home on leave. We had a lovely time and I for one was sorry when they all had to disperse and return to their respective jobs of work in all different parts of the country.

Grandad Smith, 1941, in the garden of 23 Dumbreck Road

1941: Edna, Alf and Peggy (the dog) in the garden of 23 Dumbreck Road

I seem to have put the cart before the horse rather for it was Saturday night that we had our 'visitors' with their 'Br br br' droning overhead. Usually when Don comes home for the weekend he comes to see me on Saturday, spends the day with me, staying at my house for Saturday night, and then we both go over to his house and spend Sunday with his people. This week however, as his brother was expected back late Saturday evening, we went over there then and left home about ten thirty. The 'Alert' sounded when we were halfway on our journey, but it wasn't until we were just turning into the gate at Don's house that I heard the first plane and the guns started. We went in and had our supper, and by then things had got very noisy. Don and his brother took their mother and father down into the dugout and made them comfortable. It was a marvellous night, the moon was riding full and high, and the clack, clack of machine gunfire overhead told us that our fighters were up there doing their stuff. While we were watching the darting flashes across the sky Don and Eric saw one plane come down in flames, like a red ball of fire in the sky. It was too cold to stand at the door 'sight-seeing' though, and we none of us have any desire to stop a machine gun bullet or a piece of shrapnel, so we built up the fire and the four of us, Don and I, brother Eric and sister Con, made ourselves cosy.

What never ceases to make me marvel is how, when you remember all the noise and terror of the night before, everything seems to look so normal in the morning and people walk about and go about their business, giving little thought to the inconveniences of being without gas, water and electricity for a while, and having to walk around bomb craters and put up with windows that are boarded up.

20th May 1941

Sorry for the long gap but I have been on the sick list for a few days and have only just righted myself and my work again. It wasn't anything very much, just a cold with sickness, but I felt pretty low while it lasted. I think last Saturday might have had something to do with it for although I am not scared I really think that the people who are are better off, for the shock on your nervous system has got to come out somewhere, and it hits me right in the pit of my stomach, and every shock now makes me feel terribly sick.

It was a lovely weekend, bright and sunny, and as I saw Don as well this made it complete. I had knitted a new jumper, and this with the aid of a new pair of gloves, a button hole, last year's hat, and the year before that's costume, made quite a decent looking outfit to greet the sun with. As the only time I get out my glad rags these days is when I see Don, it is scarcely worth spending money buying new clothes which you are likely to lose any minute by a present from the heavens.

It is London's War Weapons Week this week and it looks as though Peace has come for everyone has got out their flags and old Coronation decorations, and it really is a tonic to see everything looking so gay. London is aiming to collect as much as all the other big cities put together and I don't really think we will have much difficulty in obtaining our objective. London, as you no doubt know, is made up of many boroughs, which are like small towns on their own, but all join one another. Eltham, for instance, is not big enough to be a borough on its own, so it is part of the borough of Woolwich. Woolwich's objective was to raise £500,000 for the week, which is an awful lot of money, but it raised £400,000 on the first day. Other boroughs have various objectives. One is aiming to buy a destroyer, another so many tanks or so many bombers, but all in all London aims at £100,000,000, which will help pay for some of those 'tools' you are letting us have. I told you we were saving for our peace party, didn't I? Well, we thought that the money must be mounting up in the tin now, so as War Weapons Week was as good as any, we are going to empty the tin this week and buy War Savings Certificates with it. Who knows, that money might pay for just that extra A.A. shell, which will bring down the last bomber necessary to end the war.

By the way, Donna, do you know the last letter I received from you was written early in January, and it certainly looks as though some of your letters have gone to the bottom of the sea? So write soon please, for I love to hear from you.

On Saturday I saw a very good film, which had a very misleading title, 'Arise My Love'. No doubt, if you have seen this yourself, you will know that it is not just another silly picture but quite an up-to-date record of events. It is rather like putting salt on the wound however, to see such recent tragedies as the sinking of the 'Athenia' and the collapse of France depicted in a purely fictitious story, but nevertheless I enjoyed.

Well Donna, I seem to have come to a full stop with my news but I'll wait a couple of days in case I remember anything important I meant to say or in case I hear from you, so cheerio for now.

By the way I hope you got my last letter where I explained the idea of numbering my letters so you can check up whether or not any get lost.

22nd May 1941

Such wonderful news. Little did I think when I finished the last paragraph saying I had run out of news that this would be the next item I would have to give you. It makes me want to tear up the rest of my letter, for the war and everything else slips into the background against this. Sit down, hold onto something tight and listen. I am going to be married on the 15th of June. Yes really, after all these years. I feel so excited, it was all so sudden, Don just wrote and said 'Let's get married' and I wrote back and said 'Yes Sir-r-r' and that's that. I am hoping to see Don at the weekend and get everything straight, for at the moment I am very much in the dark, and everyone is firing questions at me. As far as I know, he hopes to get a few days' leave, so we will have a honeymoon even if it isn't the nice long one we have always planned on. I shall be married in white, but it will not be a very elaborate affair, for although I have always enjoyed myself at other people's weddings, both Don and I prefer to have ours very quiet. I shall probably have just my sister as a bridesmaid. We will live at home, since it would be foolish to furnish a place that we can only be together in for a weekend now and then, for I must keep my job, I couldn't be idle in war time and Don too has a war on his hands. As soon as the war is over however, we will have our own little home we have always planned and everything in the garden will be lovely. There seems so much I should write about, but my brain is in a whirl, so I think I will close now and write you another letter later with all the definite news.

Cheerio now,
Yours very excitedly,
with tons of love,
      Win

There seems to be a long gap between the letters written on 22nd May 1941 and 23rd July 1941.

This means that the vital letter with all the details of my wedding on 15th June 1941 was lost.

I am therefore having to write about this day from a distance of 62 years, instead of on the spot as it were.

Our decision to get married was finally based on the fact that Don got a job on the permanent staff at Farnham in Hampshire as a Driving Instructor. I had got used to travelling at weekends, to and fro from Farnham, and it was near enough for Don to often hitch a ride home and save me the journey. Being made up to the Permanent staff meant that Don stood a good chance of being there for the duration.

As soon as the decision to get married was made, we had just three weeks in which to organise everything, so one Saturday early in June, Edna and I went out shopping armed with my savings book which contained all of £10. We bought my wedding dress, a bridesmaid dress for Edna, and a going away dress and a wool coat, all in turquoise. I also managed to buy a long white nightdress to wear under the wedding dress as a slip.

We awoke the following morning to hear that clothes were on ration forthwith. We had spent the day before more points than we would have been allowed for a whole year. Weren't we lucky?

The weather was pretty awful for the week preceding the wedding, but on Sunday 15th June, the sun shone and a heatwave started. I remember little about the wedding breakfast as such, but knowing my parents I am sure they pulled out all the stops and made it a good spread. There was a baker's shop near Don's shop, and as one retailer to another they made us a wonderful wedding cake. This at a time when brides were having to make do with a cardboard cut-out over a meagre sponge cake. Photographs were taken in the back garden and after the reception my brother George drove us to a main-line station where we caught a train to Bournemouth. We booked into a hotel in the town centre, and ate most of our meals in a restaurant called 'Bobbies' atop the largest department store in the town. Don had just three days' leave. Of course we couldn't get on the beach as this was mined and covered with barbed wire, but someone had had the wit to shift a vast amount of sand up on to the prom, and put out deck chairs, so there we sat most of the day, gazing out over the barbed wire to the sea, enjoying the sunshine. Whilst we were walking along the prom Don stopped to take a picture of me standing outside a boarded-up refreshment kiosk, and almost had his Box Brownie confiscated by an efficient policeman. Don was wearing civvies, but I think we managed to convince the policeman he was in the forces and on his honeymoon, and not a spy.

Just a week later on Sunday 22nd June 1941 Hitler marched into Russia, and the whole situation changed dramatically. What affected us the most was the ruling that from then on no one under the age of 30 and physically A1 could be on the permanent staff. Within weeks Don was transferred north and gone were his cosy job and our weekends of meeting up, in one fell swoop.

In the P.S. dated 6th August, at the end of the letter which started on 23rd July 1941, I mention that I had just spent a weekend with Don and would write about it more fully later. Again, many letters must have been lost for there is another gap between 23rd July 1941 and 25th November 1941.

Again I have to rely on memory. However, I remember very clearly that weekend away for August Bank Holiday. I remember queuing for the ticket for the train, queuing for the train and then standing for hours in the corridor before arriving at my destination, which was Harrogate in North Yorkshire. Don met me at the station late on the Saturday evening, and I had to travel back home on Monday early so that I could go to work on Tuesday.

Writing this now from a distance of 62 years, it seems so strange that for the past 20 years my daughter has lived in Harrogate. Don and I drove many times up the M1 to visit her (who ever heard of a motorway in 1941?), and I well remember when newly widowed I made my first trip to Harrogate by train, how short the journey seemed, for that long-ago journey was still seared on my memory.

Another family event that was not reported due to the lost letters was the arrival of my brother Alf's second son, David, on the 8th October 1941. A brother for little 2-year-old Alfie. Both these boys are now into their sixties.

Just two days after the happy news of young David's arrival on 8th October 1941 came the sad news of Grandad's death on 10th – he was 79.

23rd July 1941

My Dear Donna,

I have delayed writing to you sooner, because I had hoped that I should be able to send you the promised wedding photographs, but as yet they haven't put in an appearance.

Your parcel and the newspapers arrived about a fortnight ago, for which I offer you my sincerest thanks. The panties were lovely, and most acceptable, especially in these rationed days. I am firing away with my stripy blanket, for I want to use it for a bedspread while I am on my own, then my best gold one can come into its own when Don is home, and in the happier days that lie ahead. The rust and green wool consisted of such large quantities, it seemed a waste to use them for a blanket of odd wool, so I am going to have a go at transforming these into a bolero of rust and green squares, with a green border. It sounds all right in theory, but I have yet to see how my idea will work out in practice. Anyway, how proud I shall be, if I can flaunt it before envious eyes with the fateful words 'no coupons'. By the way, whilst on the subject of wool, I had occasion recently to use a skein of wool which you sent me last Christmas, and inside the label, I found Christmas

Our wedding day, 15th June 1941, outside the church

Our wedding day, 15th June 1941, in the garden at 23 Dumbreck Road: (left to right) Don's Dad, Don's Mum, Edna, Don, Win, George, Dad, Mum

Greetings from Mrs. A.H. Matthews, 305 N-5, Lamar, so, although it is rather late in the day, may I ask you to please be good enough to thank her for me. She must have thought me very ungrateful not to have acknowledged her gift before, but naturally, until I removed the label, I hadn't the slightest idea there was anything inside it. I must certainly pay her a visit when I come, and then I can thank her personally.

The newspapers caused much amusement amongst my friends, and even I found it hard to believe that such utter rot ever flowed from my pen. Reading them now, in the light of experience, and when time has erased most of the details, and left those far away days and nights of 'Blitz' nothing but rather dim memories, it seems hard to realise that all those things actually did happen. If I had not recorded them on paper at the time like I did, I should have been helpless to do so now, for until I read those papers, most of the contents of my previous letters had completely gone from my memory. How we laughed at the one that recalled our foolishness in walking home through the shrapnel carrying the one and only tin hat, because neither would wear it, and it was really amusing to hear the little gasps of 'I remember that', and the chuckles against ourselves when we were reminded of how an Air Raid used to

June 1941: on honeymoon in Bournemouth

send us scurrying for shelter. To think that I ever wrote such drivel to you amazes me, and the only excuse I can find for myself is that in nearly every case those letters were written immediately after the bad 'Blitzes', and they must have unconsciously conveyed my rage, indignation, and frame of mind at those moments, or they would never have been written.

I am feeling a little lost at the moment, for Don has been moved further away, not out of the country, but far enough to make his weekend visits home, and my visits to him, absolutely out of the question. I have yet to fully realise what this means, for I have been so much luckier than most of my friends up till now that I never stopped to think what it was like for those who only saw their husbands or boy friends once now and again, when a brief seven days' leave became due. We are having August Bank Holiday Monday off this year though, so with the advantage of the extra day, I shall be able to go and see him for this weekend. After this I must content myself with waiting for his next leave to become due, which is a very long way off, and hoping against hope that something will happen to bring him nearer home. Please don't think I am moaning, I realise that I am still very much luckier than many.

One of the girls has had good news today. Her sailor boy friend, who was wounded and has been in hospital abroad, is now home. She hasn't seen him for two years, so you can imagine how excited she is.

Yesterday evening I went to the pictures with a friend from the office, who also has a husband stationed a long way off, and although we had a good time, and enjoyed the programme very much, there is always that little something missing when Don isn't there, and I don't think I shall ever get used to going places without him. The pictures were very good, 'That Uncertain Feeling' with stodgy Melvyn Douglas, and Deanna Durbin's 'Nice Girl?' I do so love her voice, and her rendering of 'There'll Always be an England', at the end, was lovely. Maybe you didn't hear this, for I imagine this was tacked on at the end for our benefit. All in all it wasn't a bad evening, and we rounded it off with a slap up supper when we got home, as I spent the night with her. Her mother-in-law who shares house with her had gone away for a couple of days, so she spent the previous night at my house.

24th July 1941

Quite the most exciting thing recently was Quentin Reynolds' postscript to the nine o'clock news one Sunday a few weeks back. I don't know whether you heard about this, but in case not, even though I cannot hope to make it sound half so good in plain black and white as he did over the air, I will give you a brief outline of it. He was supposedly reading a letter to Doctor G, whom he met some years ago in Germany, and here are a few of the things he told him. Firstly about Hess, 'We American journalists, doctor, have our own ideas as to how to deal with Hess. We would like to see him thrown by parachute over Berlin, but of course, we should also require the job of folding the parachute. Now don't get us wrong doctor, we're only neutrals.' About us (your country and mine) 'The Americans and the English only disagree on one subject, doctor. The English drive on the left hand side of the road, and the Americans drive on the right hand side, but that won't worry us, for the road to Berlin is a broad one, and we'll go swinging along together, the English on the left hand side and the Americans on the right hand, and we'll be seeing you. Maybe not this summer, or next fall, but we'll be seeing you and when we do, we're warning you to be in very good health.' If you didn't hear him, nothing I can say can convey the feeling, and the sneer in his voice, that captured the imagination of everyone. Speeches won't win the war, who should know that better than we, but propaganda of this kind is very easy to take, and entertaining too.

It is a lovely day, and it looks as though the good weather has come back, it has certainly been a marvellous summer so far. The June that broke all records at the beginning for being the coldest for many years changed on our wedding day, and finished up by smashing all the heat wave records for June or any other month. After about a month of the continual heat, we had just about had enough, for it seemed to sap every ounce of energy out of you, and everyone was feeling a bit worn down. Now, after a week of rather cooler weather, it looks as though the sunshine is returning.

Phyllis is home. It would take a very long while to go into all the details as to how and why, but it seems like old times to have her back. I hadn't seen her for over a year, but she doesn't seem to have changed very much in that time, except for her speech. She says 'they' for 'them' or 'those', and 'us', for 'we', and she talks in a sing-songy sort of voice gradually going a bit higher up the scale as the sentence continues. Imagine what it sounded like when whilst we were going home on the bus the other evening a shrill voice piped up 'Is us going home the same way as us did when us came?' – I ask you. Still I expect after a few months at home, she will soon get back into her normal way of talking, but at the moment it is causing us much amusement.

My girl friend Win was home last weekend, and we had quite a time jawing away nineteen to the dozen as is our usual wont when we meet after a long while. All her former London friends are now married, and I think it adds to her 'out of it' feeling, being so far away, and realising that when she does come home everything will be so different. Still, if the war lasts some while yet, and though we hope it won't, we must be prepared for the fact that it might, she may also be joining the clan.

25th July 1941

I was right about the heat wave. It is hotter than ever today, all my clothes are sticking to me, and I feel fit just to plunge into a cold bath. Have you ever tried this? I felt just the same way a couple of weeks ago, and in spite of the jeers from the rest of the family, I calmly filled the bath with cold water, but it was no good, I couldn't face it, I had to turn the hot water on, just enough to take the chill off. I hoped no-one would hear the tap running, but a joyful 'So you couldn't take it' from the other side of the door, proved that my weakness hadn't gone unnoticed.

Yesterday evening I went with Don's mother and sister to the local theatre and saw quite a good comedy play, straight from town, called 'Good Men Sleep at Home'. Sounds all right, doesn't it? It was screamingly funny and I thoroughly enjoyed it. These sort of plays usually have a good run in town with well known actors and actresses, and are then put on in the suburbs later by a local company of players, the only difference being a very much lower price to pay for the seats.

Enclosed with this letter is a little birthday gift I hope you will like. It is a little late I know, but these flowers are made by a friend of my sister, who sends all the proceeds to the Red Cross or the Spitfire Fund, and as her books are crammed full of orders, I have had to wait for mine. By the way, Eltham had a Spitfire week last week, a week much after the same style as War Weapons Week, but this one only affected Eltham, and not the whole of London, of which Eltham is but a very small part. Anyway, we raised enough money to buy our second Spitfire, so that wasn't bad going. There were dances and competitions, stirrup pump relay races, and more or less all the fun of the fair, so we killed two birds with one stone, by having a good time, and helping the war effort at the same time. Don's sisters have been making some button holes of suede, and they raised quite a bit of money for the Red Cross, by selling these at a local dancing display, all the proceeds of which went to the Red Cross.

I have just managed to secure a tin large enough to contain the top of my wedding cake, so I am going to pack this up carefully, seal it down, and hope that it won't be long before we are cutting it at our Peace Party. Our Peace Party money box is growing heavier week by week, gosh won't we have a do.

28th July, 1941

Wonders will never cease, we actually had an Air Raid last night, just when we were beginning to forget what a siren sounded like. The barrage seemed heavier than ever, and I just couldn't get to sleep. I had a funny feeling inside me, as though I was hungry, and no matter how I tried, I couldn't get to sleep. I heard the rattle of tea cups downstairs, for Mum and Dad were up, they can't rest upstairs if it is very noisy. I went down and had a cup of tea, and amazed Mum by tucking in to bread and butter and biscuits at half past three in the morning. I went back to bed but it was no good, the sick feeling still persisted, and it was long after the 'All Clear' that I finally dropped off. Phyll wasn't a bit scared and seemed more annoyed by the fact that I kept her awake because she could hear me talking downstairs, than anything else. How anyone could compare even my voice with the terrific bangs and crashes and the vibrations that seem to lift the house out of its very foundations, I don't know. The mobile guns are the worst, for they pop up at unexpected times in unexpected places, and make you jump out of your skin. They all sound as though they are in your own back garden, the noise they make. The baby didn't like it. It was all right last year when he was younger, but he is old enough now to be frightened by bangs and flashes. Still, he is going away next month, and although he will be better off, we shall all miss him very much.

Despite the fact that I have just had a really hearty mid-day meal, I still feel dreadfully sick, I guess I must have caught a chill last week. One day it was so hot, I was taking nearly all my clothes off, and the next it would be cold enough for a heavy coat.

As you can imagine, I am getting very excited at the prospect of going to see Don next weekend, for it is the longest time we have gone without seeing each other since he joined up.

Well Donna, there is very little else of interest to write about. Hoping to hear from you soon,

I'll close with tons of love,

Win xxxxxxx

...-...-...-...-...-...-...-...-...-...-...-...-...-...-...-
V...-V...-V...-V...-V...-V...-V...-V...-V...-V... V...-V...-V...-

[*This letter ends with the letter V in Morse Code repeated across the page. At this time we were all very conscious of the 'V for Victory' sign. Brave people in occupied Europe took great risks to listen to news broadcasts from the BBC and the dot-dot-dot-dash signal assured them that they were tuned to the right station.*]

6th August 1941

Hallo again, so sorry about the delay, but I have been waiting for time to tie up the parcel, which I hope arrives intact.

I saw Don at the weekend, and had a marvellous time, but more about that in a later letter.

25th Nov. 1941

Dear Donna,

I wrote to you a couple of weeks back, but I was in such a hurry to get it posted in time for Christmas, I didn't really give you much news, so here goes.

Edna goes into the W.A.A.F.s tomorrow and I must confess to a tiny feeling of envy. I'd love to be starting out on something new like that, although the Navy would be my choice. Still I may get my chance yet, for I am thinking that all us younger girls will soon be released, even though we are reserved. At the moment though I couldn't leave if I wanted to. I'm tied down to this desk, till the Powers that be decide otherwise.

Do you remember I told you some while ago that we were practising for a Stirrup Pump competition? Well, Dumbreck Road entered two teams, and believe it or not, our two teams came first and second out of the whole borough. It sure was a proud day for Dumbreck Rd. and the silver cup prize is being presented at a dance early in the New Year. There'll be high jinks that night, I'm thinking. Still our teams deserved to win, for not only were they very good, but they put in lots of time practising. Our ladies team was not entered, as Dad didn't think we would stand a fair chance against men, but after he saw the others at the camp, he reckoned that our ladies team could have beaten the others also. Incidentally our first team went in first and beat all the previous competitors, and then when our second team went in later, it knocked spots off our first team, although our first team was still second best. (Very complicated sounding all this, I hope you get the gist of it.)

Yesterday Edna took Mum up to town to see Vic Oliver's latest show 'Get a Load of This' and they both thoroughly enjoyed it, except for the fact that Edna, scatterbrain that she is, forgot to take any money. Mum, not knowing this, spent what she had booking up some seats for her and Dad to see another show on Saturday. Anyway, they had some lunch first. Edna had enough for this and was naturally thinking Mum had some on her, and promised to introduce Mum to a hamburger when they came out. They got into the theatre and imagine their mortification when they found they had only 3d between them, not even enough to buy a programme. They felt such fools when they had to refuse, but saw the funny side of it, although it made it difficult to follow the show without one. When they came out of the theatre about five, a hamburger was naturally out of the question without any money, so they made straight for the station, as luckily they had bought return tickets. When they got there they learned that they couldn't use these tickets till half past six, as the rush hour was restricted to workers only (which is quite right, says she, being one of them, eh?). They were properly in a mess now, for had they had any money they could either have gone and had something to eat or come home by bus. As it was, they were faced with an hour and a half's wait, so they decided to start walking to kill time, and catch the train further down the line. They looked at their 3d and tossed up as to whether they should spend it having a 1½d ride each on the bus, or spend a penny each, at the place one generally spends a penny. We were in fits at home when they told this tale, especially when they said they decided on the latter course. Mum said that all the while they were walking Edna kept saying, 'I've got plenty of money at home,' as if that helped, but anyway they had a good time. Still, as Mum says, Edna will have to cure herself or be cured of her scatterbrains now that she is in uniform.

Our local warden's post had a meeting last night, and Dad agreed on my behalf that I should run the Savings group for the road, and at the same time canvass them for the 'Aid to Russia' fund which has been running some time, and closes at the end of the year. I already collect the Red Cross Penny-a-week at the office, so it looks as if my father intends to see that I don't have any time on my hands with which to muse on my grass widowhood.

Doris and the babies are coming home on Saturday as David's eyes are bad again. (I told you he had an operation when he was a week old, didn't I?) The country may be safer, but I think he will be better off when he gets treatment from a proper London hospital. Poor little mite, it seems so terrible to think of a tiny baby with bad eyes. This certainly is one point against having children in war time. It's bound to leave its mark somewhere. Doris spent night after night down in the dug-out through some of the worst of the raids, before he was born, and although she didn't show it, it must have had some effect on her. I don't mind confessing that many's the time my tummy turned over, and I'm young and in the best of health.

4th December 1941

Hallo again there. Sorry for the long break which, as my best business voice is so used to saying, was due to 'pressure of business.'

Well, it's been quite a week. Edna has now been in the Air Force over a week, Doris and the babies are home, and I have learnt that I am classed as an immobile woman, in this conscription bill.

Still, one thing at a time. Edna first. We had a letter saying she had arrived safely, but as the place she went to first was only a depot where they are rigged out with uniform and kit, we expect to get another when she is settled at her training depot. All her 'civvy' clothes came home yesterday, so she must have her uniform by now. Old Peggy, the dog, misses her so, and when Mother undid the parcel she knew the coat and her tail started wagging, and off she went all over the house to look for her.

David is sweet, but naturally being so young he is mostly sleeping and not to the age yet when you can really get acquainted. Alf, on the contrary, is growing up fast, and is a proper little boy now. When he went away, he was very noisy, always up to something, and could only say a few words, but he is quieter and more serious now, although he is a real little tough guy and looks as though he will always be able to hold his own with the other boys. He talks quite a bit too, with quite longish sentences sometimes, and although he didn't remember any of us, he is slowly beginning to get used to us all again now. He loves David, takes all his toys to show him, and says in such a sweet voice 'Look David' or 'Hallo David', and kisses him. He certainly belies everything I said about war-time babies, for he is a fine, sturdy little chap.

The new conscription bill has been the talk of the week, and as far as women are concerned the gist of it seems to be conscription to the forces for women between 18–30, single women, that is. The married women are classed as either mobile or immobile. If your husband is in a reserved job and you have no children under 14 you are mobile, and although not liable for conscription into the forces, liable for conscription into war work, which may mean being sent away from home. If on the other hand you have children under 14, or your husband is in any of the armed forces or merchant navy, you are immobile, and not liable to either conscription or being sent away from home, although you are liable to part-time war work. Well, with Don in the army I fall into this class, but I am already doing a full-time war job in a reserved occupation, so it seems that even if I were unmarried, I still wouldn't be liable for conscription anyway. I am glad Edna volunteered, for this new call-up would include her, as she is just eighteen, and it is better to be a volunteer than a conscript, for you can get more or less where you like, and choose your own job, provided you are suitable. There is one thing about being in the Forces, the actual job is a fine life for anyone, but off-duty miles from home life is what you make it, and for the single girls this means dances and pictures and plenty of escorts, but that kind of life wouldn't be much fun for me, as I wouldn't want to be out dancing, not without Don, and the prospect of spending every evening off duty alone in a billet doesn't present a very happy picture. Being at home though, it is different. There is so much I can do, and although I don't go out a lot, staying in by your own fireside isn't such a bad prospect. Edna will enjoy herself though. She's only young (hark at me, I'm only twenty-one, although I feel ninety sometimes; if only Don were home, I'd show them whether I was still young or not) and full of life, and terribly keen. So for me, it's just the same old grindstone, with perhaps more work when the single girls go, although as I said before, I don't think even the single ones from our office will be called, as they are already doing war work.

Don, 1940: The 'boy' who went into the army

Wonder of wonders, Don is still here, although I haven't seen him since he went back. Every day he still writes just as before, and I can hardly believe that it is true, that he hasn't gone yet. He is going to write to you by the way; apparently the idea came to him, maybe he thinks you get too much sob stuff from me, as I'm nearly always either happy because he's home, or sad because he's gone away, and need a man's point of view, still you'll see when he writes.

Last night a fellow grass widow from the office and I went off to the pictures together. I still can't get used to this going out alone, and feel like an old maid for the evening. Still it was a very good programme, Joan Bennett in 'She Knew All the Answers' and Ann Southern in one of her Maisie pictures 'Cash and Carry'. They were both light airy pictures that take you out of yourself and I found myself giggling away at quite petty things.

I expect it will be a very lonely Christmas this year, as we are having just one day's break from work, and none of the boys will be home. What a far cry from those wonderful parties of ours in the old days when the whole house went haywire for two or three days, and laughter and fun were the order of the day. Don wasn't home for Christmas last year and I had hoped that maybe he would be this year, still miracles do happen.

I am sending you some newspapers as promised, and I hope they arrive safely. Some of the newspapers are general ones by the way and others are just local ones, with not a lot of interest in them. The story of the woman who got the B.E.M. for bravery when a ship on which she was stewardess was sunk by an enemy raider is interesting though, for she lives in the house almost opposite. It really brings it home to you when you hear stories like this of people you know.

I made Don some cakes last weekend and I have yet to receive the verdict from him. They laugh, and tell me I shall be in a quandary now, for if I don't hear, I shall not know whether it is because he has gone abroad, or because my cooking has done its worst. Still I'm not as bad as all that, and there is certainly one thing about a soldier, anything and everything tastes good that comes from or has any connection with home, even though in 'civvy street' he may have been terribly fussy.

Well, Donna, I have racked my brain, but cannot think of anything else very interesting to write about. The war goes on. The Russians and Germans are wiping each other up in the East; British and Germans are doing the same in Libya. They've sunk our 'Ark Royal' and we're sinking their convoys in the Mediterranean. Your ships are now going to cross the Atlantic, Japan is stirring up trouble in the Pacific. What a mad crazy world this is. Will things ever get back to normal again? I sometimes wonder what the end of it all will be. It will be victory for us, I know, I've never doubted that, but what a price, all the millions of lives that are being sacrificed. If their sacrifice is not to be in vain, those of us who come through it all, must spend the rest of our lives repairing the damage of these mad years. We've got to make sure it can't happen again. The world just can't stand all this upheaval at regular intervals every twenty years indefinitely.

A letter from you would be most welcome you know. That promise I made for you of one a month hasn't materialized yet, but I'm still hoping. Tell me all about your new life at college, won't you, I'm longing to hear.

9th December 1941

Hallo again,
I have been holding the newspapers and my letter up at home for a couple of days, so as to really do them up properly when I get a free minute, and then things have certainly got weaving since I last signed off.

Last night we listened to President Roosevelt's formal declaration of war on Japan, after the dastardly bombing of the Pacific Isles. How our hearts went out to those poor souls who lost their lives in this sudden new form of brutal attack. What a shock it must have been to them too, for Honolulu and those South Sea Isles always present such a picture of peace and security. It seems wicked for them to have been bombed. Still it was wicked for Coventry to be bombed, and Plymouth and Rotterdam, and Belgrade, to say nothing of dear old London, and I guess too it is wicked for us to bomb Berlin etc., but I can't really feel that anything we do to them is wicked enough, they are so black-hearted.

As soon as I heard the news I thought of you, but was relieved to realise that you are fairly in the middle of the continent, and therefore the danger of air raids is practically nil – let's hope so anyway. Maybe it won't affect your life very much – I sincerely hope not, for I have had enough of it myself to wish to spare anyone else.

Anyway, from President Roosevelt's speech it was evident that you are as determined to smash up these violators of human decency as we are, and as confident that the end could never be anything else but absolute victory.

We over here used to get a trifle riled sometimes when you seemed so slow to act, so slow to learn from our past mistakes, but that's all over now, we won't get riled any more. We're with you, as we are with the Russians, and all the other free men, who form the league of nations in these islands with you, till we've all won through, with you till peace is with us again, and yet again after that when we get down to getting this war-weary world back on its feet again.

Hoping to hear from you soon,
I'll close with tons of love,
    Win xxxxxxx

Dvr. D. Wyatt,
82nd/l3th A/Tank Regt.R.A.
c/o G.P.O. Hull.

1.12.41

Dear Donna,
Having on many occasions enjoyed reading your letters to Win, I thought it was about time I wrote a few words of appreciation.

First, let me ask you to excuse the scrawl but at the moment I am writing under difficulty. I am doing my weekly turn of guard, and as there are two of us writing on this small rickety table, I have some excuse for the bad writing.

Guard is a 24-hour duty, each one doing two hours on, four hours off, and then two hours on again. While actually patrolling you guard the vehicles, watch for bad black-outs in the billets, and challenge anyone who approaches your beat and who appears to act suspiciously.

As you may notice, I am at present stationed in Hull, which as you may know has suffered several bad blitzes. In spite of this though the same cheerful spirit prevails – in fact I think every raid increases rather than decreases the determination of the people to see it through to our certain victory. Make no mistake about it, we don't doubt for a moment the successful conclusion of this terrible mess, which was not of our asking.

As I write our boys in Libya are doing very well but this is only the prelude and when we are good and ready (there will be no half-hearted measures this time) we shall give 'Adolph' more than he ever dreamed possible.

Naturally I cannot give you any details about this Anti-Tank Regt to which I now belong, but I would like to try and tell you how effective our guns are. Sunday we were on the firing ranges for practice and one of our chaps fired 15 shots in 45 seconds scoring 14 direct hits on a moving tank (I hope this passes with the censor's approval). We are all trained in the use of small arms such as Bren guns, Tommy guns, rifles etc. Then of course we get the usual route marches, cross country runs and P.T. (Physical Training). All these are of the 'kill or cure' variety and you can take it from me that by the time you have finished you have reached as near to perfect physical fitness as you are ever likely to do.

I have gone in for the transport side of the problem. About a week ago now I had a Driver Mechanics test. This consisted of various jobs such as decarbonising a lorry, stripping a back axle to replace a broken differential, rectifying faulty steering etc. If I pass (and I have a fair idea that I did) I will be put in charge of the Troop's lorries, and it will be my job to effect such minor repairs as are necessary to keep the lorries in running order.

Well, it will soon be 10 o'clock, which is my turn to go on, 10 till midnight, so I suppose I had better get ready and go out in the cold. Before I started writing, I thought I had a lot to tell you, but now I find there is not so much I can write that will not be censored. Perhaps while I am out for a couple of hours I will be able to think of something else of interest.

2.12.41

Hallo again — many hours have elapsed since I broke off. As is usual, things didn't work out quite according to plan. When I came off at mid-night I was feeling cold and rather tired, so I decided to catch a couple of hours' sleep before I went on again at 4 o'clock. Since then there has been the usual routine to carry on, and it is now after dinner, so I have a couple of hours to spare before I do my last duty.

I had another letter from Win this morning — she keeps me very well supplied with the latest news from home — and she, like me, is anxiously waiting the day when I am home again for good. You would be surprised how grand it is to do the ordinary everyday things of life, which normally in peace time you don't appreciate. Just sitting in an armchair, wearing slippers, shaving in hot water, sleeping between sheets and on a soft mattress, and all the other common place things which we so easily take for granted. Don't think I am 'ticking' (an Army expression for grumbling or grousing), far from it — we could be a hell of a lot worse off than we are now.

I think Win has told you of our intention to visit America if we possibly can. No doubt it will be sometime after the war before this is possible, because apart from waiting for demobilisation I shall naturally have to pay some attention to my shop which my sister is so successfully carrying on for me.

Reading this, you might say to yourself 'He writes as if the war is over already' — well as I said before the result is a foregone conclusion and without wishing to appear over optimistic and leaving out the 'wishful thinkers' I can honestly tell you that there are many of us who believe that it will be finished within six months.

Well, I guess that will have to be about all for now. Once again I ask you to excuse the alterations and writing — I have had so many interruptions that it is nearly impossible to concentrate.

So cheerio for the present, good health and good luck to yourself and family.

Yours sincerely,
    Donald Wyatt.

P.S. I hope I have spelt your name correctly — I only have your address with me.

1942

16th January 1942

My Dear Donna,

At long last I have found time to write to you again. It seems such ages since I did, but I just haven't had a minute to spare, for as fast as you finish one job at the office, another crowds in on you, so much so, that I sometimes wonder whether I am coming or going.

Christmas came and went before we hardly knew anything about it. We spent the day just quietly at home, but Boxing Day saw us back at the old grind, still with the Christmas spirit in our systems, even if it was coupled with a slightly thwarted feeling, that we'd been done out of the one excuse of the year to go really gay. For the second Christmas, Don wasn't home, but he made up for it, by coming home for 48 hours the following weekend. This was the first time I had seen him for a couple of months, so you can imagine what a weekend it was. Incidentally the original arrangement I wrote about before seems to have been cancelled, and that is why he was still here and able to get home for a few hours. I'm not kidding myself though, for it won't be long now, before that final (final till the end of the war, that is) break must come, but I cling to each week that goes by, and never cease to thank my lucky stars for being so good as to keep him with me this long. Of course, he might just as well have been a million miles away these last couple of months, for all I've seen of him, but the knowledge that he is still on this side of the water, seems to give you some sort of hope, even if you don't see him.

He came in about 7 o'clock on Saturday, dirty and grimy, tired and hungry, but he soon hopped out of his uniform, washed his hair, had a good bath, a change of underclothes, and a good meal, and felt to quote his own words 'human again'. We went over to see his mother on Sunday, and actually didn't do very much with the weekend – we couldn't really for time was so short. He was there, home again for a few hours, and that's all that seemed to matter. I went to the station with him when he went back, and of course as usual the train was packed with returning troops. We walked along the whole length of the platform, and at last spied a seat in the very last carriage. He hopped in quickly to put his respirator on the seat to bag it and then come back, but he had no sooner got in, when the train started to move. I hadn't kissed him goodbye or anything, and I was just conscious of saying out loud to nobody in particular, 'It's going'. I looked up and saw Don tearing along the corridor, banging open a window, and in a matter of seconds he was leaning out and almost dragging me along the platform. I just heard him yell his familiar, 'Chin up, be seeing you soon, darling' as I landed my feet breathlessly back on the platform again. I waved and waved until the little figure suspended from the window was out of sight, then gulping back that persistent lump that will come to my throat on these occasions, turned on my heel, and ran and ran without stopping till I was out of the station and back in the road again.

It always gives me a funny feeling in the pit of my stomach to go back to our room after he has gone too, for whilst I am on my own, just using it for sleeping, as I am out at work all day, it is the model of neatness, never a speck of dust or a thing out of place, but when Don comes home it seems to come to life. Suddenly there are suits hanging from the side of the wardrobe, ties and collars wound round the books, and the dressing table is littered with empty cigarette cartons, combs and old letters. Socks and shoes seem to be everywhere, and the cut-glass ash tray, which is usually just polished, comes into its own, and is filled with tobacco ash. Then, when he has gone back again, I am faced with the job of folding and putting away, and my mind is filled with the thoughts as to how long it will be this time, before they come out again, but when it is all done and the room is back to normal again, some of the hurt goes, and I become reconciled to this 'half-living' of which I have had so much practice these last couple of years.

Edna loves the Air Force, and wouldn't change it for anything now, she says. She has passed the first stage of her training, i.e. marching, drilling, saluting etc., and is now well under way on her training for her special job. It is quite a long course, with a pretty stiff exam at the end, but if she passes this, she will not only have a very interesting and instructive job, but she will have the satisfaction that she is doing a real man's job, and really hitting back directly. When she finishes her training, she will get some leave before being posted on her new job, and we have decided that if by any chance she and Don can get home together, we are going to have a party to make up for Christmas, for she wasn't home either. Of course it's a very faint hope, and nothing short of a miracle can make it come true, but there's nothing like hoping. Incidentally our peace party money, which we have been saving week by week, has now reached over £10, and although we all hope it doesn't have the chance to grow much more before it is spent, it isn't a bad effort, and we'd have a simply wonderful time on this amount you can bet.

I'm afraid though, much as we hope for it, peace party days are still very far distant. Everything seems to be in such a muddle and even though we know that after all is over and done, right will triumph in the end, after two and a half years of war, we will not be sorry to get it over. Sometimes I do see a chink of light in the distance, that gives me hope, and then something happens, and we are back in the blackness again, still struggling hard to get to the light. That's one thing though, we'll never stop struggling, until that chink of light becomes a blaze, and we really see the end in view, we'll never stop working and as we were tried once and not found wanting, so, when the time for us to be tried again comes, we will not let down those who rely on us and have faith.

How does it feel to be an Ally? Not very much different I suppose, for although our two countries may not have seen eye to eye on some things, we have always been of the same mind when it came to the real fundamentals.

23rd January 1942

So sorry for the long break but I just haven't had a minute's breathing space for the past week.

I am going to stay with one of Don's sisters straight from the office tomorrow, and will stay there for the whole weekend and come straight to work from her house on Monday. This means that I have got to dash home from work tonight, and do my savings group collecting in the black-out, instead of Saturday afternoon as usual. In addition I have to iron Don's washing and get it packed up and posted off, get together the few things I shall need for the weekend, and have a bath, so as usual I shall be dashing around all evening. The day I get the chance just to have a quiet evening at home in which to knit and read I shan't know what to make of it, for these days I am always out, either visiting, doing my canteen work, collecting savings or Red Cross, but it's the way I like it. I never have any time to stop and think.

We are all walking about today looking as though we've got putty medals for we have just received our badge. All firms that are on Government work wear them for identification entering and leaving the place, and for the sake of those men who might be subjected to nasty remarks from that minority of individuals whose warped minds still tell them that any man out of uniform deserves a white feather. This is a ridiculous practice which went out of fashion with the last war, and is even more silly today when the munition makers on the home front are as vital as the soldier in the firing line. Still, as I said, there are still a few small-minded individuals about unfortunately, and I think that although the badges are mainly for identification purposes, they are also to stop this other business. These badges differ in wording, size and colour with the names of the different firms but ours is a rather large one with the name of the company in large letters and then in small letters underneath 'On National Service'.

I went to see 'It Started with Eve' last Friday and think that Charles Laughton as the lovable old man almost stole the picture from Deanna Durbin. On Saturday Mum and Dad were out so, as I had promised, I took Phyll to the pictures, 'When Ladies Meet' with Joan Crawford and Robert Taylor, which was fairly good, and another awful thing about the foreign legion with Paul Kelly, which was nothing more or less than a load of tripe. I couldn't see any sense in it.

I was a very lucky girl at Christmas and outside of having Don home, got everything that I wanted most. This was especially wonderful as most things are hard to get now. George bought me a new fountain pen and Dad a new powder compact. Both these articles are almost extinct now, so I count myself even luckier that they managed to get me these. Mum bought me an oven heat resistant glass casserole, Don's mother a powder puff and a box of chocolates (another almost extinct luxury). My friend Win bought me a set of tray cloth, serviette and tea cosy to match, to use with a 'breakfast in bed set', and a couple of my closest friends at the office also bought me presents, although owing to the difficulty of getting stuff and the coupons we cut out presents all round this year. I had two records from one girl.

My other present from the office was a marmalade jar and some cigarettes, and oh I almost forgot a silver toast rack from the boss.

It has been bitterly cold this last couple of weeks, and it takes me about half an hour to thaw out when I get home in the evenings, after spending ages queuing for a tram home. I never remember seeing so much snow about either, and although I like the look of it from the comfort of a warm room, it isn't so good trudging out in it early in the morning or late at night when I get back from the canteen. Still they're much worse off in Russia, so it isn't for us to grumble, although I for one feel the need of a little sunshine sometimes. Often on a cold and miserable day we fall to talking about our previous summer holidays, the sand and the sea, the sunshine, sea bathing and sun bathing, walking and cycle rides through the country, picnics, ice-creams, and moonlit happy days.

I've just read this through and it doesn't seem to make much sense, but you must forgive someone who hasn't anything really interesting to write about. Now you for instance, you are the one, you should be able to write me pages and pages of interesting news, so how's about it eh?

For the present then, cheerio, all the best, keep your chin up,
Tons of love,
      Win

19th February 1942

My Dear Donna,

Such a wonderful surprise to get your lovely long and welcome letter and photograph, which arrived on the 17th. I was thrilled with the photograph, and it will have a place of honour along with all the others that help to make our one-roomed 'home' as we call our room, look real homelike. You certainly sound as though college life is wonderful, and although I can't ski myself, it sounded so inviting when you wrote of your wonderful times, it made me wish that I could do the same. Still, who knows, maybe I shall have the opportunity one day, when we grow rich, for next to coming to see you, I've always longed to go to Switzerland at Christmas time. What day dreams I do get, but if you don't make up your mind that sometime in your life you're going to do all the things you've always wanted to do, what chance is there of it ever coming true?

After quite a spell of uneventful jogging along the same old way, this last month has been pretty tightly packed with activity. So, it seems the best thing to do is to once again revert to the usual practice of taking things in order as they happened, although in this case, the most important will be at the end.

I think I wrote last time that Edna was expected home on leave shortly. Well, her leave has come and gone, and she is now back on the job. We were expecting her late on Friday evening, but about teatime her boy friend came round saying that she had written to him saying she would be home early. He sat and waited whilst we all had our meal, and then when it was cleared away, time rolled on, and Edna didn't come and poor old Doug (he's the latest one by the way, maybe it will be John tomorrow) just sat and sat. I was bustling around, for the previous evening I had had a 'phone call from Don, saying he had booked up, and would I go and see him for the weekend. This was the first opportunity since he was last home that he had been near enough for me to visit him during the weekend, so naturally, as soon as he moved in, he made arrangements for me to go down. I spent the evening packing up a parcel of eats to last us over the weekend, for you never know whether you are going to be able to find anywhere to get a meal on Sunday in these provincial towns, and it is not easy to get the local people to give you anything, when they have only their own rations. I finished all my jobs and wanted to get to bed early, but felt I ought to wait up for Edna, so as to just see her as I would be away for a couple of days of her leave. She eventually arrived about half past eleven, complete with kitbag, and all the usual stuff, and looked very well. For the next couple of hours we all sat round the fire, bombarding her with questions: how did she like it? what was it like? was the food good? was the work interesting? Doug made us all laugh by dressing in her uniform. He is a tall thin chap, and could just about get the coat buttoned round him, and with the hat sitting on the top of his head, he looked like a Nazi prisoner, only more pleasant. I tried her uniform on, and although they all said it suited me, still prefer the Navy. I should love to tell you all the interesting things she told us, but of course that is impossible. Suffice it to say she thinks life in the Air Force wonderful and to quote her own words 'wouldn't come back to Civvie Street for anything'. I can hardly say the same for Don though, for I know he'd come back tomorrow if only the war were over.

I went into the office in the morning and rushed away at lunchtime to catch my train, which, although it started on time, just seemed to crawl along all the way. I sat there patiently knitting and reading for a while, until my pride gave way to my hunger and I got my sandwiches out. I always hate eating in a crowded carriage, always feel I ought to pass the bag round. I felt especially so on this occasion, as my companions were a sailor, two soldiers and two airmen, off home for 48 hours' leave, and I knew it was pretty certain that none of them would have anything with them to eat on the journey. I ate in silence for a while, but at last I could stand it no longer and said in a very small voice to the airman beside me 'Would you like a sandwich?' and the moment I saw the look that leaped into his eyes I was glad I had plucked up courage enough to offer them. He munched away gratefully, whilst the others all eyed him enviously, so it wasn't long before the bag had gone all round the carriage and we were all eating and talking together. I learnt quite a bit from them all also, for apparently they were all experienced travellers on a line I knew nothing about, and they warned me that it wasn't the slightest use taking any notice of the time they had told me the train would arrive, for it was always anything between one and two hours late. I started to get worried then, for I knew that Don would wait but he had said that if he was on guard, he'd send someone else to meet me, and I couldn't imagine anyone else waiting one to two hours for a train. They tried to console me by saying that he'd be all the more pleased to see me when I did arrive etc., etc. and boy was I relieved when we finally arrived an hour and a quarter late, to see Don patiently striding up and down the platform.

He didn't mind about the train being late, oh no, and he didn't mind waiting, but as he was stationed at a village some 15 miles from the town, and the last bus had left some 15 minutes before I got there, we were in a bit of a fix. There was nothing for it though but to get on the road, and try to hitch hike, although by now it was dark, and there didn't seem to be much traffic about. Don had had something to eat whilst waiting for me, and as I was sure we would get a lift, I wouldn't bother to stop and get anything in the town. We were lucky at first: we got a car that took us a couple of miles, then a local bus from one of the neighbouring villages which took us seven miles along the road, and then forked off in the opposite direction. We started to walk along the road, it was a beautiful moonlight night, and we had so much to talk about not having seen each other for so long, that at first I didn't realise that I was tired and hungry. We trudged along quite happily for a bit, then gradually as the distance lengthened I began to get thirsty. We opened up the case and got out some chocolate biscuits. I knew they would make us more thirsty but as Don put it 'They gave us a different taste in our mouths'. It was getting on for eleven o'clock by now, and nothing had stopped to give us a lift. I began to despair, and even though Don kept assuring me that we were nearly there, I felt as though my legs just would not carry me another step.

When we came within, as we thought, about a mile of our destination, we saw an inn, the first signs of habitation we had seen along the whole road. It was after hours, but we knocked them up and explained that we had walked five miles and were very thirsty, and they told us that we had another three miles to do to get to the village. This shook me, and I just gave up, saying I was sure I couldn't possibly walk another three miles without a drink, and I think the woman realised that I wasn't feeling so good, asked us both in, gave us a drink, and let us rest for a while by the fire. We stayed until we had thawed out for a bit, for it was terribly cold and I already had Don's gloves on top of mine, and then we got out on the road again. Our luck had changed though, for as soon as we got outside, a car came along and stopped for us, and within a short space of time we had rattled off the last three miles and were outside the door of the house Don had booked a room at. Then our troubles started again, for by now it was past midnight, and Don had told them we would be along early in the evening, as we would have, had we not missed the bus, so, naturally, they had thought we weren't coming and gone to bed. We hammered on the door for quite a while, and it seemed that except for the sentry marching up and down, the whole village, civilians and soldiers alike, had been asleep for hours. After a bit the people in the house awoke, and I was soon pouring out the whole story of our journey in front of the remains of the fire in the drawing room. Whilst Don went off to the Guardroom to report, she made us a hot drink and some eats, and we soon forgot about all the trouble we had had to get there, and felt thankful for the car that had given us a lift, and tried to imagine what it would be like to be out there still trudging along.

When we awoke next morning we found that there had been a heavy fall of snow, and as it always seems to snow harder in the country than in the town, we were almost snowed up, and no buses were running through from the town. I was giving vent to my feelings as to how anyone could live in such a one-eyed place, miles from civilisation, from choice, for it was bad enough Don being there when he hadn't any say in the matter, but Don was quite happy about the snow, and hoping I would be snowed up and have to stay there a week or so. Don went on parade quite early, so I had an extra hour in bed, then a late breakfast, and spent the time by the fire until he returned. I was thanking my lucky stars I had brought some food with me, for there was nothing for it but to stay there for dinner. I had it all ready when Don returned, and after a chin-wag around the fire, we went out to see if there was any hope of a bus. The first one came through about half past three in the afternoon, which got us into the town about four. I didn't much relish catching a train back at that time, for it would probably have landed me in London in the small hours, after having been snowed up on the way, and I didn't fancy the job of getting home across London in the middle of the night, so we went and had some tea and went to the pictures. I had booked up at a hotel near the station for the night, and arranged to catch the first train back in the morning. It was a very miserable girl that said 'Goodbye' to Don as he caught the bus back, and wended her lonely way back to the Hotel. I had some supper, then set the alarm for 6 a.m. and crept between the sheets. Not a soul was up in the hotel when I left, and it seemed so queer letting myself out, and walking along the roads of a strange town in the pitch black of the early morning, but I caught the train, which luckily made good time, and I was back in the office by lunchtime. The boss was very nice about it when I explained the whole story, and although the travelling was pretty hard, I was glad I had gone, for it was worth a little bit of hardship to spend a few hours with Don, after so long.

On the following Wednesday, as it was Edna's leave, Dad had booked seats for a show in town, for himself and Mum, Edna, Phyll and me, and I thoroughly enjoyed it. It was Arthur Askey's pantomime with Florence Desmond, and I was doubled up with laughter the whole time.

It was either the fruits of laughing so much, or a cold that I caught over the weekend just coming out, but I woke up with a terrific headache on Thursday morning. I didn't pay much attention to it, thinking it would pass off when I got out in the air, but by the time I got to the office, I was alternately freezing cold and hot and dizzy. I stuck it all day, but decided that instead of staying the night at Don's mother's, as I usually do on Thursdays, I'd just call in to see her, then go home to bed. She wouldn't hear of me going home though, and said that if I sat by the fire quietly and had a game of cards as usual, I'd forget all about it, and be better in the morning. Don's father called me at getting up time, and I felt glad I had taken her advice, for I felt much better and my headache had gone, but as I stood washing myself in the bathroom my head suddenly began to reel, and I just managed to dry myself and creep back into bed. My back and my legs and arms ached all over, my headache had returned, and I felt terribly sick, and it was then pretty obvious that I was in for a bout of gastric 'flu, of which there was so much about. Don's mother was very good to me, wouldn't hear of me going out in the snow to go home, and for three days she was running up and down stairs looking after me, whilst I just lay there being sick and sick, and curling up at the very sight of food.

Mum came to see me on Saturday morning, and we arranged that I should go home if I was better by Tues or Weds, but early on Monday morning, Mum rang up to say that Don had arrived home during the night on 48 hours' leave. His brother, by the way was home on Embarkation leave, and Don had been granted 48 hours' leave to come home and see his brother before he went. He didn't know anything about my being ill, and it must have been a proper anti-climax after a tiring journey home, to arrive and find I wasn't there. He came over early though and I was almost glad I was ill, for if I hadn't been, I'd have been at work, and wouldn't have seen much of him. He spent Monday jawing away to his brother, and as his presence had made me feel better, we went home in the evening. He was due back early on Wednesday morning, and caught the midnight train from town, so imagine my surprise when in the middle of Wednesday night, I once again heard the old familiar tramp tramp of army boots up the stairs. He had arrived back on Wednesday morning from his 48 hours' leave, only to learn that he had been granted seven days' leave starting from that evening.

I was a bit wary at first, thinking of that other time he had come home unexpectedly with the news that it was embarkation leave, but he assured me it was nothing like that. I was still feeling a bit queer on Thursday, having only just started to eat again, but we went over to see his mother in the afternoon. I walked in on my own, and although they commented on the fact that I was all dressed up in my best clothes, and my best stockings, they were taken back when a few minutes later Don put in an appearance. We stayed there the night and on Friday I felt so much better that we went up to town and saw Ben Lyon, Bebe Daniels, Tommy Trinder and Teddy Brown in their latest show 'Gangway'. This really was a super show and we both enjoyed it immensely. One of the wisecracks might have appealed to you. Ben Lyon had been messing around doing something or other, and Tommy Trinder said 'All right, all right, don't get cocky, just because your country's conquered Ulster'. Incidentally, remember how I used to tell you how thrilling it was to go up to town and see all the different nationalities of soldiers etc. on leave? Well, before we went into the show, we saw yet another nation's representatives – two American soldiers, evidently spending leave in London. It is a pity they are stationed in Ireland and not here, for we'd love to make them welcome, but I expect they will find the Irish people good company.

Saturday we spent with one of Don's sisters, and Sunday at home. Don went out with my brother and played billiards and snooker in the morning, then spent the afternoon playing Dad at draughts, much to Dad's pleasure, for no-one else ever gives him a game, and cards and darts. In fact he said that by the end of the day he had played practically everything, and thoroughly enjoyed the day, I know. On Monday, it took an awful lot of effort, but I went into the office. I had to go for I had been away over a week, and although Don was home, I was feeling better, and didn't want the work to pile up too much. I gave all the girls much pleasure watching me take my medicine which is horrible stuff, but I am pleased to say that it must be doing me good, for if I don't make a pig of myself and eat too much, I can now eat normal food again without getting a pain after it. On Monday we spent the evening with Don's mother, Tuesday we went to see 'Sergeant York' and on Wednesday, his last evening, we stayed home. I don't think I have seen a film for many a month to come up to the standard of 'Sergeant York', I thought it was really super, but then it couldn't very well have been anything else, with Gary Cooper as the star.

20th February 1942

Don went back yesterday, and although I feel a bit miserable and a trifle lost, knowing that he won't be there when I get home tonight, it seemed a nice long leave, for having those two days, then going back just for one, and coming home again, makes it seem as though he was home all last week as well as half of this. Goodness knows when I shall see him again, but I'm not grumbling for I realise that a few months back when we thought he was going away, I thought I wouldn't see him again until after the war, and instead of that I have been down to see him, and he has come home again for a while, so we are very lucky really.

Your letter came by the early morning post on Tuesday, the first letter I have had before leaving for the office for months and months, as Don's usually come during the afternoon. Don lay in bed and read part of it aloud to me while I was getting ready, then I left him to finish it while I had my breakfast, and then finished it myself on the way to work. He was pleased you had got his letter, and I think if you had a spare minute he'd like to hear from you, you know how they look forward to letters when they are away from home. I don't know whether he gave you his address when he wrote, or whether he was allowed to or not, but if he did and you address it there, they always follow them round and catch up with them in the end. I could give you his latest address now, but I don't know whether I should or not, so if you could either address it to the one he gave you, if he did, or address it home, and I will re-address it when it arrives. This is all if you want to write to him, that's all.

It was funny your letter arriving when it did, for I had made up my mind to write to you. Singapore had just fallen, and I remembered how I only seemed to write about the good news, so I thought that I'd write now, while we are still smarting under yet another terrific blow, to let you know that terrible as it is, we're not giving up, we're determined that we are coming out on top in the end, and that one day the tide of battle will flow in our favour for a change. It is very hard though, for so many people you know around you have husbands, sons, brothers or sweethearts in Singapore, and the only comfort you can give them is your silence, and by remembering not to talk about the war while they are around, and not to let them see the newspapers too much. Young Phyll's teacher has his son there, and she said the other day his wife came up during school time with a telegram from him saying that he had got away safely, so, all we can hope is that many more of the poor souls get similar good news.

George is helping the war effort by keeping rabbits, although

Phyll and Mum are generally the ones who look after them and feed them. Now that the snow has cleared, Dad is getting to work on his allotment, digging for victory again, for you may be sure that we're not going to go short of food just for the sake of growing it ourselves. By the way, quite a bit of American food sent under the lease lend is on sale in the shops now, and we are getting quite familiar with fatty bacon, spam and all the rest of them.

Baby David grows more chubby and more sweet every day, and luckily all the trouble with his eyes has passed now. Alf grows a sturdy little chap and a proper boy, and it is so pretty to hear him talking, he says such quaint things. Generally, when he sees a picture of an aeroplane he says 'Bomber' or 'German', but if you show him a picture and say 'is it a German?', nine times out of ten he says 'No, ours.' He doesn't understand what he's saying of course, but he sounds so old fashioned.

On Saturday, the cup that we won for the Stirrup Pump Competition is being presented at a dance, and on Sunday Sook & Doris whom we haven't seen for months are coming over for the day, so my weekend looks like being full enough for me not to be thinking all the while about 'This time last week' for that doesn't do.

Some months ago I bought a really smashing grey flannel skirt, pleated all round, with the inverts of each pleat in a different plaid. It is a beauty, and swings out showing all the plaids as you walk, so I am going to see if the shop from which I bought it will make me a jacket to match, and this way I shall have not only a cheap spring outfit, but one that suits my coupons for they are getting terribly low, and have to last me until the end of May, although there seems to be heaps of things I need. Still, that's war, we've got used to going without, and I don't really think that for the first year of rationing we have planned out coupons too badly, although next year we shall have a little more knowledge as to what to buy and what not to buy, if we don't want to finish the year with nothing to wear. I spent some of Alf's for him last week, and got enough wool to knit him a couple of suits. Mum is buying the wool for one, and me the other, for we didn't get him anything for his birthday as he was away at the time, and I have waited until now to find time to knit them. They are just plain, with a cable yoke to the jerseys, one in navy with red in the collar and red buttons, and one in red with navy buttons and navy on the collar. I am longing to get them finished and see how he looks in them.

The latest item to be rationed – soap – has pleased all the small boys, and hasn't worried the rest of us very much either, for the ration seems quite generous, and will only mean that we will have to be careful how we use it, but then who wouldn't be, when the poor devils risk their lives to bring it across. You know, although quite a few things are rationed now, and other non-essentials are either extinct or very hard to get, I never cease to wonder that after two and a half years of war, we are still living in the comparative comfort we are. When you realise that practically all our food, and other essentials are brought here by sea, that we are an island, and a very small one at that, with a huge continent overrun by the enemy (he is 'the enemy' now, not just 'our enemy') towering over us just twenty miles away, it certainly is a feat to be marvelled at. With all the mistakes that are made, and all the criticisms, many of which I am afraid I have to agree with, this thing always remains in my mind, and I try to never forget the hardships of the seamen who have kept us going all this long while.

Well Donna, I seem to have at last dried up of news, and as the work has been piling itself up while I have been writing, I think the best thing to do is close, and start slashing into it, so as to get it all done by the end of the afternoon.

I cannot post this until I get home, for I can't remember your new address, but unless I remember anything else I wanted to say, I will post it off first thing in the morning. Don't forget to write soon, for I do so look forward to getting letters from you often. Thanks again anyway for the one I have just received.

Cheerio for now, keep smiling,
tons of love,
Win xxxxx

P.S. Many thanks for the stamps, and although I don't understand much about them myself, Grandad left me his stamp album when he died, so they will find their way to the rightful place.

[*Note: the long walk described in this letter was from Cheltenham to Northleach*]

20th March 1942

My Dear Donna,

I haven't a lot of news, but I thought I'd start a letter to you, as it is about a month since I last wrote.

I'm not feeling very happy at the moment, as Don has just been home unexpectedly on three days' leave, and we rather fear the worst, he really is going this time. I should have been prepared for it, of course, for I knew it was bound to happen months ago, but it always is a shock when it actually comes to the point. Of course there is only one way to look at it: we've been far luckier than most, and when I think of where he might be, or what might be happening to him now, had he gone when we first thought he would, I realize that we really have a lot to be thankful for. I shudder when I think what I am going to do with my life in these years (for I rather fear it will be years) we are apart, but I guess there is nothing for me to do, but be like everyone else – work hard, and just keep as cheerful as possible, so that when he comes back he won't find me very different from when he went away. Well enough about that. I mustn't go making you miserable, and anyway I don't want to talk about it very much.

Here's something that might interest you. There was a programme on the wireless about a place where they build ships, thousands of miles from the sea. This caught our interest, of course, for being such a small country, and with the sea all round us, we are all almost brought up on it as you might say, and find it hard to imagine a place 'thousands of miles from the sea', but imagine how I felt when they told us that this place was Denver. There were several workmen's voices recorded, telling us how they used to make all sorts of peace-time machines but how on the outbreak of war they switched over to ship building. We do need ships so terribly badly. We need so many because they are our only life-line. They bring us everything we need to keep us going, and as long as we can get these ships to make up for our losses, we shall have no difficulty in filling them with men, men whose courage and powers of seamanship no one could question. It seems to bring you nearer to us and makes us realize more acutely that you are in it with us when we hear of ships being built at Denver.

There are quite a few American soldiers in London now and I meant to tell you before that if anyone you know comes over, tell them to be sure and look us up; what with rationing and wartime restrictions, we'd be only too happy to welcome them and make them feel at home.

Edna has finished her training and passed her exams, and is now a fully fledged balloon operator, on an actual site. She says they cause quite a bit of excitement as they are the first girls to operate a balloon completely alone in this particular town. The local people turn out to watch every time the 'balloon goes up'. She has more exams in a few weeks' time, and it wouldn't surprise me if we don't see her with some stripes on her arm very shortly, as she is so terribly keen. You may be interested to know that her work is so skilled and so definitely a 'man's job' that they are the highest paid trade in the W.A.A.F. That's what she wanted when she went in though, not the high pay, but she really wanted to do a man's job and to know that by doing it she was releasing a man for a more active job.

Sunday sees the start of London's Warships Week. Do you remember I told you about War Weapons Week we had about this time last year? All the rest of the country practically have had their own individual Warships Week, and now it is up to London to top the list. Every conceivable building and wall is covered with posters, telling us we must save as much as we possibly can to buy warships. As you know, I run the savings group in our road, so I am expecting a bumper collection when I go round with the stamps. We have a big poster in the front room window, all brightly coloured with warships on it, and right through the centre run four flags, each one the naval signal for S.A.V.E., and the words, 'The signal is "SAVE"'. London is aiming at £125,000,000, and what portion of this Woolwich (that's our borough and includes Eltham) is aiming at I don't know but whatever it is, you can bet your life we'll beat it.

The last day of Don's three day leave I had off from the office, and we went up to town. We had seen most of the shows that appealed to us, so we just went to the pictures and saw Jeanette

MacDonald in 'Smiling Through'. It was rather the wrong type to have gone to see on an occasion like this, for it made you feel it more acutely, and I'm not ashamed to admit that I cried. It was a lovely picture though, and came especially new to me as I had not previously seen the other versions of it, although I believe there have been two, and so didn't know the story. I loved Jeanette MacDonald's rendering of 'Just a little love, a little kiss' and 'Smiling Thru', but with typical English prejudice I thought she sang 'Land of Hope and Glory' just a little too fast and too 'swingy', if I could use the word. We sing 'Land of Hope and Glory' quite slowly, every word coming out forcefully and distinctly, for it is very popular and used almost as much as the national anthem. Whenever I hear it, I remember Empire Day when I was at school, when we all used to parade in the playground in our white frocks, with red, blue and white rosettes and bows on our hair, and sing 'Jerusalem', 'I vow to thee my Country' and always finished with 'Land of Hope and glory'. I've not a lot of patience with this idle flag-waving sort of patriotism in these days. I believe in getting on with the job, but somehow 'Land of Hope and Glory' always stirs something inside me.

I had planned to go and see Don at Easter and am making a red jumper to wear with my new red coat and grey skirt. I expect there will be little opportunity of my being able to go now, as heaven knows what will have happened, and when or where he will move to. Perhaps the good fortune that has shadowed us so far may last a while longer, and everything will turn out as planned. Who knows? I'll just have to wait and see and not make any plans until the last minute.

Did I tell you that as yet another spare-time war effort my brother has gone in for breeding rabbits? He's determined we shan't starve. All his free time at the weekends he spends building hutches, and he is thinking of finding somewhere to pack the tandem away, and turn the bike shed into still more hutches. Young Alfie loves them, and spends hours standing in front of the hutches talking to them and laughing at their antics. He will insist too on going right up to the bars and kissing them. I'm sure one of them will bite his nose one day. His younger brother, David, now nearly six-months-old, is a lovely kid, and good as gold, quite a different fellow from Alf, who is a proper boy, up to every kind of mischief going. He loves to come upstairs with me whilst I am dusting and often picks up Don's photograph and quite unconsciously talks to it, something like this, 'That's Uncle Don, hallo Uncle Don, Auntie Win's Uncle Don, he's a soldier, hallo Uncle Don, etc.' Whilst Don was home he was upstairs with us one day and picked up the photograph and started off on the same old routine. I said, 'You're screwy, Alf. Uncle Don's here', and this tickled him, so now every time he sees me it's, 'I'm not screwy, Auntie Win'. He's still a bit nervous of bangs and crashes, although (touch wood) his young life hasn't been pestered with any for quite a few months now, but the other day when we had an 'Alert' (quite an event this, as we had almost forgotten what old moaning Minnie sounded like) he was with Mum and said, 'What's that, Nanna?' She said, 'That's only the whistle for dinner' which satisfied him, but he's going to think we have dinner at a lot of peculiar times if ever the raids come back. He was much younger last time, of course, and couldn't talk, so we never had the problem of telling him what it was all about. He just knew enough to know that the 'Alert' was something strange, because it made his Mummy pick him up and take him down into the shelter, and the crashes that followed made his 'Nanna' wince and his Daddy or Auntie Win say funny things like 'duck' or 'that was a near one'.

There is great excitement in the office this afternoon, for one of the girls is getting married tomorrow. Her husband-to-be came home last night and has seven days' leave, so naturally she is thrilled to pieces. We are nearly all marrieds now, and the old stagers like me with nine months behind me, have been getting excited all over again, as if it were us. She chose cutlery for her wedding present from the office, same as I did, although like everything else, it is very hard to get. We all seem to favour the Army, for in all we have eight marrieds with husbands in the Army, two girls engaged to soldiers, and one had a sailor boyfriend. No one represents the Air Force, for all the rest of the girls are 'unattached'.

Well this seems rather a short letter to post, but I am afraid I haven't much more news at the moment, so I will hold it up a day or two in case anything turns up. Cheerio for now.

8th April 1942

Quite a long stretch from the 20th March until the 8th April, isn't it? But there really hasn't been much news of importance since then, and I had been spending most of my time swotting away at my new jumper in the hope that I might be able to go and see Don at Easter. Well, Easter has come and gone, and the Gods smiled on us once more, for I was able to spend the weekend with him, and I've never had such a wonderful weekend in my life. It has to be that way though, for it was the last we shall have together for many a long while I'm afraid, for he's actually gone by now, and at the moment I do not know where he is, or where he is bound for. I've just got to pray he'll have a safe passage and that when he gets into the thick of it, the powers that be, that have looked after us so well this far, will keep a watchful eye on him, and send him back to me safe and sound. He's written a letter to me, he says, which he'll send, but on no account must I open it until he comes back, so every time I see that letter in my bag, I shall be curious to know what's in it, but it will give me faith to know that when I do know, it will mean that it is all over, and he is home again.

It was a lovely weekend though. He took me up to his billet to meet the rest of his gang, and they are the happiest, craziest lot I've ever come across. I took some snaps of them all, and as soon as I get them done I will send you some. I had got my new jumper finished, and really felt the queen of the castle in my new outfit. Don liked it all, he liked the hat, and the coat and the skirt, in fact the whole rig-out, so you can imagine how good this made me feel, for I wanted him to keep a memory of me looking fairly presentable. I've never laughed as much in all my life as I did this weekend, we just didn't let the prospect of his going away impede our happiness then the slightest bit. We went for long walks around the beautiful countryside, and the wind blew my hair into a million tangles, but I felt full of health and vigour, and on top of the world. As is always the case, the time simply flew, and we just had time for me to dash to the station and catch my train when we came out of the pictures on Monday. We saw 'Helzapopin' which really rounded us off by yet another couple of hours' laughter. I waved and waved as the train drew out, until I couldn't see which of the khaki-clad mass left on the platform was Don. My heart was bubbling over like a kettle, but I felt so proud of myself, for I didn't cry. I just said 'Cheerio' as if I'd be back again next week, and it wasn't until I got home, that I really realized he had gone.

Edna is coming home on leave on Friday and Dad has booked for us to all go and see a show in town, so we should have quite a happy time. We are having one of our A.R.P. dances on Saturday, so she will just be home in time for this, which I am pleased of, for I don't like to go alone. I'm having a perm in the afternoon, a long overdue one I'm afraid, but perms, like every other luxury are hard to get, as the material is very short, and I had to book for this months ago.

I used my last remaining coupon yesterday and it's a couple of months before we get our new ones, so I mustn't want anything else. I had an ounce of wool left over from my red jumper, and I spent my last coupon getting an ounce of black and ounce of grey, so this will make black and red gloves and a black, grey and red turban to wear as an alternative with my outfit.

17th April 1942

Hallo again. Well Edna's leave has come and gone, she goes back tonight, and I have heard that Don has gone. He didn't write, of course, for that would not be right, but his friends in the village waited until a sufficient gap had passed so as not to give away 'information to the enemy' and then sent me a telegram. I can't say anything about it at the moment, for I just don't feel anything. I am kind of numb inside, and don't really realize yet that no longer is there any chance of his 'just popping home for the weekend.' I try to console myself by saying it won't be long, for after all we're all out for victory this year, and although it will be sometime after the war before he comes home again, it will be something to know it is all over, and he is no longer in any danger.

It was the day we had arranged to go up to town to see a show that the telegram arrived, and Mum didn't tell me about it until I got home, for she didn't want to spoil my evening. We saw Lupino Lane in 'Twenty to One', and although it was only slapstick comedy, the whole house was screaming with laughter from start to finish, and after all that is all that is important these days, to make people laugh. I say 'only' slapstick comedy, but although a lot of it was just silly nonsense it was very clever nonetheless.

We had our local dance on Saturday and although I thoroughly enjoyed myself, Edna professed to be bored stiff. I guess I must be getting a trifle easy to please nowadays, for after all a jolly good laugh and a dance with people you know is more fun to a 'grass widow' than a sophisticated dance full of eligible young men. I won a packet of chocolate in an elimination dance, so all in all it was a good evening for me.

After tearing away at my red jumper I have now decided to have a rest from knitting and catch up on my reading. I am also anxious to get my rug finished and done with, before it gets dirty. I gave 'the home', as we call our one little room, a real good spring clean last weekend, swept and dusted from top to bottom, washed the floor, dusted all the shelves in the wardrobe, and did one or two running repairs on my clothes, so it is now quite a treat to walk in and find the room clean and sweet. We have had such glorious weather too, these last couple of weeks, and it really makes you think we are being compensated for the hard long winter we have just come through.

Well Donna, I really think it is about time I closed this letter and got it posted off. I am sorry I haven't your new address on me, so it will have to go to your home. Don't forget to write soon and often and let me know all the news. I shall look forward to your letters even more now that I shan't have my daily from Don to look forward to.

Cheerio for now then, write soon.

Tons of love,
    Win

20th April 1942

My Dear Donna,

Hallo again, and how is the world using you these days? It seems I always start a letter to you lately with 'When am I going to hear from you' but yet again I feel I must write for it seems ages since I last had a line.

1942

Nothing very exciting has happened since I last wrote. I've been spending my time, apart from my work, my savings group and the canteen, on the usual round of visiting, or visits to the flicks with my colleagues from the office. I have had one letter from Don since he went away, written on a boat. Naturally, he gave no news as to how long he had been afloat, or of his possible destination, for it was only one page, undated, but it started off, "Tis rather difficult to write, propped up as I am in a hammock.' It was very good to hear though, for whilst he was in England I had a letter every day, and the time just seemed to drag by after he left, when no word came through. I am now anxiously awaiting the next letter, and the news that he has reached his destination safely, although I expect I shall have to wait quite a while yet.

Last weekend I spent with one of Don's sisters, and as it was Youth Sunday, being the nearest to St George's Day, we went to a special Youth service on Sunday afternoon, held especially for the scouts. It really seemed like old times to hear the jolly old Scouts' band start up, and see the boys marching down the road. I always think there is something magnetic about their bugles, for you always have to follow the sound and see them. We also listened in to a joint service held at Westminster Abbey and the Cathedral at Washington, in honour of our patron saint, St. George. I think it brings us even closer together when we realize that apart from all the other ways in which we are alike, we also sing the same old hymns.

I was listening to a talk on the radio last night, and the speaker said that the only way for the American people to really get to know us for what we really are, and not from a lot of anti-British propaganda, is for the American man-in-the-street to get into personal contact with the British man-in-the-street. We could have told them this years ago, couldn't we? If all our fellow countrymen had a friendship like ours, the propagandists might just as well retire, for because we know differently, we both are able to pick out the truth of what we hear about one another, and people who are able to know when they are being misled, are no good for the propaganda merchants, for the seeds of doubt can be sown only where first-hand knowledge is unobtainable. I think I've told you before how I dream that one day, our kind of friendship may spread all over the world, for you know of our love of peace and hatred of war, because we are able to let you know it. I wonder how much of the present suffering in the world could have been avoided if myself and thousands of others like me had had a friend in all the enemy countries. It seems terrible to me, that we hate like we do, but I don't think that hatred will ever leave us now; it has been fostered by bestial deed upon deed, and it will take us many years to forget.

You no doubt heard of the bombing of Bath and Norwich, as reprisals for the RAF's smashing raids on the German industrial centres. It must have been terrible for the inhabitants of these two undefended towns, for they had no means of retaliation, and we know how much it helped us through when we heard the crash of the Ack-Ack guns giving it to 'em back, during the raids on London. My girl friend has been at Bath since the outbreak of war, and I had a letter from her, saying she was O.K. after the first big raid, but haven't heard anything since.

The topic on everyone's mind at the moment is the 'fuel rationing scheme'. Whether or not it will be put into effect, time alone will tell, but the very fact that it has been considered, has been enough to help bring home to some people the sacrifices we must make, for a total war effort. Those of us who have seen our loved ones sail away haven't needed anything to bring it home to us, and I for one am glad of the new, more Spartan kind of life that is necessary, and will be necessary in the near future. The cost of living is high, and so is the income tax, so we've no spare money to spend on non-essentials, which is as it should be. Food isn't dear, but almost everything is rationed now, so everyone gets his fair share. Clothes rationing makes us wear thick stockings and unpick old knitted jumpers, but if it saves shipping space, then we go without gladly. Travelling is difficult for passenger transport is scarce, but it leaves more fuel and space for essentials of war, so although we exercise our privilege to grumble, we know in our heart that this is the right thing and anyway we are ever the 'Pollyannas' for we say, what's the good of travelling when there is nowhere to go, for the seaside is absolutely out of the question, being inhabited almost solely by those manning the defences, and when I haven't any coupons, and cannot dress up, I think, 'Well, what's the use anyway if Don isn't here to see me.' My income tax too, oh boy, I grumble about this too, but I pay up, for what good would a few more pounds in the bank do me if Hitler came here?

Our rabbits are coming along fine. We have quite a number now, and they are becoming quite a full-time job for George. It is a pleasing sight also, to look from the bedroom window and see all the vegetables coming up in the garden. It has been a wonderful spring, with biting cold winds, but wonderful sunshine that has brought out all the fruit blossoms and spring flowers to perfection. Daffodils are everywhere this year, and I know of no better tonic for a dark day than a gay bowl of yellow daffodils.

I've had a letter from Edna, my sister, since she returned, and she said that although she enjoyed being home for seven days, it was somehow good to get back again amongst the girls. Incidentally a girl Ack Ack gun crew brought down one of the bombers that raided Bath.

I have been catching up on my reading these last few weeks and giving knitting a rest, but I must start again, for Doris wants me to knit David a new outfit. I've used up some scraps of wool and made myself a pair of gloves with red backs and black inside, to wear with my red jacket, and a pair for Mum out of two shades of mauve. I have also been doing quite a bit of my rug, for I am anxious to get it packed away.

Well, Donna, I seem to have come to a full-stop in my news at the moment, but I will hold this over for a bit in case anything turns up, although I am hoping to spend a quiet weekend, catching up on some of my jobs. This is the first time in weeks that I have been slack enough to break off this long to write to you, for work has been pouring fast and furious, and I am thinking that there is quite a bit piling up somewhere for me at this moment, and I'd better be prepared for a mad rush. My, I never did think I could slap this old machine along at the rate I do these days, but it just goes to show that you never know what you can do till you try. The office now consists of almost all women and young boys, apart from a couple of essentials, for the last of the young men went into the Air Force a couple of weeks ago. He is going to be an air gunner, and his farewell note is still on the notice board, saying he is longing for the day when his training will be completed and he flies over Germany, and he promises to think of each one of us, as he drops his load.

It is almost lunch-time, so I must close now, so as to get out on the dot, for I have a lot of shopping to get for Mum. There are some things that we can't get at home, but are obtainable in this district, so I have half the ration books, and do my darnedest with them here, whilst Mum gets the rest at home.

Cheerio for the present then, be back later.

6th May 1942

Hallo again.

At the present moment the air in the office is blue with smoke, for a curtain or something caught alight downstairs, and they've just been putting it out. Those of us left in the office have a good laugh every time the door opens for somebody or other comes in with a blackened face. My eyes are still smarting, partly with the smoke and partly with the tale that has just come up that the office boy squirted the hose accidentally over the one person we can't imagine in such an undignified position. The laughter has died down now, and everyone is settling down to his work again, but I can't resist a little chuckle every time I think of 'Old Mac' with the hose being squirted at him.

Did I tell you that we have lost all the iron railings from the front of the house? Personally I was glad to see them go and think the houses look more modern without the railings, and it certainly makes my job of running in and out the houses with my savings stamps much easier now there are no gates to open and shut. I say no gates, actually there weren't at first, but the old ones have been gone some weeks now, and gradually new wooden ones are taking the place of the iron ones. This gives plenty of scope for individuality, for everyone is making a gate to his own special liking and size, and out of the half dozen or so already up, not one is the same size or design as the other. When anything like this is in the offing, our house usually takes the lead and everyone else follows suit, but Dad has been so busy gardening he hasn't bothered about the gate yet, and we can just imagine that when they look at our gate-less front garden, they shake their heads and say 'The Hellewells are slipping.' Actually Dad is convinced that when he does get it done it will knock all the others into a cocked hat, for he has the design in his mind's eye. What a game, there is a life-and-death struggle raging, and yet it is still a matter of personal pride to keep your house looking as nice as possible. I suppose it is a good thing we are like this in a way, for it is our homes, and the right to do just what we like, even though it may be something as trivial as this, that we are fighting to preserve.

Last Sunday I went out with about half a dozen other girls for a hike, for we have been having some simply marvellous weather lately, and we really must make the most of it, after the long dark winter. We didn't go until after dinner, and met at a central point about 2 o'clock in the afternoon, caught a train to a certain little village not far out, and spent the afternoon tramping across fields and climbing through woodlands and hedges. It was glorious. We saw primroses, violets and bluebells, and the trees were at a marvellous stage of beauty. At one point we just stood breathless at the top of a hill, and drank in the wonder of the view and the surrounding countryside. Someone said, 'It's worth preserving, isn't it?' No one answered, for our answer was in our silence as our eyes roamed over the beauty of it all. It was the first day it had been warm enough to just sit about, so we spent an hour lying in the sunshine, chewing grass and dreamily looking up at the sky. We ate our tea by a haystack, and then went into the village for a cup of tea. It was a typical Kentish village that we used to visit often on our bikes, and it seemed little changed by the war. The old mill stream still ran through the centre of the village, as no doubt it has run for centuries past, and will run for centuries to come, and we felt at peace with all, as we gazed into the clear running water. It really was the best time of the day for actual walking, after we had had our tea, so we started off again and walked on to the next village. It was too early to go home, and yet we hadn't really got time to walk on to the next one, which was quite a distance away, so we spent and hour or so, chasing a ball, playing with a dog, or just lazing around in the cool of the evening. We caught the train back about 9, and about 10 I arrived home, a very tired, but happy girl. It does make a lovely break to get out like that at the weekend after being cooped up in the office all the week.

The open air baths in the local park are opening next week, and it is my intention to go quite a bit in the evenings this summer. I always liked swimming but gave it up because Don didn't swim, and when in the last few years he did learn, there was always our cycling, and somehow the two didn't really seem to mix, and we really never did get time for a lot. Now that I am on my own though, there is nothing to stop me taking it up seriously, and I'm going to see if I can get quite a good standard.

The wheels have been taken out of the tandem and it has been packed away in the loft, for the cycle shed is being made into a home for the rabbits now that the size of their families is increasing by leaps and bounds. All I hope is that the war is over before I am too old to ride it again.

Nothing has been arranged yet, but I think it is being generally understood that all workers are to have just one week's holiday this year, and although I felt I needed one, I had been wondering just where and how to spend it. Home seems to be about the best place, for there aren't many places to go these days, and I've never had to spend a holiday without Don yet. The brain-wave struck me this morning though, that I could perhaps fix it up when Edna is on leave and we could then go swimming, walking, or up to town together.

I've managed to get down to my knitting again, and have made quite a good start on David's new pram set, although I'm afraid the rug has been neglected again. I can sit out in the open and knit, but I need to be indoors with a table for the rug, and it seems sinful to waste time indoors this lovely weather.

I'm having my hair set tonight, for next week seems to be fairly well booked up. On Wednesday our Home Guard at the works here are holding a dance, and a crowd of us from the office are going to keep up the old tradition. If I know these H.G. affairs it'll be a bit of a rough house, but so long as we have fun and raise a laugh, what matters?

Our office poet has just composed the following on the spur of the moment. It is her description of the happenings of half an hour ago:

> Shouting 'Fire' Dave rushed the door
> Through which smoke began to pour.
> Mr B. and Mr S.
> Rushing aft to stop the mess.

>   Mr H. made a good third
>   Whilst crackling flames outside were heard.
>   Poor old Mac went blithely sweeping
>   Innocent that flames were leaping.
>   Initiative came to David's aid so
>   Down on Mac came a tornado
>   Of water flung from David's pail
>   And from Mac there came a hail
>   Of reproach (louder than speaking)
>   That his 'Trousers now were leaking.'
>   In and out for quite a spell
>   Men were rushing (not pell mell)
>   Methodically with more wet stuff
>   'Til the fire had had enough.
>   Slowly then, the men came back
>   With eye rims red and faces black,
>   Weeping softly, having won,
>   Feeling 'that's another job well done.'

It's not wonderful poetry, but she's quite a genius of sorts, I think. You may be sure I'll write and let you know as soon as I hear where Don is, and that he is safe and well, although I expect it will be some weeks yet.

Cheerio for now, keep smiling, and write soon.

Tons of love,

Win

1st June 1942

My Dear Donna,

Hallo again, at long last I have found time to sit down and knock off a few lines to you. It seems quite a while since I last wrote, and I have quite a bit of news, both grave and gay. I think the best thing will be to start at the beginning.

I think I have told you before about Don's brother Eric, who gained his commission about this time last year. He came through Dunkirk without a scratch, and spent most of his time in Ireland until he 'took a boat trip' to see some more active service just a short while before Don went too. It was awful both of them leaving so close together, and we suffered agonies of mind whilst they were both on the water and we didn't hear a word for weeks and weeks. Then, the first sign of life came in a cable from Eric saying he was safe and well, and a letter in which he said he was very happy, he'd just eaten an orange and opened a packet of cigarettes wrapped in cellophane which gave him a marvellous pre-war feeling. He ended by saying what a wonderful night it was, and that he couldn't imagine why he felt so happy but he wasn't going to analyse it, it was enough that he felt that way. Imagine then the awful blow when less than a couple of days later his mother received that dreaded telegram from the War Office saying Eric had been killed in action at Madagascar. It knocked us all cold, we just couldn't realise it, and I kept puzzling and trying to conceive how it had happened. It seemed so awful, such a brainy young fellow, he'd have been 23 a fortnight ago, just the very sort we shall need after the war, to have been cut off like that.

The most ironic thing too was that he was so anxious to go, he wanted to get another smack at them, and then he wasn't killed by the Germans or the Japs, but the French, or rather French subjects. We couldn't understand it at first, we kept asking ourselves 'why' why he had to be spared to come through the Hell of Dunkirk, just to live another couple of years of war, and then be killed. We have got over the first shock of it now though, and as his mother said, someone had to do that job, it might easily have been someone else's son, and although it is awful to think that our former allies should have resisted us, if he had died at Dunkirk, it would have been in vain, but he did a good job of work, and the occupation of Madagascar must ultimately mean some thing towards the winning of the war. He is but one of thousands we know, and we are but a few of millions that are grieving all over the world, but there is more truth than ever now in the saying that you never really understand anything until it hits you personally. I for one will never ever be able to realise that Eric is dead; he was so young, and so very much alive, I shall always think of him as being away at the war still, and that I shall see him again when his leave is due.

The whole blow was made much harder though as we hadn't heard from Don, and didn't know how or where he was. For a week I lived in dread, I thought any moment a similar telegram was coming to me, he seemed so far away and out of touch, and I felt so helpless here, miles away from him. His sister had rung me to tell me the news about Eric, and I had avoided 'phones like the plague after that. I dreaded to pick up a receiver lest I should hear more bad news. For a week I got by, no-one rang me at the office, and I was just beginning to think clearly again when one afternoon the telephone operator called me, and said there was a call for me. Instead of just saying 'O.K.' and jumping up as usual, I just gazed at her blankly, and felt something within me go thump as I dully said 'For me?' If she had said 'No, it's a mistake, no-body wants you', I'd have been overjoyed, but as it was I gingerly picked up the receiver, and heard Don's sister's voice. I held my breath until I heard her say 'I thought you'd like to know we've just received a cable from Don, he's safe and well'. I managed to keep on my feet until I had put the receiver back, then as I turned and saw the eyes of the whole office eagerly on me, I managed to stumble out through a mist of tears 'He's safe and well'. Then followed such a hustle of 'I'm so glad' and 'That's good' or 'Glad you've good news' whilst I was laughing and crying all at the same time. I suddenly went weak at the knees and collapsed into the nearest chair. I think it was the

Mum with David, Dad with Alfie and Phyllis in her Guide uniform (in the garden at 23 Dumbreck Road)

strain of all those weary weeks of waiting, the reaction from the shock about Eric, and relief that Don was safe, but I just felt all the strength ooze out of me. I tried to light a cigarette but in the excitement burnt the tip of my nose which made everybody laugh, for it came up so red, and they had visions of a blister forming. I ran from one desk to the other throughout the office, saying 'I've heard from Don, he's safe and well', and it was quite a while before I could settle down again and concentrate on my work. Someone said very aptly 'He's thousands of miles away, and he still has the power to send her weak at the knees – what a man.'

I hurried home as I guessed there would be a cable for me also, and couldn't really understand why Mum hadn't rung me and told me. It appeared though that when it arrived and she saw the telegram envelope, naturally, having the news of Eric fresh in her mind, she immediately thought the worst and dreaded opening it. She said she shook like a leaf when the boy handed it to her, and was so overcome with relief when instead of the words she dreaded, she saw Don's name at the bottom, and his old stock phrase 'Keep smiling, my thoughts are with you, all my love – Don', that it just didn't occur to her to let me know, so if Con hadn't rung and told me about the one his mother had received, I should have to have waited another two hours before I knew. Believe me too, two hours is a saving when you have been on tenterhooks for weeks, and living in absolute dread for the best part of a week. I feel settled again now though about Don, and have regained my faith that he will come through it all. All I long for now is a letter, which may still be quite a while, but at least we know that he is somewhere on his journey, still safe.

Edna is doing remarkably well in the W.A.A.F. In just over six months she has passed from one exam to the next with flying colours, and now tells us that she has been recommended for a corporal, and has to go for a month's training as an acting-corporal, at the end of which there will be an exam. If she passes this it will mean she will have two stripes on her arm and be entirely in charge of a site of her own. Not bad going is it for a girl of 19? It proves also that if your heart and soul are in your job, as hers is, success is inevitable, for she is as keen as mustard. Mum is so proud of her, we all are in fact, and although this new training period will mean her leave will be put back, we are all going to try and have our holidays together, that is, Dad, Edna and I, then with Mum and Phyll we can go places together, although of course there is no question of going away to the sea or anywhere like that. I expect we shall find pleasure enough in going swimming and walking together, or visiting the shows in town.

Talking of shows, Don's sister, two of my pals from the office, and I are celebrating our wedding anniversary in a fortnight's time, by going to see Vivien Leigh in 'The Doctor's Dilemma' which is now showing in town. I am looking forward to this, for although I have seen Vivien Leigh on the films, this will be the first time I'll have seen her in person on the stage. It doesn't seem possible does it, that it is almost a year since we were married? To think that this time last year I was in the throes of working out dresses and cakes, and Don was dashing home every weekend, happy as a sand boy. It is almost unbelievable that so much could happen in a year. Who'd have thought this time last year that he'd be so far away now? Still, let's hope it will be the last anniversary we shall spend apart, and as I tell him, we'll soon make up for it afterwards.

Whitsun brought it all back to me too, for I kept thinking of last year. Don got home for the weekend, and I remember how we went shopping on the Saturday and I bought the finishing touches of my clothes, right down to gloves and a scarf and all my wedding outfit and my going away clothes were completed. Don and George were up bright and early on Sunday morning, and I can see them now in their white coats, painting what was formerly known as my room, and is now referred to as 'our home', it being the only home we have until after the war. I remember Don calling me about seven and asking me to go and make them a cup of tea, and I remember the whoops of joy that came from Edna and me as we picked the morning paper up from the mat, and saw splashed across the front page that clothes rationing started from that day. We weren't overjoyed about the clothes rationing, but the wonderful good fortune that had made us decide to get married just when we did, and thus be able to have a white wedding and all the trimmings without the worry of coupons. I can see Don leaning over the banisters telling us to make less noise, lest we awaken the whole household – happy days.

This Whitsun was very different, although under the circumstances I enjoyed it quite well. I had arranged to spend it with Don's sister Doreen, but naturally, with the news of Eric fresh in our minds, we didn't feel like doing anything very invigorating. We mostly sat about lazing and resting, for we were all getting over the first shock of it, and managed to get a few walks in, a couple of visits to relations and a visit to the pictures.

We had a good day out a few weeks back when we visited another branch of our firm in the country. We had a marvellous time going over the place, and were treated as guests of honour, being referred to as 'the people from London works'. We had a good, first-rate show in the canteen afterwards, and finally arrived home in the small hours, after sampling very well some fine old English port wine in a lovely little country pub. It may have been fine old English port, but it was a little too fine for me, and I felt my head reeling after only one, and decided that literally my head should rule my heart, and I stuck to shandy after that, although even shandy seems to have a different flavour when you drink it in the country. When we all arrived at the office on Monday morning, many and varied were the tales that were told of 'what happened on Saturday night'.

It just occurs to me that the censor may not pass all I have written about Eric, but I don't see why not, for everyone knows that we had casualties at Madagascar, even if they were only a few, and the fact that one of these was my brother-in-law, wouldn't mean anything to anyone else. I've been very careful too not to give you any dates, so I think it will be all right. Boy, what a lot I shall have to write about after the war.

Talking of writing, it also occurs to me that it is some while since I heard from Donna, and I ask myself why she hasn't written to me. Perhaps she is busy I think, but then I think again that she knows how I look forward to her letters, and would surely write to me a few lines now and again. Then I think again, but I can find no reason, so I just say 'Please write soon and often, Donna, for I do love to hear from you.'

9th June 1942

Not very much news again, although the most important thing of all is that I got a letter from Don last week. It was very old, written in April, so naturally, what news he was able to give me, is rather stale now. He says he has been writing a log of the journey, and just as soon as he reaches port, he will post it home to me, and as he didn't want to repeat in his letter anything that he had written in the log, he hadn't really a lot of news. He said they had all settled down quite happily to life on board ship, although they were longing for the sight of a few hills and dales again. He said the spirit of the boys was just as bright as ever. One of the wise cracks being, after days at sea, with no other view from the deck but, water, water, water, 'This place has changed since I was here last, they've chopped the trees down'. They're a grand crowd and Don said himself he would rather go with them than with any others, for even in the darkest hour, they managed to have a joke. I expect in intervals of several weeks I shall get still more letters written on the boat, although I expect by now he has safely got his feet on dry land again. It's a peculiar feeling you know to have a husband some where in the world, but not knowing exactly where. Incidentally, Don's mother received a letter from Eric last week, it was one written while he was at sea. I expect too there may be more to follow from him also. It gave me such a queer feeling in the pit of my stomach as I read it, for I couldn't believe that the boy who had penned those words had now been killed. Oh, will the world never come to its senses, will people never realise that war brings nothing but suffering and no good to anyone? It's up to us Donna you know, it's up to our generation to see that things are run a whole heap differently than they were after the last lot. In twenty years' time, we mustn't have it on our conscience that through our shortsightedness our children are suffering, as is the youth of today, for the mistakes of a generation ago.

Some friends we haven't seen for years came to tea on Sunday, and as they were interested, I got down those newspapers that you sent me, and we had quite a good laugh re-reading them again. It made my mouth water when I read that I had once lunched off 'Chicken salad, followed by fresh fruit salad and ice-cream', the chance would be a fine thing these days. I remember that day well though, it was the day before Don joined up, and he bought me my tweed coat – happy days.

Well, Donna, nothing else of importance seems to have turned up, so I think I'll close this letter and get it posted off. By the way, I am enclosing a few shots of my latest Polyfoto. It isn't particularly good, but Don took a fancy to that hat, it was the last one he saw me in before he went away, and wrote asking me to have my photograph taken in it.

Cheerio for now then, don't forget, write soon,
tons of love,
    Win xxxxx

P.S. I know I am late with my good wishes, but my thoughts were with you on your birthday, and I did wish you then a mental 'Many Happy Returns' – let's hope the next one is in peace.

13th June 1942

P.P.S. Just about to mail this, but must tell you that I have had an Airgraph from Don and he's very fit and well, and having a fine time enjoying the countryside of one of his ports of call. More about this in my next letter.

13th August 1942

My Dear Donna,
You will probably be surprised to hear from me after all this while, only I have been waiting to hear from you, but as it is months and months now since I last heard, I thought I had better write you a short note to find out what is wrong, and why I haven't heard for so long.

I don't have time to write long letters at the office these days I am afraid, for nearly all the men are gone from the office now, and there is so much to do, it is just one long rush all the while. Personally I don't mind this though for it makes the time go quickly, and after all, each day that passes is one day nearer the end of all this, and Don's home coming. It barely seems possible that it is four months today that I last heard from him in England, and longer than that since I last saw him. In this time he has travelled all round the world almost, and now, after much travelling around to quote his own words, he is 'In the land where the sun shines on both sides of the hedges, and the sand gets in everything'. He hasn't had a word from home yet, which must be awful for him, cut off from the world like that for all those months. I am at last beginning to hear from him fairly quickly by Airgraph, the last one I received being written on the 26th of last month. He says he prefers the desert to India, where he was before, as the climate is drier. I bet he looks brown now, I bet I'll hardly know him when he comes home, which please God won't be long now.

My sister in the W.A.A.F. is now a corporal, and got engaged a few weeks back to the boy she met at the town where she is stationed. They won't be married until after the war of course, but naturally she is thrilled to pieces. We have only seen him once, as Edna got a 24 hour leave for them both to come down and meet us and get Mum and Dad's consent to their engagement. He has been discharged from the Army, having come through Dunkirk, and is now on munitions so it isn't possible for him to get down again until he gets his next annual holiday.

I think I was just about the luckiest one in the office this year. You see the Works close down for the first week in August for everyone to have a holiday. The boss wanted me in that week however to attend to anything that might come up, so I had the choice to have my week when I liked. I wasn't feeling terribly thrilled about it, for with Don gone there was nowhere and no one with whom to spend a holiday, then, out of the blue in June came an invitation from Don's sister and her husband to make a foursome with a friend of theirs for a week in Devon. Despite the fact that it was the first holiday in seven years I have spent without Don, I can honestly say I had the time of my life. Before we went I was just beginning to get to the end of my tether, what with the awful news of the death of Don's brother, then the endless weeks of waiting whilst Don was at sea, not knowing where or how he was, then we had that lovely week. We were so lucky, for seven days the sun shone ceaselessly, and I came home brown as a berry, feeling fit to face the world for another twelve months. We spent every minute in the open, walking, bathing or just lazing on the sand. The part of the coast we went to was very rugged, but unhampered by barbed wire, and it sure was good to get into the good old salt sea again. We rowed a lot too, and one particular day, the six of us (we met another couple there and became friendly) were just returning from a row, when we saw quite a crowd watching us from the pier. Each with an oar, we kept at our task determined that none of us should miss a stroke and shame us in the eyes of the watchers. We rounded the pier in perfect time, pulling like a boat race team, and we must have looked good us six sunburnt happy holiday-makers, for as we alighted a cheer went up, and we knew that from a distance we must have looked better than we really were, for we weren't any of us expert rowers.

For those seven days too, apart from wishing all the while that Don was with us, we forgot the war. We didn't listen to the radio or look at a newspaper. It was heaven, and after all, a week out of three years of war isn't much to have asked. I wish I could describe the wonderful country we explored, for it isn't possible for me to send you any views, but I will bring with me all the snap shots I took, when I come to see you after the war.

My younger brother goes into the Army next month. He was in a reserved job, but as one by one his pals all joined up, and then Don went overseas, he got steadily more and more browned off, and volunteered. They wouldn't take him at first, but they have agreed to release him now, and to his delight he goes on the 19th of next month. He is like a dog with two tails, although naturally Mum isn't too pleased at the prospect of his going. It will seem strange at home, for there will only be Phyll and I there with Mum and Dad after George has gone.

Our wedding anniversary has come and gone, and it hardly seems possible that already it is fourteen months since we were married. I took half a dozen of my pals up to town to see a show by way of celebration, and a few weeks back I heard from Don that he had planned to take the boys out, but was on guard. Nevertheless he said this gave him ample time to let his mind travel back thousands of miles to that happy day at home a year ago, and we hope that he will be home again for the next anniversary. It was his birthday on the 11th of this month, and we celebrated it (a couple of my office pals and I) by going up to town again, where we saw 'No Orchids for Miss Blandish'. We had a drink before we went in, drank Don's health and hoped that where ever he was, he was enjoying himself too, so I've yet to hear from him how he spent his birthday. The show we saw was super. It is a long while since I have seen such a thrilling play, wonderfully acted, and packed full of wisecracks. It was set way back in 1933 too, so there was no mention of the war, which made it doubly good entertainment. I don't know whether or not you have read the book, but needless to say the play isn't quite the same, although the gist of the story was there. The show we saw for our anniversary was Vivien Leigh in Bernard Shaw's 'The Doctor's Dilemma', which was very good, and I was agreeably surprised to find that Vivien Leigh is as pretty in the flesh as on the screen.

Well, Donna, this isn't a very long letter, just a brief summary of the news, but I do so hope you will write soon, giving me all your news, and letting me know you are still in the land of the living. Although London is cram full of Yankee soldiers we haven't had a visit to '23' of any of your friends yet, but as I said before, don't forget to give our address to anyone you know who comes over.

Cheerio for now then, write soon now, and IT WON'T BE LONG,

tons of love,

Win xxx

14th October 1942

I have not heard from your friend (Lt Edward Smartt of Lamar who is with U.S. forces in England) yet, but you may be sure that if he comes to see us we will do all in our power to make him feel at home, and if he feels it isn't a waste of his leave to spend it in the company of an old married woman like me, well then, I shall show him as much as I can of London, or rather what's left of it. Still, I shouldn't say that, should I, for I realise only too well that there is a sight more left of London, than there is of Stalingrad at the moment. How do the Russians affect you? Honestly they just make me gasp more and more with wonder each day. I don't profess to know much about politics, or communism for that matter, but when I see the way they are fighting, like a people inspired, then I say to myself, 'If that's communism, let's have a basinful.' We are all so sorry that we just aren't in a position to help them more than we are right now, for in a million years we could never repay them for what they have done for us, and I don't think there is one of us who will ever forget, but then it isn't our fault that we were made such a small island with such a small population, although that is being rectified more and more each day. To the hundreds of fighting French, Belgians, Dutch, Czechs, etc., to say nothing of our brothers in arms from Canada, Australia, South Africa, India and all the other countries from the four corners of the earth that make up the British Empire, we now have added representatives from your great country. To us they are 'Doughboys' or 'Yanks', we rarely say 'Americans', and yet these terms aren't meant to be disrespectful, we use them the same way as we say 'Aussies' when we speak of the Australians, and everyone knows how much we think of our 'Aussy' cousins, for I think they are the most like us, of all the Empire.

My, what a paragraph. Will I never lose this habit of mine of running on from one subject to another? The trouble is I type everything just as it enters my head, with rather disastrous results sometimes, I'm afraid. Suffice it to say that what I meant to convey in all that rigmarole was that your friend and any more like him will always be welcome at home, to whatever we can give them in the way of entertainment under war-time conditions. I haven't had the opportunity of meeting any of your countrymen to speak to, but I have seen them by their dozens in London. Their uniform strikes me as being more 'dressy' than the heavy battle-dress and army boots of the British Tommy, but then I'm bound to be prejudiced as a very special person to me wears that self same battle-dress. I've seen them on the buses viewing the Houses of Parliament, Big Ben and the other government buildings in Whitehall. I've seen them in the snack bars, (I don't [*Several lines apparently missing here between cuttings.*] apart from such inconsequential things as saying 'lootenant' when we say 'leftenant', or 'reva-lee' when we say 'rev-aa-le'. I could go on like that indefinitely. There is 'al-u-min-ium' and 'aloom-in-um' and 'tom-a-toe' and 'tom-ar-toe', but these things don't really matter, in fact I think they give us an added interest in one another, where we might be very boring, both speaking exactly the same language.

It is now several weeks since I heard from Don, but he is quite settled down to life in the desert now. A few weeks back his log book came home. This was a diary he had kept from the day he left England until he arrived in India. (Of course he left there and went on to Egypt, but that's another story, which I haven't received yet.) It had been censored naturally and I shall have to be patient until he comes home before I know what words should be filled in the gaps, but I rather gather that it wasn't exactly a picnic. The highlight of the journey was when he stopped at Capetown, and he says the folks there were wonderful, and gave him the time of his life. How he made our mouth water with tales of chicken, fruit salad, cream, fresh fruit, milk chocolate, scones heavily laden with butter and many other lovely things that seem but a memory now.

The latest duty for me to add to my list will be fire-watching at the place where I work. I have been doing it in the street at home for a long while, but it is now compulsory, and I shall have to do it at the firm as well. I don't mind this in the least, and I have heard that as we have enough men so far to do it at night, we will only have to be on duty when the place is closed during the day. This means from eight until six on Sundays, so you can see I shall have plenty of time to answer any letters which my unknown friends might write to me. It sounds a long while, especially on a Sunday, when you look forward to a rest, but as long as we occupy our time, knitting or sewing, or writing letters, then it will pass quickly and if we watch until the end of the war, and never have a fire to fight, then we shall consider our sacrifice well worthwhile. Actually too, to be perfectly honest, I hope I'm not a coward, but I don't really fancy spending the night in the district of the office, for it got such a pasting during the 'blitz'. Still lightning never strikes in the same place twice, and let's hope it never strikes again anywhere, this particular brand of lightning, although I'm afraid that this is rather a vain hope, for I guess we've plenty more 'taking' to do before we see the end of all this 'mess', but rest assured, we'll not rest, until we are 'giving' it back, good and hard.

Our flying boys are doing this already. Really, if I didn't hate the Germans so much for the things they have done, I could feel almost sorry for them when I hear the news of our big bomber raids, for it needs little imagination to know just what it must be like. As I write this our army boys aren't doing so bad either, and I like to think that my Don out there in the desert, behind his anti-tank gun, is helping to wipe out Rommel's armoured forces. Then I mustn't forget the navy, but then who could, for the navy is always there. We couldn't do without the boys in blue, bless 'em, they literally do mean meat and drink to us.

Also at the time of writing, your boys and the Aussies are putting up a wonderful show in the Solomons, and already we have seen news reels of the raids made over Europe by your 'flying fortresses'. Your boys, along with the Canadians and ours, went to Dieppe too, and some too, never came back. I wonder if you can imagine just how we felt at the time of the Dieppe raid. You see it is so near to us, almost near enough for us to stretch out our hand across the channel and touch it, and it is very hard to remember sometimes, just how near the enemy is, when we hear the terrible stories that come through from the occupied countries. We listened hourly almost to the news commentaries about the raid, and cheered and cheered when we knew how long it had lasted, and what a great deal of good they did, but then the realness of it all raised its ugly head. The cousin of one of the girls in the office had married a Canadian soldier just three weeks beforehand, and she heard that he had been killed. Fortunately, she has since heard that he is a prisoner, which must be marvellous news after hearing he was dead, but how worrying it must be now for all those homes with prisoners of war, now that they are being treated so badly. I hope that by the time this letter reaches you, things will be a bit better in that respect. Gosh, it must be terrible enough to know that you are a prisoner, and unable to help any more in the winning of the war, and to be beholden to your enemies for the bare necessities of life, without being maltreated into the bargain.

It seems so quiet and strange at home now, for there is only my baby sister of 13 and myself at home, now that my brother also has gone into the army. My sister Edna loves her life in the W.A.A.F. though, and after all she has good reason to, for she has become engaged to a boy in the town where she is stationed. He was discharged from the army after Dunkirk, and went through a good bit there so we believe, but like all the boys he never mentions anything about it. I often think of all the news Don will have for me when he comes home, but then if I think again, I can hear him say, 'It's over now, let's forget it' and I bet I'll never get a word out of him. His pal who is out there with him and who, next to his brother who was so tragically killed in action, means more to him than any other fellow, has written to tell us that he managed to escape from Tobruk when it fell, but how he did it, of course he can't write and tell us, even if he wanted to, and I'll lay odds that his sentence 'I've seen enough fun and games to last me the rest of my life', will be all we'll ever know of his experiences. Still maybe it's as well, after all that will be the only way after the war, we'll be so busy forgetting and making up for lost time, we won't want to hear about all the horrors of a war, which we swear will never happen again.

It is six months now since I last saw Don, and, although at times I get a rather hopeless lonely feeling of wondering just where all this is going to end, I am beginning to get over the awful feeling of 'aloneness' that hung around me for the first few months. Then of course there was Eric's death. We never mention it now, for we are gradually trying to forget, although it seemed for months fresh letters kept coming from his pals who were with him. Don learnt the news from his pal John, who is also out where he is, as John's letter reached him before any from home. I didn't want him to know at first. I think I was a little afraid that he might take unnecessary risks to avenge his brother, but now that he does know, maybe he will be too fully occupied to let his thoughts dwell on it very much, although naturally he was very cut up about it.

Still, as I say, I have come through the bad patch now, and I'm beginning to sit up and take notice of things around me again. I've been going gay too, having seen most of the shows in town, been away for weekends, and generally filling every spare minute away from the office, so as not to have time to stop and think. One of the best shows was Emlyn Williams' 'Morning Star', although it was all about the London blitz, and perhaps a little too realistic for some people. Personally I couldn't help enjoying it for it was so beautifully and sincerely acted, and far from upsetting me, I had many a smile as I saw reproduced many of the silly little things that we used to say and do. The effects were very good too. I really don't know how they managed so much realism in a stage show. Another good one, which took you completely away from the war, was 'Quiet Weekend'. This was a charming piece of nonsense about a family with a ramshackle little cottage in the country to which they all retired at weekends, and the consequent noise and bustle, instead of what they intended – a 'Quiet Weekend'. I seem to stick to straight plays these days, for I never used to see very many before, as Don liked revues, and somehow I just can't bring myself to go to a revue without him, for we always did the round of them all every season.

George is in the army now, after months of trying for his release, and at the moment is going through that hard initial training which seems to break all their hearts. Still they all come through it none the worse and I am sure once he gets settled down to what he wants to do, he will be happy. He wants to get into the Tank corps, but whether he will be accepted or not, we don't know.

Well, Donna, I won't carry this on and make it a long letter because of the weight for Air Mail, but if you'll promise to write me on receipt, I promise you that there will be one crossing it, from me, mid-ocean.

Cheerio, keep your chin up,
tons of love,
    Win

4th November 1942

My Dear Donna,
This is the letter I promised by air mail should be crossing the ocean to meet yours coming this way, and I do so hope that this is so, for it has seemed ages not hearing from you.

I have been hearing quite regularly from Don, once or maybe twice in two or three weeks. He cannot give me much news, of course, except that he is fit and well, and as he puts it always 'perfectly safe'. The highlight of existence, of course, is when the mail arrives, or when they get a well deserved leave and are able to visit a town for some entertainment. I'm afraid it would break my heart to know that I was on leave, and yet not able to get home.

George is by now quite settled in the Army, having completed his initial training, and is now in the R.A.S.C. (Royal Army Service Corps), although whether or not he will stay there or carry out his original intention and volunteer for the Tanks, I don't know. He should be on his first leave in a few weeks though, so I expect we'll hear all about it then. He was originally stationed quite near Edna and did once manage to get in to see her and Bill for the day on a Sunday, but now he is miles away, so goodness knows when they will meet again, for it would be very unusual if both their leaves ever coincided.

It seems so quiet at home these days, but we just seem to settle round the fire with our knitting, listening to the wireless on the evenings when I am not out, and I have managed to get quite a bit done recently. I've sent gloves off to both Don and George, made myself some ankle socks, made a pixie hood and gloves for young Alf, and now I have the pleasing prospect before me of knitting both Alf and David a couple of vests each for Christmas. Next Sunday will see me doing my first fire-watch at the office, so I'm anticipating taking quite a lot of knitting material with me, to keep me occupied for ten hours, as I'm hoping that I won't have any fires to fight, even though this is what I'm there for.

All the crowd of us that have been hiking all the summer have continued to meet on Sunday, going just for a short walk and then winding up at one or other of our houses for tea, each of us taking our own eats, etc. Sundays spent this way, Saturdays either working or collecting for the Savings Group, a couple of evenings a week visiting, and one at the flicks, appears to be my routine these days, although it is surprising just how quickly the weeks are flying by. Here we are into November. It'll be Christmas before we can turn round, and also before you get this no doubt, and then we'll start all over again on another year, a year which I hope marks Don's homecoming, and not his leaving as this year has.

I saw last night one of the finest films I have ever seen, greater even I believe than 'Mrs Minever'. It was 'This Above All'. They were both American-made films, and both, considering that they were made so far away, very good interpretations of England, and yet of the two I think 'This Above All' was the truest, and up against it, even 'Mrs Minever' becomes rather more your country's idea of what England is like, rather than the real thing. Don't miss it if it comes your way, for it will tell you so much of what I've always tried to tell you but found it hard to put into words, and so much of it was very typical. I loved the little country pub 'The Coach and Horses' for on our cycling tours Don and I have been in very many just such places, quaint, very old, very comfortable and excellent food. The village church and the village padre were typical. The scene on the coast where the waves broke on the shore as they have always done, but at the moment only to meet barbed wire, might have been the spot where we spent our honeymoon. The W.A.A.F.s were like any that you can see in England any day, of which my sister is one, and the soldier, well, although perhaps the likes of him are the minority, he was understandable. Any soldier who came through Dunkirk must have known that state of mental confusion, and we all of us know the job on hand is to win the war. Then, we can correct past faults afterwards.

Of course at the moment the newspapers and the news reels are showing us pictures of Mrs Roosevelt's visit to this country. She seems to have been here, there and everywhere already, but as yet I haven't seen her, but then of course London is a big place.

I had yet another wedding present a few weeks back from one of Don's sisters, a beautiful water set, one of the few beautiful things left in the glass and china shop from which I chose it, and a couple of glass bowls. My passion is china, and I just can't pass a shop without the urge to look in the window, and almost as rarely resist the temptation not to come out empty handed. Nowadays, however, there isn't much to look at, for none has been made for a long while, and if you're just lucky enough to pick something up that is old stock, well you are just lucky, and it sets your purse strings back a great deal. Utility china like everything else is the vogue now, but this is built for practical use and not for show. Utility though is a good word, for I have found it stands for good quality, and of course anything that is marked 'utility', be it clothes, furniture, china or anything else, is Purchase Tax free, and therefore much easier on the pocket.

Last Sunday evening I had the most enjoyable time I can remember, for I went with Dor, Dave and Betty, remember the three whom I spent my holiday with, and saw Sir Henry Wood conducting the London Symphony Orchestra in a Tchaikovsky programme. They played the Concerto in B and the Sixth Symphony, and although I have heard both these dozens of times, and always liked them, I have never known anything to compare with the thrill of sitting in that vast audience and seeing the curtain rise to show the orchestra on the stage, and of listening, carried away by the music, then clapping till my hands were sore. When I say I enjoyed every minute of it, that would be putting it mildly for it was wonderful. As I listened to the Concerto something seemed

Please note the written comment at the bottom of the programme which says, 'Air raid during performance – everybody stayed in their seats'

to tick over inside me, and almost without knowing it my eyes filled with tears and they ran down my cheeks, it was so moving and the pianist so very good. Don bought me the record of the first movement when he was on embarkation leave, so I guess this is why I love it so much. Also I can never hear 'Just a Little Love, a Little Kiss' now, without thinking of that last day of that short leave, when we went up to town and saw 'Smiling Through'. I've bought a recording of Jeanette MacDonald singing this, and it is one of my favourite records.

Well Donna, I seem to be very hard up for news at the moment. Everyone at home is quite well and jogging along as usual. The weather this past couple of weeks has been nothing short of filthy, rain and fog almost every day, and today we have had our first real 'pea-souper', which has lasted all day. I hate to think what it is going to be like travelling home tonight, but thank goodness I know there will be a warm house and a fire waiting when I do get home. This is one of the blessings of still being at home, for it would be awful to have to go home to an empty place in the winter, and have to light a fire and prepare my own meal. I expect this war has made a good many young married girls like me say 'Thank goodness for mothers' when they return from their day's work. By the way, I have been de-reserved, this means that my particular trade (shorthand and typing) no longer automatically exempts me, but the firm have to apply for my exemption on the ground that my work is of national importance. Mum is hoping of course that I won't have to leave home also, but I don't think there is any fear of that, for there is too much work where I am.

Well, Donna, this does seem to be about all, and just in case this reaches you around the right date, a very Happy Christmas to you (it makes Don's third away from home, but of course the first in a strange country) and a bright and peaceful New Year for us all.

Cheerio for now,
it won't be long,
tons of love,
    Win

3rd December 1942

My Dear Donna,

Your very welcome letters both arrived on Friday last, thanks a lot. It was grand to hear from you after so long, and I do hope that you keep your promise not to keep me waiting so long next time. There I go, never satisfied, am I? All the same, as I said, I was very pleased to hear all the news, and certainly agree with you that one day I must sample a slice of Colorado moon and a campfire. I haven't heard anything from any of your friends who are now over here, but have no doubt I will when leave comes round.

My wandering boy has wandered off into yet another part of the world, but if you have already written to his old address I'm sure it will follow him up. If on the other hand you haven't already written, and you would like to, I could always re-address it. He tells me that he has already been in eight different countries since he left dear old England, imagine. Won't he have some stories to tell on his return? I knew most of them, and also where he is now, but I don't think I'd better tell you now, maybe later on, when it isn't so important. Suffice it to say that I hear fairly regularly from him and he always seems very bright and cheerful, and confident that 'it won't be long'.

I posted off my last letter to you just about a day before the grand news of our Middle East offensive came through. Boy has it made us feel good. You can't possibly imagine just how wonderful it is to hear good news, and good news that somehow you feel confident this time will last, after three years of defeat. Hot on the heels of the first rush of good news from Egypt came news of the American landings in French North Africa, and these two pieces of good news were almost too much to bear. I was a little doubtful at first, I thought we mustn't be too optimistic, it's happened before and we've only just built ourselves up for a big let down, but then it continued, and somehow now I do believe that this is the real thing at last. They rang the bells too, and they sounded grand, and yet although I was thankful and terribly grateful for what they'd done, and was pleased and happy for the sake of those boys who at last were getting their own back, somehow I just couldn't let myself go and rejoice. You see I'd always thought, 'When we hear the bells again, it'll be all over, no more killing, no more bloodshed, no more heartaches and separations', and yet when those bells rang the other Sunday, I couldn't feel this, for I know that even though it was a victory we were celebrating, there is going to be a lot more bloodshed before 'THE VICTORY'. Come now, I'm getting morbid and that's the last thing I want you to think I am. In fact I've never seen people quite as bright and happy as they have been these last couple of months. The news seems to have put new heart into everyone and filled everyone anew with a will to keep going until it is all finished. Just imagine the feelings of those men, going forward, after that long push last summer. John was one of those we have not heard from since the offensive started, but in Don's words, 'Never worry over John, he'll always be O.K.' We hope so anyway.

The main item of news at the moment is this new 'Beveridge Plan'. Opinions seem to be many and varied, but the general attitude seems to be – 'It's a good thing if it works out in practice as it does in theory.' It goes to show however that things are definitely going to be different after this is all over, and naturally it's up to us to see that the difference is for the better. My sister said though, 'If they change things too much, England won't be the England we know any more, and that's what we're fighting for', but she is wrong, for England will always be England, no matter how many changes take place. You can't change the fields and woodlands, the sea, the sky, the wind and the rain, cricket in the summer, football in the winter, happy crowds of cyclists riding coastwards on Bank Holiday, and all the million and one little things that are so important. It is the big things that must change, mainly amongst these, want and the threat of wars. These we must change to preserve the rest.

9th December 1942

Sorry for the long gap. During this time I have been absolutely up to my ears in work, with not a minute to spare, and have also received a couple of letters from Don. These were fairly old ones, written way back in October, but they told us that he is 'fit and well', and that is the news I always long to hear.

Edna has been taking her corporal's course recently which meant that for three weeks she was stationed down South. This week is the last week, so if she passes it will mean she might be posted anywhere, maybe not only a good way from home as she has been for over a year now, but a good way from the town where she met the fellow she is engaged to. However, she seized the opportunity whilst she was home, or near home I mean, and for the last two weekends she has come home Saturday evening and stayed until Sunday. Bill too has come down, and it has really felt like old times to have the house full again. For the first weekend my brother George was on leave also, and we all went to a dance. Gosh did I enjoy it, the first time I have really been to a dance since the war. We are getting to know Bill quite well now, and are fast getting used to his Northern English. He wants to come South after the war though, as he likes Eltham very much.

Maybe in a matter of months now I shall be in uniform, for gradually all the young girls even married ones are being taken from offices. I shan't go until they find an older woman to replace me, and how long this will take I don't know, anyway I will give you fair warning before I actually do go, for then you will have to write more than often to me, and forgive me if I don't answer very promptly. Still as I said before, more about that when the time comes.

Your letter rather surprised us all over here, when you told how you had been at college all the summer and were now staying at home until school next year. You see over here all girls from 16 to 41 are unable to leave a job, if they are sent into it, and everyone works long hours on important work, and does some kind of national service as well. If we take half a day off for no good reason we are liable to be fined, or at least warned. We don't grudge you your good fortune, please don't think that, but we do think you are very lucky, and we would all like to know how things are 'over there'. We know girls aren't compelled to do war jobs like we are, but doesn't anyone do anything? It seemed awful to us when boys of eighteen are being conscripted for the forces to hear that at 20 it is still possible for a girl to be at school, and not worrying unduly about the war. After all if we don't know we can't judge, can we? When Mrs Roosevelt was over here she said she was going to pass on to the women of her country what was happening over here, so obviously someone is interested.

George had quite a good leave, but I don't think he was really sorry to go back for there wasn't really anything much for him to come home to, for when he was home, all his pals were in the Army, and now he is in the Army himself, all his pals are overseas. He wants to go himself, as soon as they will let him, and although I don't want to see him go, I know it is what he wants.

These last two weekends when Edna and Bill and George have been home, we've been having a 'small Christmas' of our own, for we know they won't be here then. We had mince pies from a carefully hoarded jar of mince, a trifle made from a jelly which Mum managed to get, and sweets and chocolates which we had saved from our ration for Christmas; all came out and we had one grand flare up. How we are longing for our peace-party, and how we look and sigh when we think of all the wonderful parties we have had at '23'. I expect we shall spend Christmas Day quietly at home for there will only be Mum and Dad and young Phyll there besides myself, and there are no prizes offered for where our thoughts will be on that day, as always. Do you know that this will mean Don's third Christmas away from home, and his first out of England? I wonder how he will feel under the heat of the tropical sun, thinking of Christmas in England, and cold winds, holly, Christmas pudding, turkey, crackers, presents, and all the other things that make Christmas so dear. Still we can only pray that next year, the world will see sense again, and all the boys will be back home by their own firesides, telling their yarns and their adventure stories.

We over here never really understood much about Thanksgiving Day before. I had heard you mention it once or twice, but I didn't understand. It took a war, and the arrival of your boys to really teach us, for this year they held a service in Westminster Abbey. We heard all about it on the radio, and one party of soldiers even went to a school and told the children all about what Thanksgiving Day really meant. Somebody was telling me that American soldiers love our children as they think they are younger than American children, more childish sort of, if that doesn't sound too absurd.

I have worked most Saturday afternoons for the past two months, but despite this I have managed somehow to procure time in which to search the shops for things for all my nephews and nieces. You see I have Don's three nieces, as well as my own brother's two boys. I sent Don's parcel off in August, so I'm hoping it will reach him by Christmas.

I am enclosing some snaps that were taken in the summer when we were out hiking. Don't take any notice of our 'glad rags', we never cared what we wore. The Betty I have named was the girl who came on holiday with me this year, and is in the W.A.A.F. Although they all look a happy enough crowd, they all have some sort of tragedy in their lives: Jessie's boyfriend was killed in the Far East; June hasn't heard from her husband since the fall of Malaya a year ago; Betty has lost her boyfriend, for he was Don's brother Eric, and Con is Don's sister, so she has lost a brother. The rest of us with just our husbands thousands of miles away are the lucky ones.

Whilst George was on leave we all went up to town and saw a show 'Murder Without Crime', and last Saturday evening I saw a revival of that grand film 'Dangerous Moonlight'; that Warsaw Concerto really is the tops. Apart from that I haven't seen many good films at all, for it is so dark in the evenings now, and travelling home is so difficult that the only really comfortable time to go out is on Saturdays, and of course I've been unlucky and done a lot of overtime on Saturday afternoons lately. Still I won't be working this Saturday, firstly because I'm having a perm, and secondly because I am on fire-watch at the firm on Sunday.

I don't suppose this will arrive until afterwards, but once again may I wish you and yours and also all the kind folks who ask after me, a very Merry Christmas, and Peace for us all in the New Year.

Cheerio for now,
tons of love,
    Win

1943

Most of the events described in the letters making up this book had long since been erased from my memory, and only reading the letters brought them back to life for me.

However, events described in the following letter have remained crystal clear in my memory throughout my long life. I have only to close my eyes and I am back there under that tumbled heap of girls emerging through the cloakroom door. The sight that met the eyes of that frightened girl as she looked out of the window of that top floor, at eye ball to eye ball level with the diving planes with their black crosses, has remained with me always.

We heard later that a school at Catford had been hit in that raid. Now at that time I had lived most of my life in the leafy London suburb of Eltham, and all I knew of Catford was that it was a residential suburb some three miles further in to the centre of London. I had ridden through it on the bike, en route to somewhere else, but as I didn't know anyone who lived there, I had never actually been in the area nor did I know the names of any of the roads.

The houses in the part of Catford where the school stood had been built in the latter part of the nineteenth century, into the beginning of the twentieth. In 1904, the builder of the estate built this magnificent primary school. It took up the width of two roads, so it was bounded on one side by the houses and back to back gardens of Ardgowan Road, and Minard Road. Along the fourth side ran the main road from which the school took its name – Sandhurst Road School.

I was not to know on that January day in 1943 that just six years later Don and I were to buy a house in Minard Road, or that I would still be living in that very house today, over 50 years later.

So it was that Catford replaced Eltham as my 'home town' as it were, and in 1951 my five-year-old daughter started her school days there in the infants at Sandhurst school. By then of course the school had been re-built and to this day it remains a building of two halves: one half being the architecture of a century ago, and the other half, immediate post-war modern. It was during Christine's time there in the infants that several memorial seats were dedicated in memory of those who died on that January day in 1943.

Thirty-eight children and six teachers were the victims of the bombing and machine-gunning, and in the local churchyard ten minutes down the road there is the mass grave of all these people. Also in the little chapel in the grounds of the churchyard is a memorial plaque commemorating the condolences sent at the time by the children of Mexico to the children of Catford.

Only a few years ago the school and playground underwent a 'face lift' as more class rooms were built, and at that time a corner of the playground was turned into a small memorial garden into which those earlier post-war dedicated seats were shifted.

All this information I have learned over the years as very little was readily available at the time. I am sure there are still people around today who were in Catford at the time and have their tales to tell of being chased by a machine-gunning plane.

Me, I was just a frightened girl, some three miles or so away, really thinking her last day had come.

I found this letter rather uncomfortable to read, being so disjointed with all the censored cuttings, but I decided it was such an important event, the letter should go into the book, as is, with this explanation before it.
[Note: part of the letter has been cut out by the censor and these places are bridged with the word 'censored' to show where the words are missing.]

20th January 1943

My Dear Donna

It seems I leave it for weeks and weeks without writing to you because nothing of importance seems to happen, and then just when I have a free hour this afternoon, little did I think that less than half an hour before I sat down to write, I should have all the excitement I did.

I'd better start from the beginning I think, and then you will get the idea straight. Firstly as you no doubt know we had the first air raid for almost eighteen months on Sunday night, and although there were plenty of bombs all around us, we were all right. There were two raids actually, and for the first I was with friends, although not very far from home. The barrage was terrific. How on earth any plane could survive that onslaught I can't possibly imagine; it was as though they were making up three-fold for all the weary months of waiting and keeping on the alert. As soon [censored] long since [censored] Don's sister Connie and I saw a fire [censored] walked, and then suddenly it seemed to be nearer than we at first imagined, and we realized it was at the bottom of the road we were walking down. I was concentrating my eyes on the fire, trying to work out what it was, whether it was a house or just incendiaries in the front garden, vaguely conscious of the fact that we were walking through mud and glass. Suddenly Con caught my arm, and the tone of her voice as she said, 'Oh Win, look,' made me wonder just what to expect as I turned my head. The sight of a house in ruins after so long brought it all back, for all the houses that were damaged or destroyed in the earlier raids have long ago been tidied up, and all that remains now is either shored up walls or just gaps. This experience all over again of seeing a house down like a pack of cards with all the debris piled on top was rather disturbing, although I learnt the next day that there had been no casualties, which after all is the main thing. The fire was nothing more serious than a main, although it looked much worse from the distance. We picked our way through and hurried home, much relieved to find them all safe and sound. After a brief exchange of 'bomb stories' we all went to bed, only to be rudely awakened again in the early hours by the siren. Again, guns crashed and bombs fell, and for an hour it was pretty lively, but it is uncanny the way you become used to it all again. I couldn't sleep when I got back to bed, as it was nearly time to be getting up for work anyway, but I did manage to have that last hour in the comfort of a bed, and not in the dugout. Young Alf, now three and a half, is unfortunately just old enough to be frightened of the noise, but we talk to him and do our best to keep him amused. It's funny though, you can't even fool a child of that age, for when Dad

Inscription on the memorial reads:
'Sacred to the memory of 38 children and 6 teachers who were killed when Sandhurst Road School was bombed by a lone German aeroplane on Wednesday 20th January 1943'

brought him down into the shelter I started talking to him straight away – Did he see the pretty fireworks when Grandad brought him down the garden? Didn't they make a fine bang? – but when the All Clear went and my brother came to take him back to bed, he said, 'No more guns, Daddy, eh,' so all my talk of 'pretty fireworks' had just been so much wasted time.

When the sirens sounded again on Monday, we thought we were in for another dose, but nothing came of it, and after a quiet night then and again last night, things seemed to have settled down again. Then, at lunch time today just as we were all drinking our mid-day cup of tea before going up to the canteen, the siren went. It had barely ceased, and we hadn't even had time to make up our minds whether to get below or go to lunch as usual, when suddenly there was a terrific whizz, the roar of Aero engines and the clash of guns. For a split second I couldn't imagine what was happening, it just seemed as though everything had gone haywire. It proves one thing though, habit is stronger even than instinct, for instinct should have told me to drop everything and get below (we are on the top floor) but habit told me to go and put my cup in

Hither Green Cemetery (taken in October 2003). The memorial to the victims of the bombing of Sandhurst Road School is in the foreground. Around the border it has the names and ages of the children and of one of the six teachers who were killed and are buried here. The cross in the background is in memory of all local citizens killed by enemy action.

the sink. I did this, and as I opened the door to come out of the cloakroom, the roar of planes had got louder and I automatically fell flat. All this happened in a matter of seconds. I didn't know what to think it could be, and only remember having a vague feeling 'This is it' and quite expecting to know no more. We found out later, when we all gave vent to our feelings by laughing at the things we had done in those few seconds, in the comparative safety of the shelter, that all the noise had been due to [censored] coming down. It missed the roof [censored] the noise [censored] again. After this first brief episode of excitement, we heard more planes and more guns, and more bombs were dropped, but after a while it all subsided and we went to our lunch, just about an hour late. At the moment we are all wondering how our folks are at home. Some of the girls who have heard that the bombs fell near their homes have gone home to see if everything is O.K. Somebody has already rung a friend at Eltham and apparently there was nothing doing there, and no doubt Mum knows nothing about what has been going on here. No amount of blitzes or bombs have ever given me quite the same feeling as when those diving planes zoomed overhead; it was something entirely different from anything I have ever felt before, and yet I have a faint feeling of pride, for I don't remember feeling scared or panicky. I just knew that something was happening and there wasn't anything I could do about it. I see the tea is just coming round, everyone is getting on with their work as usual, you wouldn't think that just a short while ago we were all thinking our last had come.

Isn't the news grand? The raising of the siege of Leningrad, to say nothing of the successes of our 'eighth' and the bombing of Berlin, are very heartening. We can take all his bombs on London, after all we did it once before, why not again, if only everything continues to move in the right direction.

I haven't heard from Don for quite some while, quite a long while for me, and yet I suppose it isn't really, it is just that lately I have been hearing so regularly, I am getting spoilt. Apparently life in the mystic East is going on much the same as usual, but I live for the day he returns. I think it will be the happiest day of my life, and that's saying a lot, for I've had some happy days in the past.

We've not heard from any of your friends yet, although there are plenty of your fellows here. The latest crack is 'I was talking to an English soldier in London' – 'Is there an English soldier in London?' Although it isn't quite to this extreme, there are very few certainly; they are all either flying, on the sea or in the East, it seems.

21st January 1943

Hallo again,

Now that the excitement has died down and we have all been home and heard from all the other members of our families just where and what they were doing at the time of the 'incidents' yesterday, we can laugh over some of the funny things we said and did. I think this is one of the funniest, although to appreciate it you must understand how rare an egg is. We get one every two or three months perhaps if we are lucky. At different times of the year of course we get more, but naturally during the winter an egg is a luxury. One of the girls had one, and was just cooking it for her lunch when the planes swooped on us and of course she fell flat on the floor, egg and all, and not only ruined a perfectly good pair of stockings, this is a tragedy in itself, but almost spread her egg over the entire cloak-room floor. Later on in the afternoon, her boyfriend, who is stationed some way out and who knew nothing of the 'fun and games', just rang her as he generally does, and was amazed when she said, 'I thought you might have rung sooner to find out how I was.' Of course he replied, 'What's happened then?' and she promptly told him, 'What's happened? Oh nothing to speak of, I've been dive-bombed, laddered my stockings and dropped an egg.' 'What,' says he, 'an egg, a real egg, you dropped it, now how did you come to do that, dear?' and that seemed to be as much as he worried, the dive-bombing was just of secondary importance. What tickled us all too, was the office manager's 'Blimey they're here', as he fell flat, and he assure us that that was marvellous self-control, he might have said something much worse.

Of course when it is all over we see the tragedies as well as the comical things. Dreadful things happened that I wouldn't like to give you the details of. Apart from the school that received a direct hit (it's all right to mention this, for it was in the papers) many and varied are the tales I heard of machine-gunning people running for shelter, children in the street, one moment in all innocence waving to the low-flying plane, the next a mass of machine-gun bullets. We don't talk about these things, we just store them up in our minds, and wait, for we know that one day the opportunity will come our way, and these deeds will be avenged. The most dreadful thing about the school that was hit though was that [censored] every other person it seems had a son or daughter, a niece or nephew, or the child next door, or one that lives over the way, or in the next street, in it, and we keep hearing such things as 'yes, he was saved but his nerves are in a terrible state' or 'the little girl next door was killed', 'they dug my niece out with two broken legs, but she was alive.'

Have you seen any good films lately? I haven't been this week, but last week I saw what I believe to be the finest picture of the war – Noel Coward's 'In Which We serve'. I understand it is being shown in the States (minus the very British 'nautical' language, which rather amuses us, as it does not strike me as being so terrible, and anyway the occasions on which it was used justified such), and I can't advise you strongly enough, not to miss it. The acting was superb and each character true to life in every respect, typical of anybody you might meet walking along the streets of England any day. Then of course, I have a soft spot for anything to do with the Navy. Although Don is in the Army, of which I am justly proud, there is something about a sailor, whether you see an officer looking smart and efficient in his Navy blue and gold, or an ordinary seaman in his fresh white shirt and bell-bottoms. They always look so full of life and so healthy. Of course we know only too well just what we owe to them all. This goes for the merchant lads of course, they wear no uniform but we don't admire them any the less, they are all near and dear to us.

I laughed my head off at Bing's 'The Road to Morocco' but then he always was a favourite of mine. I saw the 'Pied Piper' too recently and fell for Monty Woolly all over again as he had already won my heart in 'The Man Who Came to Dinner'.

Edna was on leave for the New Year and had quite a hectic week. She is now in charge of her own crew, and of course feeling her feet very much, although actually she has had a couple of days in bed, through failing to keep on her feet literally. Apparently the balloon caught her up in a gale and brought her down again in a lovely pile of gravel. According to her letter she is a mass of grazes but apart from being violently sick during the night, nothing more serious seems to have happened. The best part about it seems to have been that while she spent the rest of the time in bed, the crew and her other corporal were out until half past two getting the balloon down in the gale. One rather ironic little point – a friend of Edna's who passed out just a few weeks before her was posted to London, and only had her balloon and her crew a matter of weeks when her balloon was brought down in the machine-gunning of Wednesday. Edna incidentally is rather kicking herself, for she could have had a crew in London, but preferred to be in the home town of her boyfriend, so she turned down the London offer. Now she has been sent miles from either spot, as Bill's hometown had no vacancies, so she might just as well have come to London, where she could at least have spent a few hours at home now and again.

Just off to lunch, there doesn't seem much news, so I'll close down for now, with the same old words, 'Please let me hear from

you soon.' My kindest regards to all my friends in Lamar, and lots of love for yourself.
   Cheerio,
      tons of love, pal,
         Win

10 March 1943

My Dear Donna,
At last I have a few minutes to sit down and endeavour to at least get started on answering your very welcome letter which arrived last week, and to offer my very humble apologies for not having answered your other letter which came some time during January. I was more than thrilled to get them both, and can only say that the reason why I haven't written for such a long stretch is due to the fact that work has just been piling up and up since Christmas and with fewer people to do it, there just isn't even enough time to breathe almost, without attempting to start on one of my usual long epistles. All my evenings and weekends also seem to have been crammed full too, what with fire-watching and the savings and now, as if I hadn't enough to do already, I am going through a course of first aid lectures and hope to take my first exam in the summer.
   My dear Donna, I was so happy to hear your wonderful news and hope that this letter arrives in good time for the wedding. At a time like this, when you must already be surround by good wishes, there seem little for me to add, but I can only say that you know I wish you life-long happiness and luck, and without sounding too smug firmly believe that if you get halfway towards the happiness Don and I have known, and have the same faith and trust which will carry you triumphant through trials and separations such as we have known, then you will have far more in your one life, than many could hope to have in a million years. How it takes me back, when I read of all your preparations, and although maybe I do turn a slight shade of green with envy as I read of all the wonderful things you are able to buy, and then glance at my twenty clothing coupons, I'm not jealous really, but very glad for you.

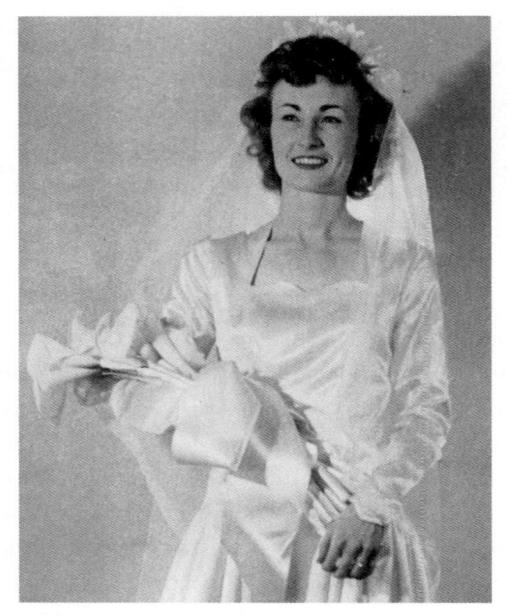

Donna on her wedding day, 21st March 1943

Your engagement party sounded terrific. I do wish I could have been there, but we must make up for this after the war. I should love to have been able to send you a present or at least a cable, but it isn't possible, so when, on your wedding day, you read of other absent friends' good wishes, imagine that the enclosed is a cable from us, and then we will bring you something for your home when we come later. Perhaps you would send a photograph of Richard. After all I've got to see whether I approve of your choice, haven't I? Your going away outfit really sounds the cat's whiskers. I should love to be able to see you in it, but I must be patient and just await your letters telling me all about everything.

    I was more than interested to hear about the war effort of your women, and far from grudging you your college education, Donna, I heartily agree with everything you say. After all, I'd be all kinds of dog in the manger to say that because it isn't possible for us over here to live in any way a normal life, then others more fortunately situated should not do so also. It's just that friendships like ours are the only way to settle these little differences of opinion that arise. I've always been perfectly frank, so I intend to be so now.

Over here many people do think, 'What are the Yanks doing?' Remember we've had almost four years of war, we realise what it means, and it is apt to rile people over here when they hear and read things that show only too clearly, at least as far as we are able to see from merely reading and hearsay, that the average American doesn't yet realise the seriousness of it all. Then you see it does rather rub salt on the wound when we hear that you people feel the same way about us, and ask, 'What are the British doing?' I read an article once, I believe I have included it in the newspapers I send to Don, or else I would have cut it out for you. It was written by an Englishman in New York, and he said the Americans couldn't be blamed for their opinion of us, for they just didn't know the half of it. We know that, as well as receiving food and munitions from you, we also send food and other munitions to you, that just as your people refuel and repair our ships, so we repair and refuel American ships in British ports, and so on, in connection with almost everything you can think of, and yet, according to this particular article the average American knows nothing of this, but thinks that it is they that are doing everything and us nothing. This of course that I tell you now, is just opinions by people on both sides, whose only contact with the opinion of the other side, is third hand, that is by means of the newspaper or the radio. We, you and I, are different; we can get our knowledge first hand. If I want to know anything about your country I ask you, and like a pal, you've always done your best to put me straight. Likewise, I have always tried to give you an accurate and true impression of not only my life and the lives of those in my family, which is a perfectly average English family, but of the little corner of the world in which I live and move, and which is 'my world'. Now, when I hear the old question come up, I can say, 'But you don't understand, why, let me read you a paragraph from a friend of mine, and then you'll understand.' Then again, if that article I read is correct, you can tell your friends about me, and what we think, and this way, in our own small capacity, we should be doing something towards that 'great understanding' which at present seems to me to be a great misunderstanding.

I will tell you about my family, most of it you know already, but if you or anyone else who reads these words would care to use it as an example to be compared to the average American at war, then I swear it to be a true picture of us over here. My father is an engineer doing a full time job, in addition to which he does his 48 hours per month compulsory fire-watching, and voluntarily fire-watches at home and is the street fire-watching captain. This means that he is responsible for the smooth running of the rota and for all the fire-fighting equipment. He grows all our vegetables in the back garden, and saves regularly in his firm's savings group. My mother works half a day, six days a week, in the local hospital, and the rest of the time, keeps house, washes and cooks for us all, collects the rations, and generally hunts for bargains and little delicacies to help our war-time rations. My elder brother, like my father, works at a skilled job all day, spends all his free time as an Air Raid Warden, is out whenever the siren goes at night, digs his garden and saves what he can. You know most of what there is to know about me. I work in the office of an engineering firm, everything we do is essential to the war. I do my compulsory business premises fire-watching like everyone else, and voluntary fire-watch at home too, also like most other people. One evening a week sees me tripping in and out of all the houses down the street, collecting their weekly savings and turning them into certificates (or, as you say, 'war bonds'). Saturday morning also sees me on a similar mission round the office, and again a few minutes after to collect their weekly contributions to the Red Cross. First Aid is a comparatively new addition to my duties, but when I am trained I will be on duty during daylight raids at the office.

Meat takes ships to bring it across the sea, so we keep rabbits, and Dad and my little sister between them carry out this job.

We all have our income tax deducted weekly, based on our previous year's earnings, and it is pretty stiff, but a portion will be repaid after the war, so it is really like extra saving. There is a tax of $33\frac{1}{3}\%$ on all luxury goods, which includes clothes other than the government utility models which are Purchase Tax free.

Many things which cost but a few shillings before the war, now cost a pound or more. Despite our war bonuses, wages haven't risen to the same extent as prices. The only thing that hasn't increased to a great extent is food, which in my opinion was a very far-sighted piece of work. Nobody could grumble at all about the food rations, they are fair, and we do pretty well, all things considered. We get twenty clothing coupons to last us approximately six whole months. If you need a full length coat, you say goodbye to 18 of these right away. Fully fashioned stockings take three a pair, and if you buy three pairs at once, and darn them and darn them, as I have done, they will last you the winter, but then if you do this, you can't have a coat too, maybe a pair of shoes for five, and a short-sleeved dress for seven, and perhaps two ounces of wool to knit a pair of gloves. Then again, if you buy a dress you can't buy undies, so we plan, and we spend our precious coupons on what we need only. We pay a lot for what we buy, if we can afford to, for we know that it has got to last. We don't grumble, in fact we get quite a kick out of 'making do' and renovations and after all we are all in the same boat, so we do not mind. There are no cars now for private use only, and only those used for strictly essential business are still on the road. Save of course for a few exceptions where disabled people in remote country places have no other means of transport. If one goes out for an evening, it means catching the last tram or bus at approximately ten o'clock, and in some places much earlier than this, or walking, and as walking in the black-out, except on a moonlit starry night, isn't exactly everybody's idea of a picnic, we mostly catch the bus.

We all have our members in the services to whom we constantly write, and who are forever in our thoughts. Their safety and their home-coming being the goal for which we are working.

There you have it, us as we really are, not particularly hard done by, or self-sacrificing really. We work hard, and compared to the freedom of our pre-war lives, I suppose we do put up with a certain amount of hardship, but we know that nothing we have ever endured is in any way to be compared with our Russian allies, so we work and fight hard to back them up, and to end just as speedily as possible this awful war. That is our main thought, all our plans say 'after the war, we will do this or that or whatever dream we have in mind.'

Is it clear, do you think you know us now, do you think we are doing all that it is possible for us to do, to win the war?

But I've been getting too serious. By the time this letter arrives you won't be interested in anything to do with the war. I know I put it out of my mind as far as humanly possible at the time I was married. So I'll get into the spirit of the thing and try to tell you some of the lighter diversions of my life during the past few weeks.

Letters from Don come frequently and speedily, for which I never cease to marvel at my good fortune. In exactly three weeks' time it will be a year since I last saw him. I've had several snapshots and photographs from him lately, and although he looks older and more serious, and naturally tanned a dark brown, he is still the same cheerful old Don. No desert could change him. He had a good Christmas, received my parcels safely, and feels convinced that he will be home for the next one.

About a fortnight ago George came home on leave, and as at this time we were all beginning to feel a little bored with the staid, steady flow of life, we decided to have a party. Much to the amazement of all our friends, who thought us crazy to attempt such a thing under present conditions, we managed it. Edna got 24 hours leave to come home and brought her boyfriend with her for the weekend. Several of my pals from the office came, George was there, of course, and Mum and Dad. We secured a precious jelly and with the aid of custard and sponge, made quite a pre-war looking trifle. We opened our last remaining pre-war tin of very tiny sardines and put these on toasted fingers of bread. We bought rolls and with the aid of fish-paste and mustard and cress made appealing eats of these, and then, best bag of all, was a bottle of port, and beer for the boys. We danced and sang and played games, and then when far into the night, Mum and Dad gave up the unequal struggle and went to bed, the rest of us kept up the party spirit all night, and somehow or other very dark eyed managed to get through Sunday as well without any sleep. Edna and Bill returned on Sunday afternoon and save for a couple all the others went home. We rounded off the weekend with a game of Monopoly, finished up the last of the port and the beer, and although I felt like nothing on earth on Monday morning at the office, the whole weekend had been a tonic to us all. We had recaptured something of our pre-war gaiety. Remember some of the grand parties we used to have at Christmas time? We are going to endeavour to have another one just like it next time George is on leave. The girls at the office are still talking about it even now, although it all happened over a week ago.

Edna should be on leave this week also, but her boyfriend is ill, so she is spending it with him, and will just come home for a couple of days before returning.

You mentioned in your last letter that you hoped I wouldn't have to join up after all. Well it rather looks now as if I shan't have to, at least for the time being. I was called for an interview, but when they heard about my work and all the circumstances, and mostly I think because I have a husband serving, they told me that for the time being I might stay where I was.

One of the office 'babies', she is only 17, got married last week as her boyfriend got embarkation leave, and another is getting married at the end of this month, so we are getting to be a real hen party.

Whilst George was home we couldn't book for a show up town, so we went locally and saw a really good variety bill, which couldn't have been beaten anywhere, so we had our evening out all together just the same as usual.

When it comes to putting down on paper just what I have been doing with myself since I last wrote, there doesn't seem to be anything to write, for life goes on much the same, most of the time. We've had a few raids, the barrage gets better and better every time, but the raids themselves are nothing to speak of. Events out East seem to be continuing very well, despite the few setbacks at first, and of course we are all hoping and praying that at last the turning point has come, and before long it will all be over.

I am sending a few polyfotos that I had taken on the express wish of that husband of mine, as he always took a very keen interest in my hats, and after I had written telling him that I had bought a new one, he would not rest until I had had my photo taken in it for him to see and pass his approval. Actually they aren't terribly good, the only time I could get to the studio being a Saturday afternoon, when it was crowded. There was only one machine and one operator, so I had an hour's wait, by which time my temper wasn't at its best, and I just didn't care how I looked, anything to get the job over and done with. However, I have ordered Don's enlargements, so I hope he doesn't think them too bad. I'm having some that he sent home to me copied, so that his mother and sisters may each have a print, and there will be one for you too.

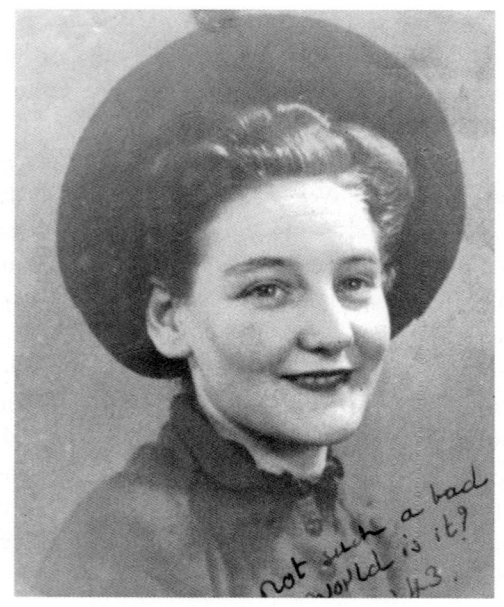

Don's favourite picture – he requested I buy a 'halo' hat as they were called. The inscription in the corner reads, 'Not such a bad world is it?'

I have been trying to get Don's log book copied, so that I might send you a copy and have been holding up my letter so as to enclose this, but judging by the length of time I have kept you waiting this time, it seems that completion of this job is a long way off. However, I will continue to stick at it in all my free time and also promise you that I will write without so much delay next time.

Once again thanking you for your letters, and wishing you and Richard all the very best, I'll sign off for now, and see about getting on with some of this work.

Cheerio, keep smiling, it won't be long now,
tons of love,
    Win

Early in 1943 the Airgraph service started for letters to the Forces overseas. The idea was to cut down on weight for mail being sent to the troops.

It worked this way. You bought an Airgraph Form at the Post Office in much the same way as you buy an air letter form today, postage was included. The Airgraph Form consisted of a sheet of shiny buff paper, slightly larger than an A4 sheet, with a printed heading to write or type in the name and address, and then you had the rest of the sheet to write or type your letter. You were not allowed to fold it, so after it was written it had to be handed over the counter at the P.O. No privacy at all. It was then processed so it was reduced in size to about 3' x 4', and you can imagine thousands could be transported very easily this way. The service was relatively quick and cheap and the tiny writing when you were on the receiving end was surprisingly easy to read.

It seems from the following letter that I had been mistakenly told I could send one to U.S.A. and had sent Donna one to show her what they were like, but it was returned. I obviously then forwarded it to her to show how much you could get on to one of these forms.

Like everything else at the time, it brought forth its jokes, and when a woman whose husband had been serving overseas for a long while, became pregnant, the joke was, 'It happened by Airgraph.'

Airgraph and letter, May 1943

Airgraph:
My Dear Donna,
Now that we can send these to your part of the world I thought perhaps you would like to receive one. I have got so used to sending these to and fro across the sea to Don that it seems strange now to write an ordinary letter. My type-writer ribbon isn't as black as it should be, so would you please let me know if this is clear enough to read when you get it, and how long it takes. Well, and how are you? It is a beautiful day today and I am keeping my fingers crossed that it may last for the weekend, as I am going away to the country. I didn't go away at Easter and I really feel now as though I do need a break and a change, if only for a few days. I am hearing just as regularly from Don, in fact, I have had seven of these and a couple of air letters in the past week, which breaks even his good record. Hearing so regularly makes all the difference. I sent an ordinary letter off a couple of weeks ago, so I am wondering whether perhaps this might arrive first. I saw a really super film last

week, 'Casablanca', and think it is one of the finest there has been for many a long day. This week's choice – 'Springtime in the Rockies' is quite good, in as much as it was light and airy and took one out of oneself, but really left me cold after the terrific impression that 'Casablanca' made on me. The news continues very good indeed. Let's hope it really won't be long now before we can all start living again – boy am I going to get tight that day. Just room to wish you and Richard and all my friends all the very best. Tons of love. Keep smiling. Win

Letter: 14th May 1943

My Dear Donna

Just a short little note, as I really haven't much news, but I find myself with half an hour to spare, up to date on my letters to Don, so I couldn't let this golden opportunity pass.

 I wrote an Airgraph last week, as I had heard that it was possible to send these to you now, and the girl in the Post Office even told me how much it cost, but it came back again marked 'no service', so I am sending it to you as it is, to let you know what the forms are like, and on the back I have pencilled the size you would have received if it had been photographed and sent to you, as those I send and receive from Don. You can imagine how much smaller the writing would be; surprisingly enough they are very easy to read.

18th May 1943

Hallo again. I'm sorry about the gap but duty called, and I haven't had a chance since Friday to come back and finish this.

 I was on fire-watch on Sunday but I met my girl friend Win (the one who has been evacuated to the country since the outbreak of the war) in town, as she was home for the weekend, and saw Joan Crawford in 'M'mselle France', which we enjoyed very much. She is staying in a very nice place, and now has a bed-sitting room with kitchen and bathroom which she shares with another girl, instead of a billet, so I am going down there in a week's time for my holiday. Only a week, but it will make a break and I feel as though I need it. Also, I prefer early June because of the nice long evenings. We have planned that I just potter around the town or the surrounding countryside during the day, and then the three of us paint the town red at night, which sounds all right to me. These provincial towns have a lot of advantage over London, in that they still carry on a reasonably normal social life, due I expect to the troops that are stationed there, so I am looking forward to the change.

It means I will be one of the skeleton staff who has to work while everyone else is on holiday in August, but actually I prefer this.

Don has moved again which now makes either nine or ten, he can't quite remember which, different countries he has been in since he left 'Blighty', but he sounds quite happy about this move as he says the country is a vast improvement on the last, although naturally he'd trade them all for dear old England. He was also very excited in his last letter, because he was going on leave the next day for the first time in fourteen months. His letters are still coming through quite O.K. and he seems to be getting mine, but I must admit I do get a little weary sometimes of all the long waiting, and wonder just how much longer I must carry on this enforced half-living with all my heart and most of my mind permanently thousands of miles away, but then I'm not the only one, lots are far worse off, but I do believe one is liable to forget this sometimes, for it doesn't really make things easier whatever folks may say, you always think your own case is the worst.

George will be home on leave for part of the week I am away, but I shall see him for the first couple of days. He loves the Army and appears to be having the time of his life, but warns my other brother, who recently gave up his Civil Defence job to join a Home Guard Ack-Ack Battery, that 'the army is a single man's job'. Still Alf is happier now that he has at last fired a gun, even if it is in the Home Guard. Anyway, they are every bit as smart as the real Army these days and if it wasn't for the name on their shoulder you wouldn't be able to tell the difference.

For the last couple of nights we have been disturbed most of the time by alert and alert, some of them longer than we have had since the blitz, but fortunately on both occasions I have been absolutely so tired that I have slept through most of it and only awoken occasionally, just long enough for the noises to penetrate to my dulled senses, then off I have drifted again to sleep. Seems a little hard to grasp that all that is starting again. Still, I expect we've got to be prepared for it.

Isn't the news terrific? It is almost unbelievable that things are actually all over in North Africa, and of course what we are all waiting for now is to find out where we will strike next. You can't imagine how after almost four years, what a blessed relief it is to know that things are under way at last, and I hope and pray that it will not be much longer now before my Don and all the other boys are home.

Edna is getting married on the 25th July, but we won't be seeing her before then, as she is saving her leave for that time. She will borrow my wedding dress and some other things as she hasn't any clothing coupons, being in the Forces, and she doesn't want to get married in her uniform. The search is now on for all we can collect in the way of good things to eat, and I have no doubt that we will manage somehow to give her a good wedding.

Not very much more in the way of news, everything at home jogs along much as usual and I continue to go places and do things as often as I can in order to save getting too deeply into a rut. So on the whole life isn't so bad.

Please write soon with all your news and tell me how you like house-keeping. I won't stop for more now as the boss is calling, so I must away. Give all my very best to Richard.

Tons of love,
    Win

21st June 1943

My Dear Donna,
As I don't seem to have heard from you since your wedding, I thought it about time I wrote you a line just to see how things are going with you. I expect you are still caught up in the turmoil of getting started on your home and housekeeping although no doubt you are very much 'much married' by now. Life here jogs along much the same as usual, with bright sparks in the form of letters

from Don arriving fairly regularly, and work ever very much to the fore. Don, who is fast developing into a regular globe trotter, has added another country to his list, and if he goes on at this rate there will be no new countries for us to visit together after the war. He says he has written to you and if I didn't mention it in my last letter, his address is the same as before except that M.E.F. is now to be substituted again for P.I.F.

I have recently returned from a week's holiday, which was followed by the Whitsun break, and another gay week in which my anniversary and my birthday fell, so naturally, now that they are all over, I find it very difficult to settle down and can't imagine that I won't have another holiday for a year.

Still, we all think the war is going to be over soon, so why worry? The weather wasn't as good as it might have been for my holiday, in fact, June has been anything but flaming this year, having put them all out with the continual rain, and only this last day or so have we had sunshine in anything like the strength it should be. However, I ceased to worry about anything, least of all the weather, the moment I put the cover on my typewriter on Saturday morning and set off for the station, labouring under the load of a terrific case, which contained 75% food and only 25% holiday attire and essentials. What a difference from peace-time.

I stayed with my friend in Somerset. Remember she has been there since the war, and recently she took a flat with another girl, so for a week, their twosome became a threesome, and I was instated as a member of the household. The Saturday afternoon I travelled and the Sunday following were wonderful days, and on the Sunday we got up early and went off to the nearest coastal town for the day, where we had the most wonderful lazy time in the sun, swimming and sunbathing, and I got a tan that is still the envy of the office. In fact I really overdid it, and had a trifle too much sun I believe for I certainly knew all about it for a couple of days afterwards. Still, it was worth it, for as I say my less fortunate (or should I say fortunate) colleagues who still have their holidays to come, aren't able to discard their stockings without slightly more trouble than I, for at least I don't have to paint my legs brown.

During the week the two girls were working, and the weather was continually wet, but I thoroughly enjoyed myself, mooching around all day, rising late, having my lunch out, and spending the afternoon curled up with a book. I was also able to give my cooking a chance, and help to make it something of a holiday for them also, by having their dinner ready by the time they got in every evening. Then the fun started, for every evening we did something or other, and although the weather changed our plans of boat trips on the river, walks and open air swimming, to more indoor activities, we nevertheless had quite a hectic time. I have never been dancing so many times in one week in my life, and really got quite good at it. We also seemed to visit every available theatre and cinema for miles around, to say nothing of restaurants and those other places where something stronger than tea can be got. Where they live is a real garrison town now, being packed choc-a-block with American troops, so I have really seen some of your boys at close quarters. What struck me more than anything, yes, even more than seeing them jitter-bug in the waltz, was their attitude towards children, and the children ever cute, seem to know this already. I never once saw a child go up and say something to a soldier, without him turning out his pockets and producing a stamp, an American cigarette, candy, or whatever was asked for. It was hard to decide who got the most fun out of this, the children or the men, for

Jeanne, Edna and their friend Paddy in WAAF uniform at Bath in 1943

whilst the children seemed to sense that these men who looked like their Daddies, and their brothers, but who talked 'funny' were friends, so the men in their turn seemed to hold the children in awe as if they hadn't ever seen children quite like them before.

My week ended with another beautiful and sunny day, and a visit from Edna, who is now stationed not far from there, and two of her mates. We had a lovely day on the river, and it was a very mournful girl who waved goodbye to the two girls and three smiling WAAFs as she steamed her way off to London again.

The snaps I enclose were taken on this day, and the one in the centre of the snap with the three of us, is my friend Win, whilst the other is her 'sleeping' partner Elsie. The other three girls are Edna and two of her WAAF friends who came with us for the day.

Edna is now on an Electrical course, which is pretty stiff, but after she is through she will be a qualified electrician, and have the thrill of actually carrying out running repairs on our aeroplanes. As this course is very long and very important, she has had to get special leave for her wedding on the 25th July, and was home last Sunday with Bill to make most of the arrangements. As she won't be home again before the day, it is on Mum and me that the many little problems will fall, but I've no doubt we shall manage to fix everything up O.K. in the end. She is borrowing my dress, a head-dress from someone else, a veil from another, and shoes from yet another, so I don't suppose there will be anything of the war bride look about her at all. In fact, she looks very lovely in white, being dark. The only thing that spoils it all is that it won't be a real family party without Don or my brother there, and in fact we look like having women outnumbering the men about ten to one, for all the men we know are in the Army, or too old to be of any interest to a bunch of very lively young WAAFs. Still, once again, we hope it will all work out, and we'll have a super wedding for them after all.

I celebrated the close of my second year as 'Mrs W.' and the second anniversary without Don, by taking three of my pals up to town to see Ivor Novello's show 'Dancing Years', which was really lovely, and for three hours or more, lost in that beautiful, slightly tragic love story, with its beautiful dresses and scenery, we completely forgot the war. Don sent me a cable which arrived right on the very day, a marvellous piece of timing this, when he is (to quote one of his letters) 3,342 miles from London, and although this may not sound much to you, it's quite a tidy way for me, when I know that this covers land and sea, not just one long stretch of land. I cabled him too, so I'm hoping that he was as lucky and got mine right on the dot. Poor Don, this is the second anniversary he has spent, not only away from me, but in a strange land, but ever hopeful, we pray that next year will see a very different state of affairs, and everyone that wished us well on the 15th, added 'May next year see you together again.' Many too admitted like I do myself, that whilst we said the same thing last year, we did rather feel it was asking too much, but somehow we can't help feeling a little more hopeful now. We know there is still a lot to do, which will take a great deal of time, but we can't help feeling that our boys who have already done such a grand job of work, must soon reap the reward which they so rightly deserve, and for which we at home all long so completely.

My birthday brought me another visit to a show for a birthday present from my pal at the office, this time a comedy, with Lupino Lane in it, which had us both curled up in our seats helpless with laughter the whole time.

Don sent word to his sister to get me some flowers, and she got together the loveliest bouquet I have ever seen, of every conceivable flower, they were truly wonderful. Don's mother gave up her own coupons, and bought me a length of material enough to make a slip, and in these days nothing could be more welcome. From Dad came a set of saucepans, those rarest of rare things, which he must have had the devil's own job to get hold of, and I understand I have another couple of presents on the way from Mum and my friend I was on holiday with, so you see I have been my usual lucky self.

You cannot often buy lace these days, but when you can it is coupon free, and I managed to get a length for a blouse some while ago, which I have recently had made up, and now have the sweetest little blouse you can imagine, and of course I have to add to everyone that admires it 'and no coupons too'.

I passed my First Aid exam, despite the fact that I had 'examination jitters', so much I made what I thought to be a couple of howling mistakes. In fact, tonight is our First Aid night, and I am writing this in the hour between finishing at the office, and the beginning of the class.

Well, I don't know, that seems to about cover all I have been doing with myself of late, save for the usual round of visiting, films, with an hour or so of knitting and reading thrown in. I have just finished a striped jumper made out of odd pieces of wool, of which I am very proud, as once again I acquired it for 'no coupons' – the things we do these days!

Work continues plentiful as ever, although there are very few of the old pre-war staff left now, most having gone off to the Forces. All the rest, save for about half a dozen of which I shall be one, go for their holiday in a month's time, whilst we six stay to 'hold the fort' and stock take.

My savings group is doing great things, and I have just doubled

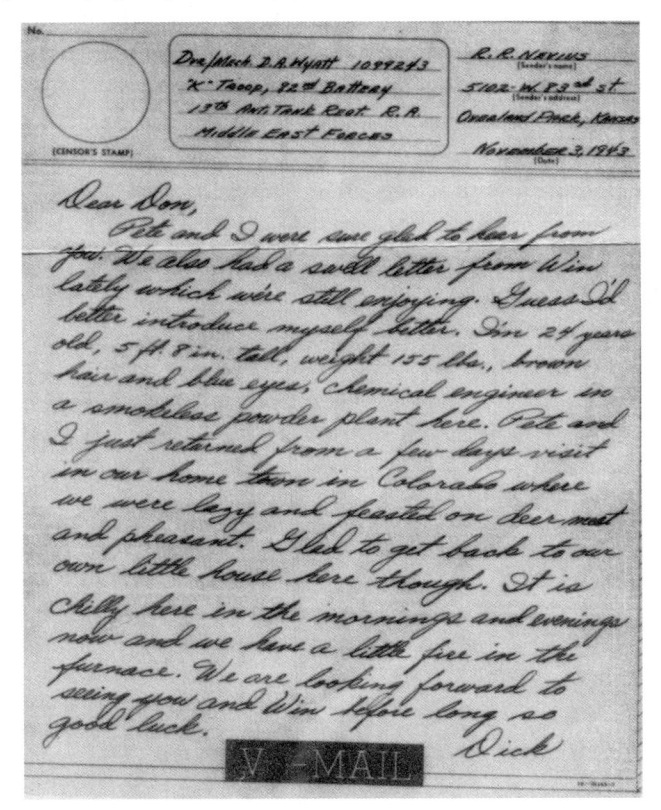

Airgraph from Dick Nevius to Don Wyatt (actual size: 4 x 5 inches)

in the first six months of this year, all that I took in the whole of last. The fun will start when we all start to spend all we are now saving, after the war. Won't we have the time of our lives? Everyone, if we are to judge by what people say, is going to be speechless for at least a week after the war, but I can't help wondering, being ever the practical minded, just where all the 'substance' to make them speechless is coming from. Still, I guess that failing all else, we will get drunk with joy.

The news is good isn't it?, and I hope that by the time you get this, it will be even better still. We all hope soon that your people will settle their strike problems too, for we can't help feeling a little worried about them over here, knowing how vital production is, and whilst I don't pretend to know sufficient about the whole affair to say whether they are justified or not, I personally can't help wondering where a lot of us would have been if during the Blitz, our rescue squads stood and argued for more money before they dug for the unfortunate victims beneath the ruins, but there, maybe the comparison is unfair. I suppose it is just that we take the war more seriously than your people perhaps, and to us, ever the main issue is to get on with it and get it over with.

Everyone at home is very well, Mum is still working at the hospital, and Dad is still putting in his good work in the garden. On Sunday we made three pounds of jam from the raspberries in the garden and our lettuces have been wonderful.

Well, Donna, time is up, and I must away to wash the grime of the day from my countenance before going off to my First Aid lecture. Don't forget to write to me soon, will you, and give me all your news, I long to hear from you.

Give all my very best regards to Richard,

Cheerio and tons of love,

Win xxxx

6th July, 1943

My Dear Donna,
I wrote the above a fortnight ago, but have been holding the letter up, as there was some muck up at the chemist about the snaps, and

instead of my own, I found myself in possession of some that belonged to someone or other who possessed a laughing sailor boy. The laughing sailor boy has gone back to his rightful owner, but I am still awaiting the return of mine. I also notice that I told you I was enclosing one with the WAAFs in, but decided after all that it wasn't very good, and might not be very interesting to you after all, so, when I do get them I will just send you the one of the two girls and myself, and perhaps one of me.

My reason for writing today is that your letter, enclosing the wedding snaps, and the newspaper cutting, arrived this morning, and you can't imagine how thrilled I was with them. I should have loved to see all those lovely rainbow dresses, I bet they looked really lovely, but what struck me most was how big Anna Mae has grown. She looks years older than my young sister Phyll, who is fourteen and starting work after the summer holidays. Of course, I'm now more than eager to see the photo's of you and Dick, for I am sure that these too will be very good. I read the account of the wedding, and thought how wonderful it must have been, but do write and tell me all about it yourself – did you have a party after the reception, and where did you go for your honeymoon?

Your new home sounds just like my idea of a dream home, and I dearly wish it were possible to hop on a boat this minute (with Don by my side of course) and come over and see it, but we definitely have a date after the war, haven't we? I'm thinking we'll have to make it soon after the war too, for otherwise if Don carries out all the plans he says he will after the war, we'll have to wait until we have a family off our hands. I don't know, but I believe I addressed one or perhaps two letters to Belinder Road, but maybe they will forward them, or send them back to me. If you were in England you'd be considered real 'Diggers for Victory' with all the stuff you have planted, and I'm sure it must keep you very busy. I should have liked you to have seen the faces of all the girls when I read out that your hens gave you two dozen eggs a day, their mouths literally watered.

Don's fond of doing things like that. He writes and raves about all the fruit he has, eggs and chips and all the other long forgotten luxuries, and then finishes with 'We all wish that home could have these things instead.' We don't think this way of course, we are only too pleased to think they get some kind of 'compensation'. The last straw, however, was when he mentioned having just eaten two banana sundaes . . .

Another thing that made me sit up was the fact that after weeks and months of searching he still hasn't been able to send me any stockings, because the only ones he has seen have been 30/- a pair. My goodness, I'd have heart failure every time I put them on, if I thought of the price, and also when I think that 30/- is either three or four weeks' pay of his. I'm not quite sure, but it is somewhere in that region. He still persists in looking though, for something to send me home for a present from the 'Mystic east', but I keep telling him that I'd be quite satisfied if he'd hurry up and bring himself home.

I can't imagine what I could have said to make my last letter be so heavily censored – for I'm sure there just isn't anything going on these days that I could write about. I guess I must have been letting off steam about something. Strange though to think that I wrote as often as I used to during the Blitz, and never a word censored – but then, isn't that just the way of the world?

George is home on embarkation leave, so it now means that he definitely won't be home for the wedding, unless something very unforeseen turns up. Mum isn't too happy about the whole thing naturally, but he is anxious to get out there and get a crack at 'Jerry', and if possible, to meet all his pals who have been out there months and years already. By the way, I have sent Don's address several times, but I guess it must have fallen 'neath the censor's scissors. Still, I'll have another go, and hope it reaches you this time:-

Dvr./Mech. D. A. Wyatt,
1099243,
'K' Troop,
82nd Battery,
13th/A/Tank Regt. R.A.
M.E.F.

If by chance you don't get it, or you can't send direct from your part of the world, if you will send it to me, I will see that he gets it. Was it an Airgraph that he sent to you? For I tried to do this but was told there wasn't any service – so I guess it is just for Forces.

I received a snapshot from him last week, taken on his leave in May, and was really thrilled with it, for he has lost that old, drawn and tired look that has been so prominent in all his photographs since he went away, and apart from being very, very deeply tanned, looks just the same happy laughing Don as he always did. I'm having a negative taken from this latest snap, so that I can have a very large copy printed for framing, and then I will send you one of the little ones.

The main topic at home these days is the big event in three weeks' time, for Edna and Bill are being married on the 25th of this month. She got a 24 hour compassionate leave last weekend, because of George being on embarkation leave, so once again Bill came down and we had quite a family party. Lots of girls that are coming, will have to catch a train back to camp early in the afternoon, so we've got to have the wedding as early as 9.30 in the morning. Imagine the running around we shall have, especially as the house will be full with all the girls who will have come up on Saturday, and Bill's family who are coming down from Manchester. They are going to Wales for their honeymoon, and then, until after the war, they will live in Manchester. At least Bill will, for his job is there, and Edna will naturally go there for her leaves. After the war, however, they intend to settle in the South, perhaps Eltham, for Bill loves this part of the country and says already with the little contact he has had with it, he makes the people at home smile when he uses some cockney phrase unknown in the North.

I'm going to try and stay in as much as possible this week, for last time George was home I was on holiday and hardly saw anything of him at all, and it may be a long while before I see him again. It is almost eighteen months since I have seen Don, and believe it or not there are times when I really have to concentrate hard to remember what he looks like or how his voice sounds, but I've no doubt all these little things will come back in a flash the moment I catch sight of him again on that crowded railway station on that great day, not too far distant, I hope.

What a lovely idea to share a house with another couple, and it must make good company when each of your respective husbands is away.

Well, that seems to be about the limit again for now, but as the snaps still haven't arrived, I will continue to hold this up until the end of the week at least, hoping that they turn up.

All the very best to you both once again and hoping to hear from you soon.

Tons of love,
  Win xxxxx

[*Note: See photograph on p. 223 which shows the Airgraph obviously written to Don by Dick Nevius in response to the sending of his address in this letter.*]

30th September 1943

My Dear Donna

Very many thanks for your welcome letter which arrived about a fortnight ago. At the same time came Dick's letter with the wedding photographs which were lovely. They were much admired by all my friends and I do really think you looked very sweet, my dear. It was my first view of your handsome husband, and well I thoroughly approve.

Your new house sounds very nice and I only wish I could see it, but I'm sure I shall some day, unless you move again. I bet it was exciting, wasn't it, collecting all your furniture and all the other necessities together.

I bet it was fun too getting everything done together, wasn't it, although I somehow manage to get quite a lot of fun out of my lone bargain-hunting. I'm aiming at getting all the odds and ends by the time Don gets home so that all we have to get when we finally settle will be the remainder of our furniture, rugs, carpets, lino, curtains. At the moment I am concentrating on kitchen stuff, and when you remember that every little thing had to be hunted for and snapped up when you see it, I believe I haven't done so badly, for I've quite a good collection of dishes and basins, cake tins and trays, a tea-strainer (these are very rare), oh, and last week a rolling pin was added to the list. Some while ago I had a right royal Saturday afternoon for I went into a shop for one thing, and saw quite a lot of other rarities that had just come in, and I came out of that shop loaded. Imagine how I looked boarding the train home armed with two enamel bowls, two earthenware storage pots, a frying pan and three pudding basins. I've got some scales too. They were bought before the war by a friend of Dad's and never used, so yours truly bought them, and they are the kitchen-to-be's proudest possession at the moment. I haunt all the hardware shops and make a point of adding something to the collection every week. Luckily I've got all the china in the way of tea and dinner sets that anyone could want, and a set of saucepans, so I'm far and away better off than most war-time brides. Then of course I've got quite a good bit of linen that I bought right at the beginning of the war, so when I do complete my kitchen equipment we will be well off, save for the big items. It's amazing though what a lot of fun you can get out of quite ordinary things when you have to buy them this way, for a pudding basin becomes a whole lot more valuable when you've hunted the shops for it, than it was in the old days when one could just walk into a hardware shop and order each and every necessary thing, and then the same afternoon a van called and delivered them all. My goodness, did such things really used to happen, it doesn't seem possible. I tell you one thing though that has completely disappeared, for although other things are scarce, if you're lucky and cute you do see them sometimes, but, I know you'll laugh, I haven't seen a colander since the war – I don't know whether you call them by this name, but they are usually round with holes in them, and are used for straining vegetables. Why these and sink baskets, which are of course similar kind of things, should have disappeared above all other things I can't say, but maybe I'm just more kitchen equipment conscious and other people would tell you of a lot more important things to them which they can't get.

I've taken up cooking a hobby too in an endeavour to get fairly proficient by the time my wandering husband returns. I make a point of making something every week, despite all the cracks from the family, and also those which I have to endure from Don. I soon silence him though by telling him that if he isn't careful I won't practise but wait and do so on him. Mum has to shut her eyes as I put the fat and the sugar in, although she doesn't mind if it turns

Don, 1943. The 'man' after four years of soldiering

out successfully. If it doesn't, I never hear the last of it all the week, while the family are on short rations. So far I have excelled at salad cream, made with powdered eggs, ginger cake, again with powdered eggs, wartime fruit cake, with no eggs at all, and steamed syrup puddings. Mum doesn't mind me making these for they don't take sugar. So far my pastry isn't anything to write home about, although it is eatable, but when you have a husband who could exist purely and simply on treacle tart and custard if he had to, these being his favourites, I shall have to learn to make good pastry. He'd eat custard, yes, just cold custard alone, not with fruit or anything, every day for his sweet and never complain, but I tell him he'll have to learn to get fond of other things, for I like variety and anyway I can't learn to make all these things for nothing, can I? Thank goodness I can at least cook him an old English dinner of roast beef, Yorkshire pudding, baked potatoes and cabbage, or roast lamb and mint sauce, or boiled beef and carrots with pease pudding, or even a steak and kidney pie – it's just the fancy things I'm not so hot on, but then I ought to be thankful I've a husband with plain tastes, didn't I?

Anyway here have I been rambling on like this and I still haven't told you that the 'old man' is quite well and happy as usual, although apart from knowing he is in the M.E.F. [Middle East Forces] I haven't the faintest idea where he is. I'm truly slipping for at one time I could always work out his various moves but lately he changes his abode far quicker than I can keep pace with. Did I tell you that he sent me home some silk from Syria for a dress? It is lovely stuff, but rather too shiny and bright for a dress, being stripes. I tossed up for a long while as to whether to have a dress or not, not wanting to disappoint him, but I finally struck on the idea of a housecoat. It is ideal for this as I can have the full beauty

Don, 1943. A lull during fighting in the desert

of the gayness without worrying about it being too bright, for the brighter the better for a thing like this, and maybe if I were really desperately in need of a new dress I should beg, borrow or steal the coupons somehow, but I know I would never spend either the coupons or the money on anything so definitely a non-essential and a luxury. It is in a long queue at the dressmaker's so I don't suppose I shall get it for some while, but I want to get it made up ready and then I don't suppose I shall wear it but save it for that second honeymoon, which Don says, 'Won't be long now.'

Our mail both ways continues speedy and regular. He wrote only this week saying that he had asked me a question on 30th August and got my reply back by the 15th September – not bad, is it?

George is still here, and at the moment on an upgrading course not far from home, so we are seeing far more of him now than we have seen for almost a year. Taking advantage of George's being near, Edna has been getting one or two weekend leaves on the strength of it, and we've had several housefuls, for when Edna comes, Bill naturally comes too, and Edna has taken to bringing a girl friend with her as well. And what's more, last time George brought a Canadian. My were we a crowd that weekend, but we had fun, making a terrific noise the whole time, and generally getting the old pre-war feeling.

Did I tell you last time I wrote that we had given up the rabbits and got two chickens? Well running true to our usual luck with our animals, one has already died and we had ruefully to see it go to the incinerator, for we didn't fancy eating it. However, Dad has been working hard and is going to get a proper run built, and then buy four more, for we did get these two rather on the spur of the moment, and had nowhere properly for them to go. The one remaining chicken at the moment is most peculiar, in fact I've never seen anyone so temperamental, she lays six eggs in seven days and then goes eight or nine without any. We've just passed through the eggless week, so we have high hope that her strike will be settled soon and she gets into production again.

Peggy the dog too has been ill with eczema, and has pulled nearly all her coat off, and as she is an overfed, very fat wire-haired terrier, you can imagine how funny she looks, quite apart from the fact that she shivers with the cold, poor thing, and has made quite nasty patches where she would persist in scratching. It was all right while someone was around, for we could stop her, but at night and when Mum wasn't there during the day, she kept undoing all the good the lotions and bandages did for her. Still she is getting better now, and apart from the fact that she won't leave the warmest spot in the room and we have to wrap her up in a blanket at night, she is almost her old self again.

I took my second First Aid exam last Tuesday, and although I broke out into a cold sweat when I entered the examination room, the result of hours of jitters beforehand, I don't really think I've done too bad, and have high hopes of passing, although of course I am scared to get too confident and then be disappointed. Let's hope the results aren't too long coming through. Provided we do pass this, it'll be all out then for our third, and our medallion which comes at the end of this, although I'm afraid there are many gruelling weeks ahead of us before we qualify for this honour.

We had rather an interesting talk the other lunchtime in the canteen — an officer who had taken part in the Tunisian fighting, and who is now home again as a result of wounds, told us of his experiences, and mighty interesting it was too. Of course the main idea was to show how really important the things we make are to the fighting men, as if we needed telling. Still the news is marvellous, isn't it, just a little while longer and all our patience will be rewarded and the black days through — four years — it seems almost a lifetime.

Did I tell you of our latest arrival — Don's sister Doreen had a baby boy on 22nd August, and he is to be plain John. He is a lovely little fellow, very thin and dark, with a sweet little face. My godchild Iris, who is the daughter of another of Don's sisters and now about four months old, grows sweeter every time I see her, and everyone says that she is the image of Don when a baby. Of course Don has heard from his mother of this likeness, and when I have been to see Iris, and write and tell him how sweet she is, he always answers that he isn't surprised since he's heard whom she takes after.

This coming Saturday I am fire-watching at work and have a

jumper to unpick in readiness for re-knitting, so I look like having quite a busy day, for I have also volunteered to cook the dinner for my two colleagues and they in turn have kindly volunteered to eat it. Also, this Saturday afternoon I'm having a perm. It seems ages since I had one, and I've been looking forward to this for ages, although the actual process of having one is agony to me, for I just can't bear having my head pulled first this way and then that. Still I've been telling them all at the office when they have commented on my hair looking as one's hair always does seem to look just before it is done, that they will all the more appreciate my beauty when I have it done, if it looks awful this week. Naturally this brings forth many more cracks all along the lines that it is a bit late now to make amends for what nature did 23 years ago, but I can take it.

I was very interested to hear how your rationing works. I don't believe I have ever told you about our food rationing, have I? Meat is worked on a money basis, and has varied since rationing started but at the moment and for some time it has been 1s 2d per head. This is roughly 23 cents. We can now take our whole ration in meat, but during the summer months we had 1/- meat and 2d corned beef. So you see the quantity depends on the price, and if you buy the expensive stuff you don't get as much as if you buy cheaper. Sausages and offal are off the ration – and we get these when they are going. Tea, margarine, butter and cooking fats are 2ozs, 4ozs, 2ozs and 2ozs respectively. Bacon is 4ozs, sugar 8ozs, cheese 2ozs. All of these are per week. We get one pound of jam per month, but sometimes during the summer we can take 1lb of sugar instead of jam, if we want to make our own, and we also get two special issues of sugar for jam making. Eggs and milk vary with the time of the year, but we have dried eggs and dried milk, which I believe are a packet or a tin per month. Almost everything else, save for vegetables and soups, and coffee and cocoa, which are off the ration, are on points, of which we get 20 a month. I'm not quite sure of all the point values and I don't do much of the shopping, but things like tinned salmon, meat and spam are pretty high in points, spam and meat being about 16 or 20 I believe and salmon about 32 for the highest grade. Biscuits vary but I think the average is 12 a pound when you can get them. Raisins and sultanas are about 12 a pound I believe, while cereals, rice etc. are quite low, being 4's and 2's. Sweets and chocolate are 12ozs a month. Soap is 4 tablets a month, or if you want soap flakes or washing powders, these are 2ozs instead of one tablet for soap flakes, or a small packet of washing powder to one tablet, a large packet instead of two tablets etc. Fish and poultry are off the ration – when you can get them, as are of course things like sauces and pudding mixtures, custard powder etc. You say too that when you travel you just take your ration book instead of food. Well we can do this, but we have to get an emergency ration card, so that the shop where you buy in the new district is credited with the extra amount and your own shop with that much less. When I go to friends I take my own rations because it saves the bother of buying them when I get there, and of course I also take a couple of tins of stuff that no points could buy, for Mum still has some of her early store-cupboard containing things that were obtainable a few years ago before rationing was thought of. When things like oranges are available the under sixes get them, and we also get some onions during the winter, although of course we grow our own. Well I think that about covers everything, and I hope I've got all the amounts right. I've checked with my pals here and they agree – I don't want to be had up for making false statements.

How I envy your learning to dive – somehow, try as I might, I can never master this, I just can't let my head go before my feet, I don't know why. Before he went away Don could hardly swim at all, and I ran circles around him at this sport, but he swims every day almost now in the Medi, and is fast becoming really proficient, and I shouldn't wonder if he isn't well ahead of me now.

Well, Donna, I seem to have rambled on quite long enough, and although I guess I could go on for ages like this, finding plenty to say, I really do want to see if I can get this letter away to you without keeping it hanging about for a long while like I generally do, so if I have forgotten anything I must write again later. Tell Dick I will answer his letter soon, although I know he would not have me neglect the 'old man', and he certainly keeps me busy answering his letters. He's gone short today though, but then I'm sure he'll understand. I am glad you are going to write to him,

I'm sure he'll be very pleased to hear. He says that no matter what anyone else may say, the mail is definitely the most important thing about the war.

1944

4 January 1944

My Dear Donna,

At long last I have a spare moment, and the opportunity to write and thank you for your wonderful present that arrived just before Christmas. It was the most wonderful surprise, for although I knew that there was something on the way, I didn't dream it could be anything so lovely. You can't imagine what the sight of something pretty and dainty did to my poor 'utility' eyes. I don't remember when I last saw lace on undies, and even the most expensive available in the shops now aren't half so pretty, and offer nothing in the way of trimmings. Much as I shall be tempted to wear it now, what with coupons and things I am going to try and save it for when Don comes home so that I have something pretty with which to gladden his war-weary heart. It wouldn't be much of a homecoming, would it, to see me clad almost entirely in 'Make Do and Mends', which are all the vogue this season. I know I can never thank you enough on paper, and also that it isn't any good saying you shouldn't have done it, but you know you shouldn't. I hope one day I shall be lucky enough to hit on something both suitable for packing and for sending to you, but as I have said before there is very little choice these days. Strangely enough, I'm sure if I did happen to find something, sure enough it will be made in U.S.A., since we've not manufactured anything in the luxury line for four and a half years, so naturally there isn't much about. Still we'll soon get cracking after the war, and then I shall be able to send you something that you'll definitely be able to remember as coming from England.

Isn't the news terrific, especially the sinking of the Sharnhorst, which came to gladden all our hearts, at what we pray was the last Christmas of the war? It is so strange the way we are all thinking great things of 1944, and the prayer in all our hearts is that we may get it all finished this year, we've had quite enough of it, and we are all dreaming now of the return of our loved ones, of the lights up again, and all the things we used to have and enjoy, for we feel somehow that we have fought and earned them back again. The fight isn't over yet though, and we've still a long way to go, so I mustn't launch off into too much wishful thinking. Anyway, at the moment the thoughts of 'when, where and how' in regard to the second front are uppermost in our minds, and it's a peculiar feeling, wanting it, and yet dreading it at the same time.

What kind of a Christmas did you have? We spent ours fairly quietly for there wasn't anyone home, but somehow we didn't seem to mind this year, for we feel so sure that there'll be high jinks next year and no mistake. We had the usual office party in the pub on the corner on Christmas Eve, where there was much dancing and singing, and I consumed more gin and oranges than I care to count, but I walked out feet first and with my head in the air, so that was O.K. (I mean orange drink in with the gin, not real oranges of course; it looks as if that is what I mean.) I spent Christmas Day at home with Mum and Dad and Phyll and the family from next door, my brother and his wife and the two boys. We had a really super Christmas dinner of chicken and pork, and Christmas pudding too, due to Mum's careful saving all through the year, and it lacked but few of its peacetime ingredients, and tasted just as good to us anyway. I guess we've an awful lot to be thankful for that it is possible for us to sit down to such a meal at our fifth war-time Christmas. Makes me feel kind of guilty to have so much when there are starving people such a short way away across the water. Still it helped us to bear yet another celebration without our loved ones, for as well as Don, neither Edna nor George was home. After we had eaten our fill of chicken, pudding and mincepies we all just flopped round the fire for an hour or two to let it digest, then we did rouse ourselves enough to play games with the children for Christmas is always the same to them. They were very lucky too, my brother had made the big one the most wonderful rocking horse you can imagine, and a smaller horse on wheels for the younger one, all out of bombed-out wood. They looked lovely and to my mind far surpassed any toys in even the peace-time shops. They had bricks too from the same source, and little wooden carts pulled by toy rabbits, and it was only necessary to supplement these with a few other toys, books and crayons, and they had as big a pillow case full of Christmas toys as any child has ever had.

My girl friend who has been away since the war was home for Christmas, as were all her family, and I spent the evening with them. Sunday I visited Don's mother and father, at the house of one of his sisters, and then on Monday I saw Win again and we went to a party together in the evening. She was home for a week and I saw her a couple of evenings before she went back but now I expect it will be some time before she is home again. Her fiancé is in Italy, and we get an awful lot of fun out of showing each other our various souvenirs they have sent home. She has a bedspread from Sicily, an Italian blouse, a German belt, and various other things, whilst for Christmas I received a dress length from Don. Boy was I thrilled with it, and this very weekend it is going off to the dressmaker's to be made up. It is a kind of cotton and wool mixture in blue, mottled with white, and as I am having it made in just a plain tailored style, it should look quite smart. I told you about the silk he sent earlier from Beirut for my birthday, didn't I. Well at long last it is finished, and is the most smashing house-coat you could wish to see. Don sent it for a dress length, but it was a trifle too bright for this, and I thought that a house-coat too would be more of a luxury. In just a plain princess style, shaped at the back and waist, with a Peter Pan collar and buttons all the way down the front, it really looks the cat's whiskers, and I know that I just dare not wear it until he comes home to see it in all its beauty. You'd never believe that a combination of orange, black and grey stripes could look so smart. He also sent his sister a dress length for Christmas, and his mother a lovely cross in Mother of Pearl, which she is thrilled to bits with.

So you see, what with your parcel and then Don's parcel arriving I had a really exciting time as far as presents were concerned and in addition I had a dustpan and brush from Mum, handkerchiefs from sister-in-law Doris (real gold dust these, since she gave up her coupons for them), the sweetest green nightdress-case from friend Win, some slippers, a powder puff, a box of powder and a face flannel from Don's mother, and a potato peeler and nutmeg scraper from Phyllis. Edna is getting a friend of hers to crochet me some table mats, so you see I have been very lucky and had some lovely things.

At the moment we are all looking forward to Edna and George's leave which, provided nothing unforeseen happens, should be somewhere around the end of this month. They are both due home together, and as they spent their last leave at Edna's in-laws, they are coming home for this, which is by way of being a special celebration for brother George is getting engaged to Edna's friend Jeanne, with whom he spent his last leave. If the almost impossible does happen again and they all do get their leaves together, there will be Edna and Bill, George and Jeanne, and all the rest of us at home, so you can bet we'll make up for Christmas and do something in the way of celebrating. It will only leave young Phyllis unattached now, so poor Mum who has been looking forward to having her house full again, after the war, will be really deserted, especially when I leave her too. Still I guess we will always go back there for our family parties.

Don is very well and happy as usual, although he is still not staying in one place long enough for me to know exactly where he is. If I had realised when he first went away, just what the expanse of two years without seeing him was really like to endure, I don't think I could have stood it, but surprisingly enough the days, weeks and months slip by hardly without notice, and we are both confident that the end of this year will see him home again. I have so many things to show him that I have bought, that I'm sure this will take almost a week, and as for all the news I have to catch up with, with him, well I guess we won't ever stop talking. I had a lovely photograph come just before Christmas taken on the leave when he was lucky enough to meet his friend John, and they do both look well. They are separated now by as many miles as ever they were, but they are both content now that they have actually met. I should very much have liked to be a little fly on the wall as they talked, for they too had two years of experiences to impart to one another, things that I, and the rest of us, will never know until it is all over.

I have been very busy these last few months with my knitting, as I undertook to knit the two boys a couple of jerseys each for the winter, especially as young Alf was to start school this week. That's been put off however, as he has the 'flu', but surprisingly enough he is anxious to go to school, which is very unusual, and I think he will get on well when he does start. He is a big boy, although he is only four, and knows almost as much about aeroplanes and bombers as I do. I am now on the second set, having made them one each, and after these are done, must really get cracking on some for myself, as I have been putting off and off the knitting up of some cherished pre-war wool, so as to get the last ounce out of those I have. Now, however, I have got to the stage when if I don't knit myself something so that I may look a little more respectable, I shall be really miserable. Still I can at least say I have been patriotic and worn my old clothes, when it has been a real effort for me to drag myself away from the shop windows.

By the way I forgot to tell you that Don says he has received an Airgraph from Dick, but maybe you have already had an answer since he said he had to answer letters with strange addresses that he couldn't memorise promptly in view of having to destroy them. I hope you are both very well, and that you enjoyed your holiday when you went home. How is life these days? Don't forget to write soon with all the news, as I am always cheered by your letters.

I am afraid I have very little more news to offer at the moment, life still continuing its humdrum way. Still I'm not complaining, the time passes very quickly really and we get an awful lot of fun out of life under the circumstances.

A very, very Happy New Year to you both and to all your family, and my friends in Lamar. May it be a peace year for everyone.

Cheerio for now then. Write soon.

Tons of love,
  Win

11 February 1944

My Dear Donna,
I hope you won't be too surprised by this unusually quick answer

to your letter, written on the 2nd January, which arrived yesterday, but I find myself with a convenient half hour to spare, so must seize the opportunity with both hands, as such occasions rarely occur these days.

Very many thanks for your lovely long letter, must have taken you quite a while the day you sat down to write that. I'm certainly going to notice the difference after the war, when I have not got this old typewriter to use for knocking off my correspondence. Guess I shall have to get the 'old man' to treat me to one, if only for writing to you, for I bet we'll have such an awful lot to write about once we do start, I shall never be able to keep pace by pen.

I was very happy to hear all your news, and as you say the mail service is greatly improving, for your letter only took about five weeks to reach me. My, but you surprised me with your cooking achievements. Boy, what wouldn't I give to be able to claim that I could produce such a meal! Even if I had the material with which to do it. I can see that I shall have to put some hard practice in before you come to visit us, as at the moment my activities are limited to purely ordinary dinners, etc., you know, roasts, vegetables and puddings, and a few varieties of cakes. Further than this I have never ventured, but the only point in my favour is that Don likes absolutely plain things, and can't stand 'mucks and messes' as he calls them, whereas I like things that have been decorated and played around with a little. We have agreed though to compromise by my sticking to plain things during the week, and then I may splash out on my inventive powers when we have visitors. We have yet to see if this arrangement will work out in practice. Anyway, I should have loved to be a guest at your Thanksgiving dinner, it sounded delicious. It must be a grand feeling to look around afterwards at the satisfied faces of your guests and think 'alone I did it.'

Your vacation too sounded all that one could wish for, and although I guess it was lovely to see your people again, I can understand how you must have felt to be back in your own home. I've heard lots of married girls say that although they loved their homes before they were married and love to go back on visits, having once tasted the joys of being their own mistress, they could never return permanently to not doing all their jobs for themselves again. The one thing that stands out clearest in my mind, when I think of visiting Colorado, is the mountains. How I should love to see these, for pictures of them always give me a queer feeling inside. We hear that American soldiers over here get the same feeling about the greenness of the English countryside. I guess it is just seeing something that you know is peculiar to one place only that makes it especially wonderful that you have been able to experience the sight of it.

By the way, thanks for the names of three more friends of yours over here. I shall watch out for word from them, and you may be sure they will find a welcome waiting for them. It seems strange doesn't it that after all this while I still haven't been successful in meeting any of them, something has always seemed to turn up at the last minute to take them away, but there, I will not give up hoping. You ask if there is anywhere in London where I could be reached, but of course, Eltham is in London, although this may seem hard to understand. It is only five and twenty minutes by train from the centre of the West End. If you are writing to any of the boys, tell them to go to Charing Cross station, (all service men get to know this as soon as they arrive in London) and then they will be told there what time and from what platform the next train leaves for 'Eltham Park', that is the name of our station. On the other hand they can always ring me at the office between nine and half past five. If they ring from outside London, they will have to tell the exchange it is a London number – Bermondsey 2217, but if they are already in the London area, they can dial it themselves from any Call box, just B.E.R. 2217. This probably sounds all very complicated to you, but if you know the procedure you can tell anyone else who wants to know. On the other hand we don't mind in the least, just a letter or even if they knock at the door and introduce themselves, so long as they aren't shocked if they find us up to all sorts of odd things in the kitchen. It is quite often a mixture of me cooking, Mum knitting and Dad doing woodwork, but I can assure you, on the whole we are perfectly normal.

Last weekend I went down to see my girlfriend Win at Bath and had a wonderful time. The weather was glorious and although we didn't do anything really special, it made such a nice break and a change. I met on the train, believe it or not, the only two in existence I'm sure, but there were two shy American soldiers. My girl friend wouldn't believe me and said there was no such thing, and I said I'd hardly believe it myself if I hadn't seen them, but they definitely were terribly shy. After quite an awkward silence I did manage to get them to accept my magazines to look at, and then one very shyly offered me a cigarette. This was my first try at American cigarettes by the way and I found them only slightly different to ours. A trifle stronger perhaps and more loosely packed but apart from this, much the same. They did talk a little to another fellow who spoke to them, but they wouldn't accept one of my cigarettes in return or a piece of chocolate, as they said they were hard to get. They were awfully nice boys though, and I learned that they came from Boston, that they didn't mind England, but of course 'home's best', and who doesn't agree. However, as I alighted from the train I found myself wondering if like Alice through the looking glass everything was backwards, for all the previous boys I've spoken to have maintained that the English are reserved, although it was definitely the other way around this time. The funny thing is they all say they've been led to believe we are quiet and retiring, but they admit when they get to know us, we aren't a bit. Maybe it is this that takes their breath away a bit.

Don told me that he had received Dick's Airgraph and that he was replying straight away, since they mustn't keep addresses and he can't memorise every different one he gets. I'm glad anyway that his reply has reached you safely. You say his address has changed. Well it did for a bit, but he is now back in his own Regiment, and it is the same as I gave you before, 13th A-Tank Regt, R.A.M.E.F. Incidentally M.E.F. should be sufficient, but maybe from America it would help to put British M.E.F. I don't know what rank he put on his letter to you, but whilst he was in the new regiment he got another stripe, which he lost on returning to his own, purely he assures me because they were over strength and that he will get it back at the first vacancy. Anyway, at the moment his one-stripe rank is 'Lance Bombardier'.

I have not been out in the evenings at all since then, as it seems we have returned to the old days and once more it's a case of snatching your sleep where you can, thanking your stars if you wake up in the morning, and find you are still among the lucky ones, and just generally making as good a job as possible of annoying circumstances. I often wondered how we'd take it, if this state of affairs returned again, and for myself I am glad to say we still can. Everyone admits now that they don't like them, especially people of my mother's age, who have had their share, for false bravery is silly. It's the bravery of sticking it that sees you through, and of course the knowledge that what they are doing to us is but a fraction of our power upon them is very comforting, when you remember how different was the situation three years ago.

Again too now we know that by using up some of his aircraft on us, he is lowering his strength for the second front, and the fact that you are helping, helps you a lot to accept the discomforts of these disturbed nights. Several people at the office have been unlucky, and have lost their homes, or had them badly damaged, but I'm glad to say no one has been hurt. We at home are all right, and my experience the other night seems to be the only casualty we can claim, and this has brought me more laughter than sympathy.

It was like this, a couple of nights ago after lying in bed for some time, I decided I'd better get up, so I groped for my slippers and dressing-gown in the dark, and then walked smack into the wardrobe door which the gunfire must have blown open. Boy, did I give my face a crack – almost immediately a bump, the size and shape of an egg came up on my forehead, and although I wasn't conscious of any great pain when I did it, the next morning it was up bigger than ever and really ached all day, every time I moved my head even slightly. Yesterday it was much better though, a lot of the swelling had given place to blueness, and save for it still being very tender when I touch it (I haven't washed higher than my nose since Tuesday) a lot of the pain had gone, and it didn't hurt all the time. This morning however, my right eye, which has hurt faintly ever since, has turned a deep purple, and is all swollen and puffed, so you can imagine what a pretty sight I look. All this for walking into a door I didn't know was there – Hitler's got a lot to answer for.

When I was telling you earlier on about the gang being home on leave, I meant to tell you that George and Jeanne got engaged, and we now hear that they have decided to get married on their next leave, which should be some time in April. It will be at Jeanne's home in Huddersfield, and we are quite looking forward to being able to go out to a wedding, and have all the fun and excitement without the necessary work and worry beforehand. It will be a long journey though, but we don't mind this, for it will make a nice break. Strange isn't it how all the rest of the family, save yours truly, have married someone from miles away? I'm the only one that's got an out and out Londoner like myself. You should hear all the different dialects now when we are all home. There is Doris's Welsh, Bill's Lancashire and now Jeanne's Yorkshire, all different from our hard London tones. George and Jeanne's affair has been even more rapid than Edna and Bill's, but he is 31, and to quote him feels that now he has made up his mind he wants to settle down soon. His greatest hope now is to get the war over quickly and get on with the job – and so say all of us.

Not much more news from this end I'm afraid. I've been spending quite a bit of time knitting again, now that I stay in in the evenings, and at the moment I am making myself a new pink cardigan. I have also spent quite a few hours this past week unpicking an old black coat, which I have washed and turned, and tomorrow the dressmaker is having it, to try and make me a skirt and a bolero for the office. How I wish I was useful at this kind of thing, but needlework just doesn't appeal at all. This same dressmaker made up the dress length that Don sent me for Christmas, and it really looks lovely. I haven't worn it yet, keeping it for the better weather and of course hopefully wanting to have it nice for Don's return. It is only quite simple with a 'V' neck with revers and a collar, gathers at the shoulder in the front, buttons down to the waist, a fairly straight skirt and a belt. The material just makes it though, and as she has made it very well, and it fits like a glove, it looks worth quite a classy price, with its tailored air.

Well, Donna, I guess this is about the limit from here. I am enclosing a photograph I had taken last November, although it isn't very brilliant. The dress was the one I had for Edna's wedding, and the full length photograph was on the request of Don, who wanted to see the frock, but I never did like them taken this way. What's more it was taken soon after I was ill, so I had it coloured to cover up the haggard look which would have sent him scurrying home on the first mail plane, but I'm happy to say, save for the bruise and bump of the moment, I am looking and feeling very much fitter.

Cheerio to you both for now then. Don't forget to let's hear from you soon. By the way I hope this arrives in time for your anniversary, and I wish you 'many happy returns' and hope all the rest will be spent in peace. Lots of love for you both,
   Win

P.S. I meant to tell you, we have had quite a bit of excitement in the old home town for a girl was murdered near us quite recently, which caused quite a bit of a sensation in the papers. They have got someone for it apparently now though, so I guess there will be many mothers sleeping more peacefully and girls going off to late dances without fear again now. Air Raids don't bother me overmuch, but the thought of being murdered in the dark, doesn't appeal at all.
   Win

8th March 1944

Dear Donna,
Just a brief note to tell you that since I wrote this letter we have had our home shattered by a bomb. I will not stop to tell you all about it now, and in any case I shall not be able to give you the full details until after the war, but the main thing is we are all alive. Our only casualty was little Alfred next door, who has a couple of stitches in his head, but he has been a marvellous kid, and not cried or murmured once. Immediately after it happened, everything looked a pretty ghastly mess, but we shook the soot and debris from our back and got cracking. For four days we worked as we never worked before, and we now have two rooms to live in, one for sleeping and one for eating. Both of these have no windows, cracked walls and the ceilings down, but they are nevertheless an improvement on the rest of the house, now that we have cleared up and put the doors back. Still enough of this. Once I get started I'll be telling you too much and then the whole story will take pages. I'll write again soon and may be able to give you more

details. Meanwhile, if you still address letters to '23' they will reach me, provided nothing unforeseen happens and the house is condemned.

Will write again soon, don't worry about us, we always come out O.K.

Cheerio,
    Win

14th March 1944

My dear Donna,

At last I have a moment to give you a quick follow up and a few more details on our little spot of bother. I couldn't say much last time I wrote, and although I'm a little tired of it all now, I will tell you what I think will be all right and then have to give you all the other details after the war. The first amazing thing about it is that I was up when it happened, a thing I don't usually do unless I am fire-watching. Generally Mum calls and calls me urgently but not even the heaviest gunfire would make me part with the warmth and comfort of my bed. However, as you will probably remember from my last letter, I had had a nasty crack on my forehead about a week previously which came out on my right eye, making it all swollen and inflamed, and which incidentally has now given place to a small cyst, which I shall have to have removed if it grows any more. On the night it all happened it was still in the very inflamed stage and making me feel quite groggy, giving me even more reason to stay in bed, and yet, when Mum called out that night and told me to get up, as things were getting sticky, I did so without hesitation. I saw my bed too, after it had all happened, and I now believe in miracles. For a few minutes after I had got downstairs I sat moping by the fire, until I heard incendiaries falling, when at once I was on the alert. What happened in the next few minutes is still a bit vague in my memory. I know we hustled Phyll and Mum off to the shelter. Dad and I were just about to follow ourselves when we saw the roof alight with an incendiary. I got the water while Dad rushed upstairs with the stirrup pump, and then as I followed after I met him coming down. Apparently the incendiary had fallen off the roof, through the conservatory that adjoins the house, and landed on the ground, where when we reached it, it had burnt itself out.

I remember thinking to myself after this, 'What now – oh the front,' and I rushed to the front door to see if there was anything on the front of the house. I had just got it open, an act which incidentally saved the door, for it was our only remaining one, when I heard the heavies screaming down. They were almost down when I heard them, so there was nothing more I could do but fling myself flat in the hall, crawling nearer and nearer to the wall with each second that passed. It seemed hours that the stuff kept falling all around, although it couldn't have been any more than a few seconds. Then out of all the noise I heard Dad calling to me. I shouted back that I was all right, and was he, to which he replied that he was under the table. He is a bit deaf at the best of times, and with his tin hat on and being inside, the first thing he'd heard was the ceiling coming down on him, so he'd dived under the table, which had undoubtedly saved him, for he didn't have a scratch. As soon as I knew he was all right, I thought of my brother and his wife and the children next door, and as they say you always pray when you are in trouble, I can honestly say I was praying as I lay there huddled on the floor. I don't know what I was saying, but I was asking Him to take care of all those I loved, and at the same time shouting to Dad not to move until everything had stopped falling.

By the time this happened, and we had picked ourselves up and out through the debris, my brother had got all his family down into the shelter with Mum and Phyll and we met him coming back down the garden to us, his face covered with blood, which we found out later was not his, but from little Alf whom he had held in his arms. He managed to tell us that they were all all right and told me to go and see to Alf as he was hurt, so I rushed down to the shelter, where the others all sat, slightly dazed. I took him on my lap, he wasn't crying or making a sound, but the blood was just streaming from his face. Mum thought his eye had gone, but somehow in the dim candlelight I could see him blinking at me through the blood, and after wiping it away, I could see that it was all coming from two gashes on his forehead. I stopped the bleeding, and we wanted to get him round to the First Aid post, but the poor little chap, although not murmuring, clung to us and wouldn't let us take him out of the shelter. I bathed it the best way I could and tied a bandage on, and we took him to the hospital the next day. I've never known a kid so brave, never once has he cried, or said it hurt, or made any fuss at all, and he has let them put the stitches in, and later remove them at the hospital, without a murmur. I am happy to say that although he still has a plaster on his forehead and maybe it will leave a couple of nasty scars, he is well on the mend.

The rest of that night was like a terrible nightmare with happenings and thoughts all jumbled in my mind. I remember getting Dad to remove the kitchen door from the stove so that I could make tea and Mum, not realising, nagging me for getting the best cups out of the cabinet. I remember how Alf, Dad and I worked to make one room reasonable, and the way we hustled Mum and the others through so that they shouldn't see the worst of it. Everything pointed to our having to get out, but we just couldn't; it's our home and we wanted to stay, so there was nothing for it but to turn to, and boy did we work, never have I so swept and dusted and scrubbed before in all my life. My back ached as it has never ached before and I was grimed from head to foot with soot. We spent four days doing the really hard work and bit by bit we have done cupboards and drawers, sorted things out, and cleared up the washing, so that now there is nothing more we can do until the workmen come. They have already re-slated the front of the house and we have a waterproof sheet over the back. Dad has put all the doors back on their hinges, which saves a lot of the wind, and of course all the gaps where the windows were are boarded up. The fireplace and mantelpiece came out in the living room, but Dad has put this back, and somehow we've scrubbed out the soot, so if you don't look up at the ceiling sideways to where the French doors were, or at the cracks in the wall, it's still comfy. The front room too, which is now our bedroom, isn't so bad either, having only about the same amount of damage, and Mum and Dad and Phyll are sleeping on the bed settee in there, whilst I have my divan alongside. It's not a big room for four people to sleep in, but we realise how lucky we are really, so we gladly put up with the discomforts and inconveniences. I expect it will take a time, but I guess eventually when all the upstairs and everywhere else is patched up, we'll hardly be able to see from just looking at the place that anything happened.

    I should have liked you to see some of the freak things that happened. In my bedroom I found my wardrobe on top of the bed, in addition to the ceiling and heaps of glass from the window. On my desk on one corner where a pottery vase stood there was a huge lump of plaster and yet I picked that vase up from under the wardrobe uncracked. The spray off my dressing table was on the floor on the other side of the room, unbroken, and photographs and mirrors hung and stood in position, unperturbed by the merry hell that went on. Downstairs the wireless which stands on the sideboard was shot off and hung by its wires over the edge, and yet we stood it up and tried it, and there isn't a valve broken, it goes without a hitch. My scales, which stood on top of my wardrobe, were underneath everything and yet not dented nor the enamel chipped in any way. They are out of gear as far as weighing is concerned, but I guess they can be put right. The hinges were broken off my desk and it has been scratched, in common with all Mum and Dad's other furniture, but otherwise unhurt. The biggest freak of all was that the room in Alf's house where my dining-room suite is stored was the least badly damaged of the lot, and due to this and the fact that it was all covered, it is hardly touched. Alf's house is worse than ours, and they shared with us for a few days until we had time to help them, and now they too have the two downstairs rooms reasonably tidy, the same as us. It definitely hadn't got my number on it that night, for the hall is the one ceiling in the two houses that is still intact.

    Well I think that is about as much as I can tell you. I've kept it strictly to us personally, for more than this might not be passed by the censor, so I'll have to tell you later. It was an experience, one I shall never forget, and I must say there won't be any hesitation about the way I jump out of bed as soon as anything is around in future. I realize now the value of being on the alert. Mum has taken it very well, and Dad has worked with every ounce of his strength at what must have been an even more heartbreaking task for him, since it is their home – I have the future before me in which to collect mine. Young Phyll too was a marvel, keeping absolutely calm and helping to shovel up plaster and glass as if it were the most natural thing in the world. What effect it has had on the children there is no knowing of course, but outwardly little David has been quiet as a mouse, unable to understand it all, never taking his eyes off his brother's bandaged head, save to point at some damaged object and say merely, 'Bomb done that.' Little Alf, even though he is only four, seems to understand more than we give him credit for, for even as we bathed his head, he spoke of how we'd have such a mess to clear up in the morning, but never mind, he'd help. He did too, taking a delight in being given a duster, which he used to dust everything he could reach. He tells everyone he meets that his Dad is going to pay 'Old Hitler' back next time he gets on his gun. 'He'll give him what for, for spoiling our house,' he says. I'm inclined to agree with him too. I'd be sorry to be a Jerry next time Alf is on duty, I bet he doesn't miss. I've told Don a little about it, since he'd guess that something was wrong if I didn't, and of course we've had frantic letters from George and Edna, but we've had to insist that they don't come home, for we've nowhere to put them, and anyway, there is nothing anyone can do, once it has happened, it's just a case of keeping your chin up and not letting it get you down. It certainly hasn't got us down, although when I think of little Alf getting hurt, I fully realize the wickedness of it all. It's bad enough for us, but little children ought not to have to suffer for wars that grown-ups make.

Well, Donna, since it was not long since I gave you all the rest of the news from here, there isn't much more to add. George's wedding is now fixed for the 29th of next month in Huddersfield, and we are all looking forward to the pleasure of going out to a wedding with all the excitement and fun and games, with none of the work and worry. I'll be able to tell you more about this later.

Went to the flicks last Saturday for the first time in weeks and saw 'Jane Eyre' which I enjoyed very much, although I did find it a trifle sombre. We have 'This is the Army' on this week though, which I wouldn't miss for the world, and I am chancing the raids to go with a pal tomorrow.

Mail and news from Don comes through as steadily and quickly as ever, and he keeps up his good spirits despite his longing to be home.

Well, Donna, I have rather a lot of work waiting to be cleared, so I will not hang about with this letter, but get it off to you at once. I will write again soon, when I hope to have some more homely, if less exciting, news to impart. Funny isn't it, how we always apologize for our humdrum lives, but how we realize the tranquillity of them, when something happens to give them an unpleasant jolt?

Cheerio for now then, don't forget I am still waiting for more news from you, so do write soon. Love to you both.

Tons of love,
Win

11 May 1944

My Dear Donna,

It occurs to me that it is quite a while since I last wrote and even longer since I heard from you, so I am seizing this opportunity of a free half hour to write and see if everything is O.K. with you, and to get you up to date with what news there is from this end.

How are you both keeping? I often think about you, and wonder how things are going. At home here we are jogging along, still living in the battered shell of what was once our home, and gradually endeavouring to get things a bit straight. Continuing his travels, Don's address is now C.M.F., which means Italy, and he isn't finding this sun resort of the Mediterranean quite so sunny I'm thinking, and certainly a trifle cold after the heat of the desert.

Still, you know Don, he takes it all and still comes up smiling – I just don't know how he does it after all this while, and I only hope that very soon his patience will be rewarded and he will be back to the comforts of home again. Imagine my feelings, I hadn't heard from him for over two weeks and then last Monday seven letters came all at once. Was I staggered! I was on duty at eight, and only had time to get into my uniform, so I stuffed them into my pocket until I got there.

After reporting, I found a vacant chair in the rest room, and just sat there until I had waded through them. How long I've no idea, but I do know the room was full when I started and by the time I

*In the garden at 23 Dumbreck Road in ambulance uniform.
Note the patched roofs and windows.*

had finally come out of my coma, it was empty, although I just hadn't seen or heard anyone come or go.

He says the extreme poverty of the people is pitiful to see, and in true British Tommy style, his main job after fighting is feeding the kids. I only hope they remember who it was that helped them, in twenty years' time, when the kids of today are able to decide whether we shall have another war or not.

The most important home news recently was George's wedding a fortnight ago. He was very lucky and got his leave, although everything was uncertain right up to the last minute. However, everything came right in the end, and they were married in Huddersfield on the date fixed.

Jeanne looked lovely in white satin, and young Phyllis was a bridesmaid with a friend of Jeanne's. The bigger girl was in pink and Phyllis was in blue. It is wonderful how with borrowed dresses, we still have pretty weddings these days, despite coupons, even though we can't work out elaborate style or colour schemes.

We all went up there for the weekend and had a grand time. George and Jeanne spent their honeymoon in Blackpool and had a marvellous week for weather. We did just see George on his way back for he called in at home to collect his kit, but naturally he wasn't feeling too happy. I feel so sorry for them. It must have been awful to have married and had to part after such a short while, at this time more than any other.

Naturally we never know from one day to another when this invasion is going to start, but we do know when it does, it is going to be pretty awful. Although these past two years have been pretty bad for me, missing Don the way I have, I almost think I'm better off not to have the worry of his going into the second front – at least I've got over that initial stage, and can now look forward to his home-coming. Still, I mustn't get blue. It's no good crossing bridges before you come to them. We know we've got to have this second front if we ever want to get a bit of peace again, and whatever comes with it, we must take for the sake of those who have already given their lives, and for those poor devils in the occupied countries, to whom the end of the war must mean even more.

After all this while, I must admit we are getting a little browned off with our communal living at home, for although we have had a lot of repairs done, we are still waiting for the great mess which will come when they pull down what is left of the walls and ceilings and re-plaster them. What a game that will be, but we know it will never be straight until it's done. We are hoping they will come to do it soon, for I'm just longing to get back in my own room again. How I shall appreciate its comfort and privacy! Also it will be lovely to have the place clean, for no matter how we dust, it still collects all over the place, even upstairs which we haven't used since the incident. We understand they will be coming soon though, and I think the procedure is to do the top, and let us move up there, whilst they do the downstairs. I'm getting sick of the one room we live in, and the front room which has been the bedroom of all of us – Mum, Dad, Phyllis and myself – ever since. The sideboard is our only dressing table, and this is continually covered with a variety of clothes, bits and pieces belonging to both sexes.

Quite crushing this for me, for I'm over tidy in my own room as a rule, and have a place for everything. Still I'm not grumbling. We are a lot luckier than some, and we do have a roof over our head, so we must count our blessings. All the windows are back now, although we are not going to attempt to put up new curtains until the work is completed. The roof is done too, and the doors all shut now. Oh, and yesterday, we had the new French doors fitted. They are exactly the same as before. After this gap in the living room being boarded up for so long, they do seem strange.

By the next time I write, I hope I am able to tell you that the walls and ceilings have been done and we are near to being back to normal, although I think it will be some months before I can do this. One thing though, we have been lucky having the summer before us, for we can get out and get rid of the sight of the place a bit. It would have been dreadful in the black-out.

Mum has decided that she deserves a flower garden as compensation for the dullness inside, so she has cultivated a patch in the back garden and I must say it adds a touch of brightness to an otherwise drab scene. Dad in his turn has the chickens for a hobby. Did I tell you they lost their roof the night we lost ours, but that didn't stop their laying the next day – they are tough little blitz birds.

At the moment we have two dozen chicks, or I should say we had two dozen, for we've lost one, but the others all seem to be doing remarkably well, and already in the few weeks we have had them, seem to have grown out of all knowledge. It seems dreadful to think that at Christmas time they will all be somebody's dinner. I guess by then we will have forgotten how sweet they look at this moment.

I have been very busy with my knitting as usual and have just completed two little coats for my god-child Iris's birthday last month. I saw a good film last night – Ida Lupino in 'The Hard Way'. True enough it was away from the war, but one could hardly call it light, since the story was very heavy and almost tragic, but the acting was so brilliant I thoroughly enjoyed it. Haven't been much lately as there always seems plenty else to fill the time. I did see Deanna's latest, 'His Butler's Sister', which film I think Pat O'Brien stole, and more recently 'The Sullivans' which made me cry, but I thought it a lovely film. Dennis Morgan, the hero of 'The

Desert Song', really captured the hearts of my pal and me, as we sat enthralled through the picture last night, and sent our knees to jelly. In fact, we both came to the conclusion when we came out that we must be love-starved to have a film star get us like that. What a war this is. Certainly isn't fair on a girl, is it?

Did I tell you I had joined the London Auxiliary Ambulance Services? Well, I am now a fully fledged member of this organisation, and my friends tell me I look O.K. in my uniform. I will try and send you a snap sometime, if I can get hold of a film, but these just aren't obtainable now, unless you are very, very lucky.

My uniform isn't very elaborate though. Navy slacks with a navy jacket with the usual pockets and belt. The only decoration is a gold crown under the left pocket with 'Civil Defence, London' on it and a gold flash 'Ambulance' on the shoulder. I wear a blue shirt with a black tie, and a peaked hat with L.A.A.S. on it in gold completes the outfit.

I can't tell you anything about my duties, of course, but 48 hours a month I am on duty, and I thoroughly enjoy every minute of it. The gang are awfully nice and we really have fun. Sounds bad, doesn't it, when our work is so serious, but then good company always helps.

Well, Donna, I seem to have cleared up briefly most of the news I can think of at the moment, but I bet once I've sent this off, I shall think of a dozen other things I meant to tell you. If so, I'll write again soon, but please do let me hear from you. I just long to get all the news from your end. Are all your family well, and how is Dick? We are all the best of health and spirits. Oh, and little Alf's head is better now, save for the scar.

The afternoon is fast drawing to a close, so I will leave you now. Don't forget to let me hear from you soon. Meanwhile, lots of love to you both. Cheerio.

Tons of love,
Win

Again there seems to be a gap in letters which takes in a crucial time – D Day and the follow-up days as we started to gain ground in Europe.

Fortunately the events of the war are already well documented for this period, but I will endeavour to fill in the gaps of personal things that happened during this time. They must have been written about at the time of course, but somewhere along the line quite a few letters seem to have been lost.

D Day, 6th June 1944, was also the day Donna's son Gary arrived in the world. She told me when we met years later that whilst she was in the delivery room busily giving birth, all the radios were going full blast and everyone was drinking in the news of the landings as it arrived. Many years later in 1980 I was to meet Gary and his family for the first time at their home in California when Don and I finally made our visit to the States.

Also, this was an important time for my brother George. Whereas Don spent all those years fighting in almost every theatre of the Middle East and all the way up Italy without a scratch, George landed in Normandy on D Day plus 2. Almost immediately the convoy he was driving in was attacked and although he took cover under one of the lorries, he was caught by shrapnel in his back. So it was that within 48 hours of landing, he was back over the water again, on a train, bound for a military hospital in Scotland. He spent three months in hospital before being graded A1 again and sent back to his unit.

---

5 October 1944

My Dear Donna,

It seems such ages since I heard from you, that I felt I really must write again to see if everything is all right. I would have written sooner but I kept wondering whether or not the post might bring something from you. I bet I'll get a letter long before this gets to you, as there is more than likely something on the way to me now, but I wanted to write for I've got a bit of news that might interest you.

At long last one of your friends and I have actually met, and although owing to unavoidable circumstances, we didn't spend as long together as we might, we did have time for a really long chat, and hope for better things to come. It was Addison Sharp – I had a couple of letters from him asking for the correct details of how to get here etc. and then proceeded to wait. I didn't have to wait long, for he arrived two days after his second letter, on the very first evening I had spent out since the Doodle-bugs – isn't that life? My pal from the office and I always used to go every Wednesday out to a show, or the flicks, and we usually finished up at her flat, where I spent the night. During the Doodles of course we didn't go, and then last Wednesday 'The Song of Bernadette' was on, so we went, for the first time, and I stayed there all night, and knew nothing of my visitor at home until Dad rang me in the morning. However, he seemed to make himself quite at home, despite the ruins, and Mum said he was just like the other boys, Don and George, when they come home on leave – he dumped his kit in the corner and took a seat, and then everyone started talking. I managed to leave the office an hour early at go home and see him, and from five until well past twelve I don't believe we stopped talking. We touched on almost every subject under the sun, and forgot many things we meant to say – at least I know I did. I do hope he enjoyed his two day leave, although I was sorry he'd had to waste a day hanging about as it came in the middle of the week, when I was at the office. I can't tell you very much about how he enjoyed it, I expect you will hear about this from him, but we think and hope he did. He looked a little puzzled occasionally, for I guess we did strike him a trifle strange, but on the whole, we hit it off very well, and we hope he comes to see us again, if he was happy, next time he gets the opportunity, and then perhaps now that we've broken the ice, we can take him out and show him some of the sights. We were sorry that due to rationing and the house being in such a state, we weren't able to entertain him and comfortably put him up as we'd have liked, but I think he got quite attached to the ruins, and will miss them if the repairs are done by the time he next calls.

We would have had everything almost back to normal by now if it hadn't been for the Doodles, but due to the extensive damage these did to houses, nothing but First Aid has been allowed. Now that things are a little quieter though, Dad is trying to get part of the licence back at least, so that we can get the plastering of the walls and ceiling done before the winter. If this is done, we can clean up a bit, and sort the rooms out, even if the walls are bare and the painting and decorating has to come later. The temporary repairs to the roof haven't kept the rain out very well, so we are hoping to get this done again too before the winter, in which case, we shan't mind all the rest, and will believe we are in a palace, after over six months in it as it is. Still, this will sound as if I'm moaning, and believe me, I'm not, I realise all too well how lucky we really are, but it does get a trifle wearing to go on living in a muddle, and I think my nerves get a bit on edge now more than they used. No doubt this is due to the breakdown I had last winter, and then our trouble and the Doodles just added to it. I'm all right of course, but I know I get a bit bad-tempered sometimes, and get mad with myself when I do this, but it will pass, I shall soon be myself again, and then how thoroughly ashamed I shall be at writing such miserable letters, as I somehow feel I have been lately. I do hope they've not been too bad, for everything has been so wonderful really, hasn't it? The news is terrific and gets better every day, and now at long last we really do feel we are justified in believing the end is in sight. I think this is the cause of my feeling a little impatient. I want it to be all over and done with now, as soon as possible. I'm weary of it all. That's the British all over you know, it's no wonder others find it hard to understand us – when we are down and there is nothing but darkness ahead, we keep at it, and keep cheerful, never for one minute giving up hope that everything will work out in the end – then when it all does, it is a bit too much to bear, and that last little bit, is awful. Still, it's not awful really, is it, it's wonderful. Just imagine, we are back into France, through Belgium, actually into Germany – the channel ports are free, and the brave people of Dover will get no more shelling. As I write this, the battle is raging for Dunkirk – and what a different battle from the last one – and what a different outcome there will be. Of course, there is lots still to do, but with the defeat of Germany in sight, we are starting to feel that soon we can start re-building our homes again, have the lights on, and welcome the boys back, for I am hoping that Don will at least get home for a spot of leave, before going to the Far East, and of course, do you blame me, in my heart I hope he will not have to go away, but we don't know. Maybe they will have enough men without those that have already done so much going again, and maybe not, we must just wait and see, but to have him home, if even for a short while, and to see him again, would be truly wonderful.

George is completely better again, and graded A-1 as before, so we are relieved that his wounds have left no permanent effect on him. He says his back has healed so well, he just can't feel a thing now, save for his poor old feet, for he has just had a month of breaking-in training before rejoining his unit, and after nearly three months in hospitals, route marches didn't come as too pleasant a surprise. Where he will go now, we don't know, we are waiting to hear, and rather think his next letter will be from France again – after all, he only had a couple of days there before – I hope he gets a longer run this time.

Today is little Alf's birthday – he is five – it hardly seems possible, does it? David too will be three on Sunday, and a proper couple of boys they are, up to everything. They had three months in Wales during the Doodles, and even now, Alf still speaks with a really strong Welsh accent, which he seems to be taking longer to lose, than he did to pick up. He makes us laugh sometimes, the funny ways he says some things.

[*Note: The newspaper cutting says 'continued on Tuesday' but no cutting of this continuation has survived.*]

5 December 1944

My Dear Donna

They say it never rains but it pours, and this past week has certainly been that way for me, for after a few miserable weeks whilst the workmen were doing their worst, making life almost intolerable, destroying any inclination I had to go out, or do anything at all save watch intently as each hole was filled up, longing for the day we could begin to live somewhat humanly again, everything began to happen at once. To begin with, the workmen finished the plastering of all the downstairs, and we were able to move down again, after a week upstairs. This made us feel better to begin with, then Addison turned up for a 7-day leave, and we had what was for me after the quiet life I have lived of late, quite a hectic week, doing the town. Then we got the news through from Edna, and it's a girl,

Patricia Joan. Just to round off everything, your letter came on Saturday, containing all the latest snaps of you all, and especially Gary, so I've been jerked out of my apathy, well and truly, and have so much to write about I scarcely know where to begin.

I was very happy not only to hear but to see from your snaps how well you all look, although I wish I could have had one where I could see your face. I bet Gary is far and away bigger now than he was in those snaps but he looks very sweet, and I know how proud you must both be of such a lovable son.

As yet, we've only had the telegram from Bill giving us the news of Edna, which came on Friday morning, so we don't know yet whether it was a November 30 or a December 1 baby, but there was a letter from Bill for Mum when I met the postman as I left this morning, so I am anxious to get home and see what he has to say. I think Edna was the only one who didn't mind, but the rest of us definitely wanted a girl and I feel thrilled to bits about it, even though it seems hard to imagine my little sister having beaten me to it, still as you say, I'll just have to get going doubly quickly when

Patricia, born 30th November 1944 (taken on her first birthday)

I do start. We are all looking forward anxiously to seeing Patricia. We bet she'll be very dark, as both Edna and Bill are very much this way. She arrived two days early, which means that it is possible that Edna and Bill will fetch her down for Christmas. We all very much want them to come, and Edna and Bill want to come too, but we've left it for them to decide whether they'll risk the rockets. We don't want to take any responsibility.

At the moment I can't help feeling excited at a new scheme which has been started for home leave for men in Italy, and at last there does seem to be the chance of seeing Don again, after all these years. One of the girls in the office has had her brother come home for Christmas, and is so happy about it. I know now that I mustn't expect Don for Christmas, and that I really mustn't expect him soon at all, for it is all a question of chance, and with so many of them all to take a turn, he says it will take years and years for those unlucky ones who are left until last, to get home. However, it is something to look forward to and plan for, and boy, what couldn't we pack into 28 days together, after all this time. Of course it will be doubly worse saying goodbye again and seeing him go off, as too it will be so much harder for him, knowing what he is going back to, but at least we'll have the consolation of knowing that it can't be for so long the next time. After all the war can't last that long can it, or can it? Sometimes I think it will never end. Still having considered it from all angles, we've decided that we'll risk making it worse for ourselves when the second goodbye comes, and that if he is lucky enough to get the chance to come home for a month, he will do so. Just to be able to talk things over together again, side by side, and renew all those plans that for nearly three years have been merely written words, I'm sure it will give us both heart to bear the time of parting that will be left to us. At the moment then I'm just keeping my fingers crossed and planning for when the great day comes.

George hasn't had to go back yet and is now hoping to stay until after Christmas at least, which means that we may have him home for Christmas. As a matter of fact, he and Jeanne are on leave this week. Addison went back on Sunday and George arrived on Monday for ten days. He has gone up to spend a few days with Jeanne's people, but we expect them both back for the weekend and the rest of their leave. Thank goodness we have the house in a little better shape to invite them to, but as yet it looks a forlorn imitation of its former self. However, after weeks of dirt and dust and plaster, we have nearly all our 'second aid' completed. This means that by the end of the week every ceiling and wall will be renewed and replastered, and all the walls will be stripped of paper ready for 'third aid', which we understand won't be before the spring, when every room will be redecorated and painted. There are still odd jobs like window frames and woodwork to be mended, but carpenters don't make much mess, and immediately we are rid of the workmen, we are going to try systematically, bit by bit, to get each room cleaned and set out again. Of course the plain white plaster walls won't be too charming, but at least the draughts won't seep through and when we get the rugs down, curtains up again and all the knick-knacks out, it should look a little better. I don't suppose we'll do much before George and Jeanne go back, but after that it will be full steam ahead to try and get it looking something like, for Christmas. The downstairs rooms were finished save for decorating a fortnight ago, and we spent a whole Saturday and Sunday cleaning them up to make them liveable. It took us all day on Saturday to get the front room cleaned and move a lot of the bedroom furniture down, so that the workmen could have the upstairs fairly clear to work in, and then on Sunday we did the living room and bath room. It's amazing how much plaster clings, and though with the aid of linseed oil we got rid of a lot, there are still corners and little messy jobs that no one has had the heart to attempt. Still it's just a question of time now, and we should be fairly normal again. In any case we are now far better off than a lot of people, for we have every wall and ceiling sound, and boy do I cross my fingers quickly every time anything falls near, and glance up again to see if those lovely new ceilings are undamaged. I think we'd just go right up the wall if anything happened to it again now.

Anyway, all this is beside the point. At about eight o'clock on that Sunday evening, worn out with our two days' hard work, I had decided that a hot bath to get rid of the grime was the order of the day, and then to bed. It didn't work out that way though, for whilst I was wallowing in the water, there was a knock at the front door, and in walked Addison, with all his kit and seven days' leave before him. It just couldn't have been planned better, the way he came, just as we got everything more or less straight downstairs. If he had come the week before, he'd not have been able to get inside the door for dirt and mess. We fixed him up a bed in the front room, amongst an array of stacked furniture, but he didn't seem to mind, and we had a grand week together. It would take pages and pages to go into detail about all we did and saw, in fact it was just as much of a holiday (sorry, I now know that I must say 'vacation') to me. I saw places I hadn't bothered to visit since my school days, and even places I don't remember ever having seen before. It polished up my history too, for you don't realise how little you know until you try to tell somebody else, but all in all, bearing in mind I left my school days behind over ten years ago (doesn't it make me sound ancient?) I didn't do so badly.

Wednesday afternoon, 5th December 1944

Hello again.
Duty called yesterday, and I had to turn my attention to work – that awful word – but I'm hoping now to be left in peace to finish this letter. According to Bill's letter, Patricia is very dark, weighed 7lbs at birth, and is the most wonderful baby in the world – aren't they all? He swears she winked at him when she first saw him. He says any hopes he had for a son vanished when he saw his daughter. He thinks she is wonderful. We are all more anxious than ever to see her now, and I've got to get busy, as I've been waiting before knitting anything for Christmas and now it can be a pretty dress. This will be quite a change for me. I've knitted so many boys' suits. The two boys next door are naturally all talk about Christmas at the moment and my brother has been busy for weeks, making toys, so it looks as though yet one more war-time Christmas will pass without their realizing that there is a toy shortage. They are very lucky to have such a clever Daddy.

We had a shock on Monday. We thought we'd lost our dog, Peggy. She was missing all night and we didn't any of us get any sleep, although Phyll had walked the streets for hours in the blackout searching in vain and George had been to the police station.

We just couldn't imagine being without her and Dad was convinced she'd been run over or something, as, until the workmen came, she never went out alone at all, especially in the dark. Of course it has been impossible to keep her in whilst we've had the workmen in, as the front door is continually open, but she hadn't ever gone far away before. Imagine my delight last night when I put my key in the lock and heard the familiar patter, patter, patter, coming to greet me. It seems she followed one of the workmen home, although he tried to send her back, and as he was going out that evening he couldn't bring her back so had to keep her all night and bring her with him in the morning. We were all so relieved that she was safe and Mum said she really sulked yesterday when she was made to stay in all day. I guess her night out has given her the urge for a high life for it seems they looked after her well and spoiled her the way we've always done. The times I've called her fat and lazy and useless and yet I was as miserable as all the others when I thought something had happened to her. Home just would not be home without her.

I noticed in your letter that you had received the snaps I sent recently but you don't mention the one in uniform and it suddenly struck me that maybe this one didn't get through as it had bomb damage in the background and I just didn't think of the censor when I sent it. Have you had it?

What am I going to do with you, for I see you say there is a package on the way. It's useless saying, 'You shouldn't have done it' after you have done it, but you shouldn't have really. Naturally though I am eagerly awaiting its arrival. I love surprise packages and I'm looking forward to the time I can send you something really nice for I enjoy packing them up and sending them off just as much. It's an impossibility though until after the war. You should see the rubbish the shops have for display. I just won't buy anything that isn't strictly necessary on principle, except of course for the children. I've eight nieces and nephews now, including Don's, – and nine with Gary. As you say, it really does make me feel left behind, but never fear, I've every confidence I shall leave you all standing when I do get going, and then you'll all have the laugh on me.

Well, Donna, I really must close down. I've heaps of work to catch up on and it's nearly tea-time already, which means the afternoon will be gone if I don't get cracking. It was lovely hearing all your news and naturally now, being greedy, I'm looking forward to the next one. By the time you get this, Christmas will be over and I hope you had a really wonderful time. I wonder how Gary will react to his first Christmas. How marvellous it must be to be that age and not have a care in the world. Still, life's not so bad, is it, and there's every prospect of the New Year really seeing all our dreams come true. We've just got to keep hoping and smiling a while longer.

Loads of love to you all then, and an especially big kiss for Gary. Take care of yourselves and write soon, will you?
     Win

Parcels

In the Autumn of 1944 readers of The Lamar Daily News *suggested that it would be a good idea if they sent in money to the paper to be used to send luxuries and other unobtainable items to me in London.*

Money flooded in and a committee of four matrons of the town, headed by Donna's mother Mrs Pivonka, undertook to spend this money for the benefit of all my family and to tie up and post the parcels.

The following three letters are my immediate response to this news. There is a general letter sent direct to the paper, starting 'My Dear Friends', another to Mrs Pivonka personally as she had sent personal news of Donna and her family, no longer living in Lamar, and the final letter in February when the last of the parcels had arrived. Again this letter starts, 'My Dear Friends'.

9 December 1944

My Dear Friends
Gosh, what am I to say, where can I begin – never in all my life have I had a task such as this to perform. I'm at a loss to find a way to sort out all the hundred and one thoughts that keep tearing through my brain, and my emotions are so mixed, I don't know whether to laugh or cry.

How can I thank you, what am I to say, in the face of your lovely letter, and the magnificent news contained therein? What you have all done for me is the most wonderful thing I've ever known, and I keep asking myself, 'Why should it be I?' I'm such a fearfully ordinary person. I'm not great or clever or anything special, and yet you have seen it in your hearts to do this great and wonderful thing. No words I can ever write, can really express what I feel. My heart is so full of happiness and gratitude at the realisation that this strange world we live in can raise such kind and generous folk, amidst all the hate and strife that is around us. Naturally I shall not rest now until your packages arrive, and the list of contents has been sufficient to set my imagination rolling. I'm just dying to really see all these lovely things. There is nothing you could have done to please me more, apart from the fact that all the lovely things you are sending have long since been very scarce luxuries here. When I think of all the thought and work behind your effort, and what it must have cost you in time and energy, I'm just breathless. I can't say what I feel. Remember, I'm British. I'm no good at expressing my feelings, yet believe me, deep down in my heart are all those words I want so much to say, but cannot do so.

It's such a shame that duty must be so heavy on your gifts, and that you thought to cover this as well was very kind. I can imagine how thrilled and happy all the rest of the family will be when I get home at lunchtime and tell them the news. It's the most wonderful Christmas present ever.

My greatest ambition when this war is over and Don and I have sorted out our lives again, is that we should both visit you all. We will definitely do this. We have promised ourselves, so nothing will keep us away. When that great day comes, perhaps I can adequately thank you for this wonderful surprise. Meanwhile I'm helpless to do anything and thanks in cold black and white, could never really express what I feel.

You mention your boys coming to see us over here. By all means let them all come. We have little enough to offer unfortunately, owing to wartime restrictions, but what we have is theirs to share as many of them, and as often as they come. We know only too well, just what a touch of home life, even if it is a bomb-blasted house, English coffee and margarine, means to boys a long way from home, and the most we can do for them is the least they deserve. Any of your boys who are over here and want to come are welcome. Do not hesitate to give them the address. We've room for them all.

Of course, I will let you know as soon as the parcels and money order arrive. By the way, I almost didn't live to enjoy your kindness, for I was in such a daze after reading your letter on the train this morning on the way to the office that I nearly walked under a tram car, and then, when I alighted, owing to the frosty surface of the road, just fell flat. What a blow to my dignity. Right in the middle of the Old Kent Road, but I didn't notice it. I was still walking on air and even now, just can't believe that it is really true. I guess my face must have been a study to my fellow travellers, for I could almost feel my mouth dropping open more and more with amazement as I got further through the letter.

Well my friends, I don't think I can manage any more today. I'm too excited for writing.

My sincerest affection to you all then, and may you have the happiest Christmas ever, as I shall, and may we all find peace again in the New Year,
   Win

P.S. Dear Mrs Pivonka, I will answer your letter properly later on when I feel a little more coherent. At the moment I'm still walking a little on air, but just had to sit down and write these words before I could think of concentrating on work.

19 December 1944

Dear Mrs Pivonka
At long last I am seizing this opportunity to really try and answer your letter. It's been awful at the office lately, what with the Christmas rush of work, and we've been so busy at home too, trying to get the house into order for Christmas, that I really haven't had a free moment. Luckily for me though, the post arrives later in the mornings this week, due to the rush, and as I cannot get on with my other work until it does arrive, I have every excuse in the

world to be typing this, instead of concentrating on my 'war effort'. What's more, I am in extra early this morning, as I was on duty at the ambulance station all last night, and the journey straight from there is an easier one than from home, so consequently they can always rely on my being early on Tuesdays.

Although I wrote off straight away after receiving your letter, and tried the best way I could to thank you and all my good friends for their wonderful surprise, I really felt I ought to write you a letter especially for yourself, after all the interesting family news you sent me. I so enjoyed reading it all. It's all so very strange and different from the way we are and live, and yet fundamentally I guess there is but little difference in us all as individuals. I think you already know about all our family news, but just in case not, I'll tell you briefly all about us all.

Dad is an engineer, but the business of the firm he works for is leather. He has been there since he was about 20, save for his last war service, when the wives of all the men who joined up were given first opportunity on their jobs, so that when the men came back they automatically took over their work again, so you can imagine after all these years, he knows just about all there is to know about leather.

Mum is very short. We are all taller than she, even Phyll, the baby of the family who used to be such a tiny little thing. We all lead her a terrible life and I don't know how she stands us, or how she has carried on these five weary years under such conditions, but somehow she has, and we've always had plenty to eat and been well cared for.

My eldest brother is exempt from the army due to his work and although lots of these jobs that previously held men back, are releasing them now, we don't think he will go as he is over the 30 mark. He is married, with two little boys, Alfred and David. Doris, my sister-in-law, comes from Wales, and after years in London still lapses into her Welsh accents sometimes. Alf is five and has recently started school, which he loves. He can draw almost any type of aeroplane or tank, etc., there is, and rattles off the names of both Allied and enemy planes, far quicker than I can. Some of these German words sound so funny in his baby voice too. Poor little chap, I'm afraid he will carry two scars on his forehead as a reminder of this

Alf, Doris, Alfie and David

dreadful war, long after many of us have tried to forget it, but considering what he went through, his nerve is remarkably strong again, and he takes things very calmly now, outwardly at least. I think the fact that he never seems really well these days is due to the inward shock all these bombs and rockets give him. There is nothing that makes me madder than when I think of little children so young having to suffer. David is a sturdy little chap of three, who does not give a damn for anything or anyone. Nothing bothers him, he's always happy, and luckily still young enough not to know what it is all about. They all live next door to us, so we naturally see quite a bit of them, and tonight Dad and I are going to decorate their Christmas tree, the first they've ever had, and although we've tried to explain it to them, I don't think they really get the idea, and I'm longing to see their faces when they see it all lit up. Alf, my brother, has been busy for weeks past and now up in the spare room there is a lovely array of toys, engines, trucks, cars and a barrow for Dave. He's been on about this barrow he wants for Christmas for months, and when you ask him why he wants it, he just says, 'To put loads of dirt in.' I can see there being potholes all over the garden once he is let loose with this and a shovel.

Eltham as you know is a residential suburb of London, right on the borders, and whilst half an hour on the train takes us to the centre of the city, half an hour by bus in the other direction and we are in Kent, the loveliest county in England, and well deserving of its name, 'The Garden of England'. Whilst our postal district is London, Eltham is called by many Eltham, Kent, and too whilst we now have a big High Street with every type of shop imaginable, several other large shopping streets, three cinemas, and almost every kind of entertainment, the older people still call it 'the village'. Fifty years ago it was apparently a very pretty little village of Kent, with country lanes where there are now main roads, and our lovely old parish church and many old houses serve as a reminder of those days of not so long ago. Dating back further of course to the sixteenth century we had a Palace in Eltham, which was the country home of the kings, which has earned for Eltham the title of Royal Eltham, which still sticks. Of the palace, the banqueting hall still remains, or least it did until way back in 1940 when it was damaged in a raid. I haven't been over it lately but I think they saved it pretty well. We also have exhibits in the public library, a Roman urn and pot, which were dug up in Eltham not many years back, and it is hard to realise that way back in the years before Christ Romans walked over the same path we traverse today. So much for Eltham. I think it's a lovely spot to live in, being so handy for the country on the one hand, the town on the other if we want to see an especially new film or see a first class show, and even if you only want to go walking distance there is plenty of entertainment. Most of us travel by train to the heart of the city for our work, or at least to one of the other more industrial suburbs nearer to the centre, but I'm always glad to breathe the pure air of Eltham again when I get out of the train at night.

I love the country and the sea, and before the war, there wasn't a weekend that passed when we weren't out on our bikes into the heart of the countryside, taking in the most wonderful scenery of all, or down to the coast to smell the sea air and feel the salt breeze on our faces. We've Old Father Thames too; he looks very dirty in the centre of town, but out in the country he flows among the quiet hills, and it was lovely to take a trip by boat down the river to the sea, or up the river to Windsor and the other beauty spots. Life was very sweet in those long ago days. I wonder if we really realised how lucky we were, but one thing is certain, we shall appreciate our good fortune even more so, having been without these simple pleasures for so long, when they do return, as return they will when this wicked war is over. It's been everything Churchill said it would be – blood, toil, sweat and tears – but it is coming to a close now. Soon we shall have the tremendous task of righting everything again, and in comparison with our task of putting our house back in order again, what a colossal task this will be. That's how we felt when the workmen were in and we could not turn round at home, but we put our backs into it, and we've broken the back of the work already. So will it be with the peace. We'll just have to put as much into winning this, as we have the war. Then, and only then, can we hope ever to have unity and friendship amongst the nations in this war-weary world.

I seem to have wandered on. In fact, I hardly know how I got started, or what I set out to write. I only know that I was so happy to hear from Donna's Mum after all the years we have known each other, and that I wanted to try and thank you for your lovely letter to me and the grand news it contained. I have received your duplicate copy. It came last week, and now, well, as you can guess, now I am eagerly awaiting those exciting packages. Please give all my love and thanks to my very good friends yet once more for me, won't you? I do wish I could thank them all personally but this really isn't possible.

If I don't close down now, I shall just ramble on and on thinking of more and more to say, and as the post is now in, and someone has just planted my morning cup of tea on my desk, I guess I had better get down to the business of the day. I hope I haven't bored you with this long epistle. I'd like to send my love to Ponkey and Anna Mae and Mr Pivonka and yourself. I feel I know you all so well, and I hope that one day we shall all meet, and really seal this bond of friendship. Christmas, which is now just five days off, will be a thing of the past when this letter arrives, but we'll be into the New Year, so may it be the Victory Year we all want so badly, and by next Christmas let us hope that all the boys all over the world will be home again, and that it really will be 'Peace on Earth'.

Lots of love to you, and many thanks again for all you have done.

    Win

1945

28 February, 1945

My Dear Friends

I really must apologize for the long delay in writing to you, only I wanted to wait until all your parcels had arrived before I wrote, and then just as the last one did arrive so I went down with gastric 'flu, and then I've had a fortnight off from the office. I knew it was no good trying to write all I wanted to say to you whilst I was home and without the aid of my typewriter, but now, on my first day back I'm here to tell you all about it, and I hope you will forgive the delay.

I think the best thing is to start right at the beginning, eh – then I shan't get muddled. The money order for the customs duty arrived a couple of days before Christmas and of course I duly cashed it, and sat back breathlessly to await the arrival of the parcels. Then on Christmas Day came your envelope containing the names of all my good friends – what better day for it to arrive, and what more could I ask to make what was a very happy Christmas very much happier?

How I would love to be able to write to you all personally, but even if this were possible I'm sure I couldn't think of that many ways to say the same thing, so I'm going to try and say it all once, and hope that you are all able to read these words and feel that I am writing to each and every one of you personally. I do somehow feel as though I know you, for when Harley Davidson called to see us, he went down the list with me and was able to describe quite a lot of you to me, so that I could almost visualize you all. Anyway,

I shall keep this list always. It will be one of my most treasured possessions, until I can come and visit you all, and really see you face to face.

The first parcel arrived about the second week in January, and was the one containing my suit. You can imagine how my fingers all became thumbs as I tried to undo the string, and finally forgot all about shortages and economy, and just used a knife. I was stunned, it's simply wonderful, and what a lovely colour. I generally wear quite a bit of black, and in fact for the last few years, have had black, red and grey as almost my entire colour scheme, so you can imagine how wonderful a complete change feels. It was a trifle big for me, but at the moment it is in the hands of the dress-maker, who after practically covering me with pins, is altering it to my size for me, and I can see it is going to look really terrific.

The hat which came later fits and, even though I do say so myself, really suits me. This again is a complete change for me, and it's lovely to have a hat that really feels as though it will stop on. I have altered my hair to suit it, and I must say both this and the suit together really look, what Don would say 'smashing'.

Shall I tell you what I've done to complete the outfit? Well, Don sent me some money to buy myself a Christmas present so I hunted high and low and I finally found the one and only pair of non-utility shoes a shop had to offer. They are what we consider really lovely for these days, although maybe before the war, they'd have passed as just 'good'. Anyway, they cost the earth, and I think they are wonderful, and the very least my new outfit, and the super stockings Donna sent me, call for. I looked out my brown bag and gloves I had when I got married and decided that whilst the gloves are far better quality than I'd ever get now, and wouldn't disgrace my suit, the bag did look a bit far gone, so I've ordered a new one, with a long strap.

A girl at the office has a sister who makes really lovely ones, far better than any that can be bought in the shops now. Well there you have it – my outfit complete. Of course I'll keep it for high days and holidays, so that it is still new for when Don comes home, but I can just imagine the looks of envy that will follow me down the street, when I go out completely rigged from top to toe in new things, for this is something that can't be done with coupons.

The suit would have been 18 coupons, and when I tell you that 24 have to last between six and seven months, and that shoes take 7, stockings 3 (if they are fully fashioned and you can get them – if!) and a blouse 4, you will realize that no-one ever has a complete new outfit all together, and the purchase of a suit alone leaves one sadly lacking for the rest of the period – oh yes, I think I'm about the luckiest girl that ever was.

The 'Betz' parcel arrived next, on the following day, and I can't tell you how we all went into raptures over those cosmetics, they really were a treat for war-weary eyes. The lipstick cases struck me more than anything for we can only buy refills now, and I'd forgotten what a really smart case looked like. I say, we can 'only buy refills', and what refills. It isn't until you see the real thing again that you realize how wartime cosmetics differ from those we used to get in pre-war days.

I'd almost become used to rouge that faded and left me like a ghost after an hour or so, lipstick that rubbed off after one cup of tea, powder that was gone almost before it was on, and soap that had but a mere percentage of perfume and fat. Now, though, my lipstick stays put, as does my rouge and powder, and why, I almost feel like the old 1939 me again. By the way, the cold cream did not come. I guess someone thought I'd got my fair share and more of good things, and as I think so too, they are more than welcome.

Here is how we sorted them. The family agreed that I should keep the rouge, powder, one of the lipsticks and the deodorant cream and I didn't need much persuading I can tell you. I have passed the other two lipsticks on to Edna and George's wife, Jeanne, and of the soap Mum has one tablet, Don's mother has another, Alf's wife, Doris, another, and the fourth is helping to scent my drawer at this moment – I just can't bear to use it.

In this parcel too, of course, were my blouse and that pretty blue cardigan. I started to wear my cardigan almost at once, as it goes marvellously well with a blue dress I had made with some material Don sent me from Palestine. When he bought this material he had an awful business working out the length in meters and the consequence was it only worked out enough for short sleeves, although it was winter weight material. Now, this girl being the world's chilliest mortal, I just had to have a cardigan to wear over it, and hey presto, just the very thing I need arrives – I think you must all have second sight. The blouse looks lovely and fresh beneath my suit, and I'm just longing for it to be warm enough to walk out in it. The dressmaker is lifting the sleeves and taking this in for me also, so it'll then look really 'smashing'.

We went a whole fortnight before the next parcel came, and this time it was Clara Larsen's and contained my hat and Phylly's outfit. If you knew Phyll, you'd know that she never ever gets very excited about clothes, or anything for that matter, but if knowing this you'd seen her eyes when she undid the parcel, you'd have been more than rewarded for your clothes – to say she was thrilled is putting it but mildly, she was really delighted.

Off came her slacks straightaway, and on went the blouse and skirt. The blouse fitted her perfectly, and so did the skirt after we'd turned the hem up about six inches. I'd had it on before she came in, but she did not know for we packed it up again and let her untie it. It was just my length and I almost wished I was 15 again, and able to wear it. I've never seen her in anything that suits her better, and she wears it about every Sunday now, without fail. She was going to write to you herself, but had to give it up for, to quote her, 'It's so hard to say what I feel' so I said I'd try and do it for us all.

Then came a long wait for the next parcel, in fact I had almost decided not to keep you waiting any longer, but to tell you of the safe arrival of the other three, when it came, just over a fortnight ago. It looked as though it had had rather a rough trip, the box was all broken and everything was out of its wrappings, but the contents were unharmed, and after all that is the most important thing.

Mum's dress looks really lovely on her, and although it will have to be shortened just a little, it isn't nearly as long as we imagined it might be, as she is very short. Apart from this, it suits her fine, and she loves it. The slip too, she is thrilled with, and is going to keep for very special occasions, it being the first slip with lace on she has had for many a long day.

Dad was really bucked with his little package, and you couldn't have sent him anything better, for he always likes to wear a white scarf, and was needing a new one very badly. He is keeping it for his best suits but it is just his style and of course he has proudly taken it to show all his workmates. Both he and Mum too ask me to convey to you all their very best thanks and to say that whilst maybe they will never have the chance to meet you all in person, any of your boys are welcome to share our home, whilst they are over here, anytime they like, but of course you know this has always been so.

Alf just refuses to let his new hat out of his sight and once he'd tried it on we had a hard job to get it back from him to show someone. He clutched this and his card and refused to be parted from them. It fits him fine, and he tells all the boys at school that it came from America. Doris says that when they are out the bigger boys chip him about his 'baseball' hat, and he looks up at her in wonderment, not understanding what they mean. Let me explain, you see the word 'baseball' conjures up a vision immediately of America over here, just as we understand that 'tea' and 'England' go together over there. The bigger boys recognise his hat immediately as being something from 'over there'. They call it a 'baseball' hat whether it is like one or not.

Of course, Alf isn't old enough to understand this, but doesn't seem to mind them teasing him about his hat, he loves it. The ear muffs are very nobby, we never see anything like them over here. Mum has possession of the dress length at the moment and we've left it to her to decide what shall be done with it. At the moment she can't make up her mind whether to have something made for herself out of it, or something for Phyll, or whether to send it to Edna, but wherever it finishes up, you may rest assured it will be used to its full advantage.

The other item in this parcel was that pretty muslin blouse and we didn't know who was supposed to have this, as it hadn't been mentioned in the letter, and wasn't even on the label of the parcel, although of course the customs had spotted it. Now, I hope you won't think me greedy, but well, Mum doesn't wear suits, shirts or blouses, Phyll hadn't anything it went with, and it just fitted me so well, and looks so lovely with my new suit, they all said it had found its 'niche' immediately I put it on. Well, that's the way we sorted it all out, and I hope it was the way you wished it to be.

The thing that struck us more than anything was the care with which you wrapped everything, the gay wrappings, and the many pretty cards. How we wished they had all come by Christmas so that we could have added them to our rather dull war-time display, but we had another Christmas all over again when we put all your cards on the mantelpiece. Every sheet of tissue paper has been carefully folded and kept, and all this, the pretty tyings and the boxes, you can't imagine how useful even these will be.

My goodness but I almost forgot to mention the wool. At the moment I am nearly at the finish of a bolero I have knitted for Mum — in the red, and I think it is going to look really gay for her. I haven't decided what to make with the green and fawn yet, but I think some of that green will see its way into a pair of gloves before long. It is slightly thicker than our wool generally is, but I've done so much knitting, I'm well used to wangling patterns and altering sizes so that it works out O.K.

How I should have loved to share with you the job of choosing and tying up all these lovely things, for I can visualize it so well, and see you all amidst a pile of wrappings and goods, not knowing where to begin. An especial thank you to the four senders of the parcels — it must have taken ages filling all those labels and cards and getting them all addressed — but believe me, your efforts were not in vain, we all appreciated so very much every moment of your time you gave to making this wonderful gesture to us.

Now, about the money. You see, there was quite a bit of it left, after I'd paid the customs, and I didn't know at first what to do with this, or what you would wish me to do. At last I hit on this idea. How does it strike you? And do you agree? Over here we don't buy War Bonds, but Savings Certificates. These are valued at 15/- each, which is about three dollars. Well there will be just enough to buy us each one of these with the balance, and I kinda thought you'd like to know that the rest of your money was helping the war, from this side of the Atlantic, if we did this with it, and of course we'll always keep this one very specially as 'yours'. I do hope I have done the thing you'd have all wished in this respect. I can't think of a better idea, but I'll wait and hear what you have to say about it.

Well, there seems to be little I can add now, to what I have said before. You know how I feel about it all, and still I'm a little dazed and in wonderment about it all, and can't believe that all this has really happened to me. I should however, like you all to know that we will none of us ever forget your kindness and gesture of friendship, and we pray that very soon now the wickedness of the world will be wiped out, and this wonderful 'neighbourly' spirit may return to every corner of the earth.

Your little town has given an example of the spirit of a better world we all hope for in the future, that could not be beaten anywhere, not so much from the material aspect, but because you 'thought' to do all this – it's that which counts, and that is why I shall think of all of you always with the warmest affection, and as if I belong to you.

For the future then, my dear friends, may I wish you the very best of everything, may all your sons, husbands and brothers have a speedy return to you, and may you always be allowed to live your lives in peace, as you wish. I will never forget you ever.

My sincerest love to you all,
   Win

1 May 1945

[*The beginning of this letter seems to be missing. We have the paragraph below, which seems to be the end of the first day's printing and then the section 'continued from Monday'.*]

… nursing to bring them back to normal again – I realize more than ever how lucky I am that Don was never captured. The continued suspense of his being in action isn't so bad, as it would be to see him come home the way these boys have come. It just makes you mad, with a cold hard fury – you can't put it into words – rather like Don felt when he heard that his brother had been killed – he said, 'I wanted to go out and smash something up.' That's rather the way I feel when I hear these atrocity stories – you feel kind of helpless, for you know that nothing can be bad enough to punish these wrongs, yet at the same time, nothing can make amends for all that has been done. I never knew I could really hate like this, but six years of war is a long time.

(Continued)

They are starting to take the anti-splinter netting off the trams and buses now, and it is lovely to look out as you are riding along. The sandbags are disappearing, and the tank traps and the pill boxes. All that is left now to remind us is the bombed buildings, and the vast wide spaces, for they are clearing more and more sites. All around too, little colonies of pre-fabricated houses are springing up to meet the emergency housing problem, and to house the bombed-out, that is why they are clearing completely houses that are beyond repair. They are rather nice, these little temporary houses too. They are full of windows and fitted with all modern gadgets – they will certainly be like heaven for those that have to start off from scratch again, after having lost everything, and for the boys returning home after the war, for at the moment only bombed-out and servicemen are allowed to have them.

Well, there you have it, that is my city today, on the eve of victory, drab and dreary-looking with all its war scars, and everything needing a fresh coat of paint, but beautifully quiet and peaceful – no longer do those awful bangs come breaking through, sending a chill up and down your spine. Those tired strained faces too, that you meet on the street, somehow are different from the faces that once were strained with worry. It is more strain through waiting now, and I somehow feel that when the great news does come through, once we have got over the shock and really realized it, there will be all the rejoicing we've always promised ourselves. I wonder when it will come. Everyone thinks it will be some time this week but then we've had these moods before. Still, I think it is the real thing this time. The news is so wonderful from every angle, isn't it? Naturally, that which interests me most is the deeds of the famous Eighth in Italy – they've done it again. We've all been laughing about it at home, for we say Don is walking home. He's walked up Italy and now he's going to cross Europe on his way home. It doesn't seem possible that when he left these shores three years ago, he was three months on the water before he reached his destination – why now he could fly home in a day. It does seem to bring him so much nearer. For years we've dreamed of the day when Berlin would fall – and now it has fallen, and what happens – no one bats an eyelid – human nature is a funny thing, isn't it? I wonder how long it will be before this world gets back to normal again, before all those poor starving people have been taken care of, and their homes and cities are built again – and our own cities too. They are certainly knocked about a bit but at least we've not suffered anywhere nearly so bad as our gallant Dutch allies for instance – how dreadful life must have been for them these six years – I guess we'll never really realize. Thank goodness these last battles that are raging now are destroying only German homes. For them, I have not the slightest shred of pity. I did not need to see atrocity pictures to know what they were like, I've seen enough evidence with my own eyes of their evil beastliness – war's a terrible, awful thing – all this must never happen again. As long as we never forget, it never will.

It was George and Jeanne's wedding anniversary on Sunday and we did have a good time – nothing very exciting but they both got home for the weekend and we always have a good laugh when George is home. Mum got them the loveliest iced cake too. It was the first we had since the ban was lifted on icing cakes and the baker certainly excelled himself. It was delicious, and the cake itself was as good as any pre-war cake.

Edna's visit was all too short, and how we missed both her and Patricia when they went back. It seemed so strange to have the house quiet again. She is such a lovely baby and now we won't see her again until they come down for their holiday in the summer, unless of course they come for the peace party – maybe they'll come for this, or else they will wait until we have the real peace party when Don comes home. I've knitted her some booties and a sweet pink bonnet since she has been back, and now I'm busy knitting a little cardigan for Iris, who celebrated her second birthday last week. Don will certainly have to hurry home, or all these babies he has been god-father to by proxy will be babies no longer. There have been four additions to the family since he went away. Another of his sisters had a son last week, which means that each of his three married sisters has had a baby since he left – I'm fast losing count of all my many nephews and nieces, and I'm sure he must get confused when he gets news of all these people he has never met.

We had the most glorious summer spell a couple of weeks back and really made the most of every minute of it. I just lived in the garden, and got corns and back-ache with all the work I did, but it was worth it, for it looks lovely out there now – it is a pleasure to throw back the curtains and gaze at it all through my one remaining pane of glass every morning. We've had quite a bit of rain this last few days, after the long dry spell, and now the earth has got back its dark rich brown appearance, and the greenness returned to the grass and all the leaves – I can never really get used to that light grey appearance when we go any length of time without rain – somehow it doesn't seem like old England. Of course we could well do without snow at this time of the year, but this is exactly what we did have over the weekend, everything looked like a Christmas card and an icy north wind just cut you in two – this after we'd lazed around in cotton dresses just two weeks ago. No wonder they say if we can survive our climate, we can survive anything – I'm inclined to agree – but somehow I would not have it change.

I'm afraid there isn't very much more news at the moment, Donna. I haven't had any mail from Don for quite a while, but then I don't expect to, whilst the battle lasts. He did manage to have three days' leave in Florence before the offensive started though, and had a glorious time in one of the army rest camps. I'm still just waiting for him to turn up one day without any warning, although he still says there is no prospect at the moment. However, I'm confident that voice will come over the wire to me one day – and then all this waiting will be over – life will really start anew.

A good while ago Don sent me home some money to take all the family out for an evening 'on him', but they wouldn't come whilst the rockets were about. However, I've now booked for a show in town called 'Strike It Again', which everyone says just keeps you curled up with laughter the whole time. It is next Wednesday we're going, and I'm so looking forward to it, for I want Mum and Dad and Don's Mum and Dad to enjoy it, as they haven't had a night out for so long. Con and I are going too of course, making six of us, but at least we have got out a bit since last year. The bombs didn't keep us in, but the mums and dads felt they wanted to wait until it was all over before they went. The end of the bombing has meant such a lot to them. For myself, I find I get joy out of little things – things that may sound silly to you – like leaving my watch and my ring on the dressing table at night, instead of sleeping in them – as they were safer on your person than off. Like getting out my things ready for the morning before I go to bed at night, the way I always used to, and yet I wouldn't for a year after our bomb, because the things I'd left out got spoilt, and I felt I was tempting fate and just wouldn't do it. The greatest thrill though is taking a bath – since last June, until recently, I could never take a bath without a Doodlebug chugging overhead, or without that dreadful fear that a rocket might fall any minute. It's strange the way we all hate to be caught at a disadvantage, isn't it? Now, I just wallow and wallow in it for hours. By the way, I've sent you off a copy of a newspaper that gives a short account of the V-2s. I'll be able to add my own details to this later on maybe, but what's in there is all right to talk about now. The first place I've marked is very near the office, and the second is where a lot of my pals in the ambulance service were injured and many other people killed. The market that is mentioned is where Don used to go daily before the war to buy his meat.

I haven't any more news yet of that flat I mentioned I might have – I'm still hanging on hoping I might get something better. I wouldn't mind one of the new temporary houses, they are not very big, but they are self-contained, and you could make them look very nice, until things get straightened out, and permanent houses are built. Anyway, as there still isn't any prospect of Don's return for a while, I'm hanging on, then maybe something will turn up. Now that the summer is coming, I don't really want to leave the garden and go and live in an upstairs flat, especially if Don doesn't come home. I might just as well stay on at home, where I have plenty of company.

Well, Donna, this really does seem to be about the limit for today, and it is about time I wrote my wandering husband his daily dose. Do write soon, and let me have all the news. Cheerio for now then, and do write soon.

Tons of love,
    Win

16 May 1945

My Dear Donna

Isn't it wonderful – it's over, it's really and truly over, no more bombs, no more rockets, no more fighting on the western front, no more black-out, no more sirens – even yet I cannot fully realize that at last the wonderful day to which we looked forward so long has really come. To tell you how I feel, how any of us feel, would be well nigh impossible. There are no words to express the utter relief and thankfulness that we feel. We had a wonderful Victory holiday – for it was Victory, not peace. Peace will come when the Japs are finished, and now that our brief holiday is over we are all determined to work our hardest again, until the war is really over. With so many of our boys still having to fight the Japs, it was more our own deliverance we were rejoicing, but also for a great many it did mean the end of the fighting – those that have served their time are safe now, no more bullets or guns can harm them – it's just a question of time before they are home. I'm hoping that with his three years' active service behind him Don will be one of these lucky ones, but at least I know he is no longer in the fighting, and if he does go to the Jap war, I have every hope that he will come home first.

For us at home though V E Day and V E plus were the happiest days of the war, everyone really let themselves go. Especially here in London, we owe all the Allied fighting men an especial debt of gratitude for delivering us from our ordeal of fire and saving us from what we know were worse things to come. We didn't let them down, we stuck it when the going was hard, and they repaid us, for they didn't let us down. They smashed the German military might, and saved our blessed little island. Even now, I still jump at unexpected noises, and sometimes I fancy I can hear an air-raid siren, but when this happens I always tell myself, 'There is nothing that can harm us nearer than Japan now,' and you can't imagine what this means, after having the Germans and all they meant just a few miles across the water from us for so long. That's all over now though, and we are going to try and forget – not forget what it means, that we shall not and must not ever do, if we are to rid the world of wars, but in giving all our energies to building up our cities and homes again, getting ourselves back to normal life and helping those countries far worse off than ourselves, we hope that soon the terror of it all will fade slightly, and we'll be able to really know what peace means. I'm no heroine, I've known what it is to be scared to death, I've literally trembled with fear on many occasions, and sometimes felt like screaming and running a thousand miles away, but I didn't, like everybody else, there was just that something that saw me through and held me back, and now it's over I'm glad I've seen it through, terribly glad I lived to see the end, and to know that wonderful feeling on V E day – I've been wonderfully lucky. Taking stock, as a family we've come through with but few debits. George and little Alf both have scars that will stay with them always, but otherwise they are none the worse. I've a tummy that lurches continually and is always playing tricks on me, but I'm convinced that this will right itself, now that I won't have any more shocks. The house, well, it's still a bit of a wreck, but it's nothing compared to what it did look like, and anyway we've still got it, and that's more than thousands of others can say. This goes too for all Don's family. They've all had their homes damaged, but none beyond repair, and if it weren't for the fact that Eric won't be coming home, there too the storm has passed and left little visible to show. On the whole we've a lot to be thankful for, we got away with it very, very lightly, now it's up to us to show our gratitude by making this 'better world' we keep talking about an actual fact and not just a daydream. We've already made one big step towards it, and that is through the friendship and mutual aid that sprang up during the times of trouble. It was still evident in Victory, and folks that had helped each other quell the fire bombs on their homes and sweep up glass and plaster, got together, shared the good things from their cupboards carefully kept for this day, and threw dances and parties for the children in almost every street. The wonderful feeling of friendship made you just want to glow all over.

Let me tell you how we spent our holiday. I think it was typical of the way every so called 'reserved' Londoner spent it. That Monday before-hand was awful, the waiting and waiting for the news to come through – I just couldn't concentrate on my work and the boss had given me lots of long tricky technical things that needed all my concentration. Everyone felt the same and I think one girl expressed it the best way I know. She said, 'I think I know now how an expectant father feels – this waiting is awful.' Of course we laughed never having had personal experience of what an expectant father feels like, but we understood what she meant. We parted at the end of the afternoon, all feeling confident it would come through before the morning and warned each other to keep sober. Surprisingly enough, everybody did – for one thing there wasn't much to get drunk on anyway and for another thing people just didn't need it to make them let themselves go, nearly six years of waiting was a good enough excuse for most.

We spent all Monday evening decorating the front of the house and it did look good when we'd finished. We found all our old coronation decorations, and had flags of red, white and blue draped right across from our house to Alf's and out to the trees in the front. A Union Jack from every window, and three flying across the centre of the two houses, gave it a lovely splash of colour. Dad made a huge red, white and blue 'V' too, covered it with fairy lights and hung this in the centre of our two houses, right at the top – how wonderful it looked streaming out its light on V E night. We fitted up more fairy lights in the hall, and turned on lights everywhere; it was a wonderful sight.

All the rest of the houses were just the same, flags of all the Allied nations fluttered from every available spot, and there was not one house without something, and most houses were absolutely covered with decorations. People had really excelled themselves too – everyone found something red, white and blue to hang out, even if they hadn't any flags, and everyone found something of these colours in their wardrobe to wear. Every girl's hair was tied back with the gaily coloured ribbon, every lapel sported a favour. I saw one front garden studded with jam jars painted red, white and blue, and the house opposite to ours, where they are still waiting for a prisoner of war son to return, actually had red, white and blue curtains, upstairs and down. Dumbreck has never looked so gay, and it was typical of the whole of London, every street looked like fairy land.

We awoke to glorious sunshine on V E morning, and spent the time preparing for a real Victory tea, as we had nothing on hand. I baked a large fruit cake and made some peanut butter cakes. Doris made fancy cakes and jam tarts – we pooled our surplus milk and made junkets for the children, found odds and ends of lettuce, beetroot, etc. to make a salad and really had a first class spread. George arrived home just before the prime minister's speech, and after this, I took the kids out to see the decorations in all the other streets, but they were so worried that maybe they might start tea without us and that they didn't want to miss anything, that we hurried back. By the end of our walk though, little Alf could point instantly to an 'Old Glory' a 'Red Star' or the majestic flag of China, as he could when asked to point out a Union Jack. There were so many naval, army and air force flags, flags of our dominions, the Cross of Lorraine, and oh everything you could think of, goodness knows where they all came from – they appeared at the windows as if by magic. We had a grand tea, tucking in to all the good things, laughing and joking, and repeating over and over again to the amazed kids who just couldn't understand what it was all in aid of 'the war's over, the war's over'. We naturally sampled those bottles we've been keeping for so long, but in the main we have saved them for our real peace party when all the boys are home. We danced and sang for a while indoors, but as darkness fell, then the world really came to life. Every window was thrown up to let the light out, the gaily painted fairy lamps glistened all over the place, our 'V' lit up the whole street. Loudspeakers gave forth their music from wide open doors and almost every street had the biggest bonfire I've ever seen. Our two boys were really amazed by these. They've never known a bonfire and fireworks before. We had a beauty on the site where the bombs fell, and rubbish was coming out of every house as dozens of delighted kids heaped it into the flames. As we stood around the fire, we all sang, stopping now and then as a rocket soared into the sky, or a fire-cracker went off behind us.

Alf couldn't understand these either. The only rockets he knew didn't go up, they came down, and people didn't say 'Oh, aren't they pretty?' He soon got used to them though, when I remembered diplomatically to call them just fireworks – this was a new word and easy to understand. We stood around the fire until our faces were roasted and then moved off further down the main street that runs along the top of us, for in the centre of this they had started a dance. A radiogram was providing the music, and with the aid of arc lamps, hundreds were dancing in the street. It didn't seem like our old town, everything took on such a new appearance under all the light and the music, but we only knew we were enjoying life for the first time in five and a half years, and the feeling was heavenly. At about midnight we felt a bit hungry and the kids were tired, so we reluctantly broke away and took them home to bed, and made ourselves some sandwiches. My feet and legs felt as though they didn't belong to me, they'd had so much exercise, but I was more full of life than I have felt in ages and danced poor George down to his knees. At midnight the searchlight display started and we stood at the gate, munching sandwiches and gazing up at the wonderful sight – round and round they swung, making the sky a ceiling of dancing lights, then they all formed together into a dome, straight up into the sky – it was wonderful to see them. At about a quarter past twelve we started our own party in Dumbreck. Someone brought out their radiogram, and others brought out some arc lamps and we danced in the road, until worn out with happiness and laughter we were forced to stop round about two. If you've ever danced in the road you'll know it's no easy matter. I broke the heel off my only black shoes, but that didn't matter, nothing mattered. We were all so happy. We were together all of us, those same people who had been together in sorrow that March morning a year ago and cleared up the ruins of their homes, helped board up each other's windows, and shake plaster from our carpets. We were now dancing together over that same road that had held those huge piles of debris which we had swept out, and which still holds the huge white cement stains as a result. Now reluctantly we went to bed, and switched all those lights off – but we left our 'V' gleaming all night for all the world to see.

Wednesday morning saw us a little the worse for wear but we were up bright and early, and I spent the morning in the garden. We had seats booked for a show in town in the evening. I'd booked them several weeks before, never dreaming of it being 'V' holiday or anything like that, but it really did make a smashing finale to the holiday having the booked seats to go to, since it was impossible to get in anywhere unless you had previously booked. We all went, Mum and Dad, Don's mum and dad, his sister and myself, and had the front row of the dress circle. We went up to town early in the afternoon to see all the sights up there and the crowds and crowds of people. Everyone was in such a happy holiday mood, singing and laughing and raising a cheer on the slightest excuse. Once it was Churchill passing in his car, once a couple of trucks full of returning prisoners of war, and once just a band of a dozen kids headed with a flag and beating out a monotonous tune on a couple of rusty tins. Everyone is happy, now and then a loaded jeep would hoot its way through the crowd and everyone would cheer the some dozen or so hoist on top of it. They climbed everything possible to put a flag on to – we watched one soldier pick the highest tree and to the tune of the gasps from the crowd he climbed to the top and tied his flag on. I think the only thing that got them beat was Nelson's Column in Trafalgar Square. This proved a little too much and no one attempted this. The police were good-naturedly turning a 'blind eye' like Nelson, on misdeeds which would have at any other time commanded a firm hand on the shoulder. We walked around until it was time for the show to start, and then took our seats. It was a grand show, just one long laugh all the way through. Ike went to see it last night, and said he enjoyed it – according to the papers he is 'so happy to be back in a country whose language he can almost speak.' We've a great admiration for Ike, have we all, over here – the papers call him our favourite American soldier, and that just about puts it in a nutshell. Anyway to get back to the show, we laughed until we ached, and you could see the cast had all got the victory spirit and were really giving of their best all the time.

    We stayed in town until it got dark again, and saw the lights up there, the most impressive to my mind being the searchlights forming a dome over St Paul's and the floodlighting. As we left the station at Eltham Park, the strains of music reached our ears – they'd started another dance in the same spot of merriment as the night before, but we were too hungry to think about it before we'd had a meal – it was impossible to get anything in town, with queues and queues everywhere. We fully intended joining the dance again, but I was asleep in the chair before Mum had got tea made even, and so I went to bed with the music ringing in my ears. Maybe it doesn't sound much on paper, but if you could know what all that enjoyment, the lights and the decorations did for our war-weary souls, you'd know what a truly wonderful time it was. I didn't go to church on V E Day, but went last Sunday to the special thanksgiving service. It was a fitting end to a glorious week of victory, and now we are back at our desks, ready to carry on with the job again and get the Jap war over.

Gradually though little things are happening to really bring it home to us that at last it is all over. We've got used now to not drawing our curtains at night, some of the older men are being demobbed, and they say that married women will be released soon. I shall carry on anyway until Don is home for good. I'm still flat hunting, but as yet I haven't found anything – it's like looking for the proverbial needle in a haystack, now that all the evacuees are flooding back. The housing problem is really serious, so many houses have been destroyed or are still in need of repair. We guess to solve this problem is going to be our first headache in the building of this 'better world', but if we put everything into winning it, as we did the war, it'll all come right in the end.

The most wonderful sight of these days since victory has been the planes bringing home all the thousands and thousands of our prisoners. They fly over continually all day, very, very low to give the boys their first sight of the city they'd been told was 'rubbed out'. Those airmen must be in their seventh heaven, flying with no flack to worry them and knowing that they are doing such a grand job. They just seem to flit where they will across the sky, no question of formation, as we've been used to seeing them, and it's lovely to be able to listen with joy again to the roar of a plane. I didn't think I'd ever like it again, but I do. As every one goes over we say, 'More boys on their way home.' My friend's brother isn't home yet – they've heard that he is in a hospital in Russia, having worn his boots off after one of those awful death marches that the Germans sent him on. They all hope he'll be recovered and home again soon though. I haven't heard from Addison for a few weeks, so I'm wondering whether he has been busy on this job or whether he has gone home. I quite think the next time I hear it will bear an American postage stamp, but maybe not, maybe he is still here, in which case I guess he'll be knocking at the door sometime, although of course I hope for his own sake he is at home.

As far as I know, Don is still in Italy, but as yet there is no sign of his coming home, but as soon as the war finished out there he went back to his old regiment (he had been on loan for a couple of months during the last bout of fighting, and wasn't at all pleased about it, as his new regiment had only just come out there, and he had visions of his own regiment going home without him). However, to his delight, he is back again with all his pals now, and says he's as busy as he was when he was fighting, having so much to do and so much sight-seeing. His last letter spoke of a day out in Venice. Now that the censorship is lifted I'm looking forward to hearing some interesting tales about what he has been doing these past three years. I know he has been to India, Egypt, Libya, Palestine, Trans-Jordan, Syria, Iraq, Persia, Lebanon, Cyprus and Italy, to say nothing of his stop at Capetown on the way out, way back when they had to go right round the Cape to get to India. He was with the desert army at El Alamein, in the French rising in Lebanon, and has slogged his way up Italy from Toranto, but I'm hoping to get even more details now. His best pal was killed early this year, but apart from this, all the boys I waved goodbye to, and took a snapshot of that last Easter before they went away, are fit and well. Now that it is all over, it seems like only yesterday that I met them all in that tiny country village on Easter Sunday, when they knew that they were going to leave any moment.

From here, there is little that I want to talk about that I have not already told you. There have been many occasions when I've thought – if it weren't for the censor I could tell Donna about this, or that, or whatever, but now events that happened so long ago have dimmed and lost a lot of their meaning and in a way I'm glad. We lost our complete factory way back in September 1940. All the records and drawings were lost, but the patterns, the most essential point in engineering were saved, so we were able to carry on. For weeks we worked in a room over the local pub, working with every ounce of our strength, getting the records into order, whilst they put the roof back on the factory and got the machines, rusted over from the water used to put the fire out, into working order again. A whole basket of incendiaries fell on the roof. Everything was just devoured, typewriters, steel cupboards, desks, everything, there wasn't a thing left. I shall never forget that scene of desolation amongst the still smouldering ruins as I turned the corner that morning. You'd never know it had happened now. Everything is built up again, although we still have our offices in a temporary position. At this time they opened up another huge branch out in the country, and it is there, when the war is really over, that everything will carry on – by then, it won't make any difference to me where they are. We could have all gone down there to work, out of it all, in fact during the Doodles they pleaded with us to go, but every one of us decided to stay with our families and with London. We called ourselves fools, but we couldn't break away. We've had several bouts of damage since from various means, but we've always kept up production. Don's shop was very badly damaged last summer when three Doodles fell very close, but they were able to keep going – the window is still boarded up though, as they aren't allowed to put glass into shops yet, not with so many houses still needing it. I could go on and on, there are a million things to tell you, but somehow they don't seem to matter now – this is my war letter to end all war letters, from now on, there is going to be nothing but planning for the future and happiness to write about, and anyway you must be tired of hearing about the same old things as I am. A kind of unwritten law has sprung up, hardly anyone talks about the raids now. We've got to give the kids a chance to forget.

Dad has been very busy over the weekend and every evening this week putting the glass back in the conservatory. We'd forgotten how light it was with the lovely glass roof joining the house instead of the boards across that we've had to have since it was bombed. When this is done, he has got someone to help him, and he's going to start on the decorating – we want to try and get it all done before Don comes home. Now that we've taken down all the black-outs, and I've had my bedroom window put in yet again, and now thank goodness for the last time, the whole house takes on a different appearance and seems to be flooded with light – we can well imagine now how it's going to look with all its new paint.

I seem to have found all my long-lost energy since V E Day and now feel just brimming over with the joy of living all the time. I've been working very hard on the garden, and everything is coming along well. At the moment everyone is talking holidays, and where they are going, but I find it rather difficult to make plans, for to begin with I shall naturally have time out from the office while Don is home, and then, if I find a flat, I shall probably take a week then to get it in order. In any case I guess my friend and I will pop off to the sea for a week sometime during the summer if our respective males do not come home. Her boyfriend is in Greece, and she's hoping he'll come home any time. She herself is at present home again on sick leave – she's had very bad health for several months now, and is trying to get her transfer home again, so that her mother can look after her. I tell her it will really seem as if the war is over if she comes home, for she went the day the war broke out, and ever since then we've never missed a week without writing to each other. It'll be lovely having her home again, so that we can go around together the way we used to when we were both 'unattached'.

Thursday morning

Hello again,
I didn't have a chance to finish this letter yesterday and now I'm glad for guess what, Gary's photograph arrived last night – at least it was waiting on the mantelpiece for me when I got in. Donna, he's just the most wonderful baby ever, I've never seen such an adorable kid and there is nothing I would like better than for you to wrap him up in a parcel and send him to me. Isn't it a wonderful photograph too, they have caught such a lovely expression and he is sitting there as if he really knows what it is all about. All the girls at the office raved about him this morning. They love his little quiff of hair, and the general comments were, 'Isn't he a lovely kid' and 'Couldn't you love him?' It's a lovely, lovely present to have sent me. Please give Gary an especially big kiss for it. He'll take pride of place beside your photograph now in my bedroom. By the way, I couldn't decide who he is really like, but they are definitely your eyes that smile back at me – you should see the two pictures side

by side. Did I ever tell you what happened to your picture – it's the one in your black dress with the lace collar, and is several years old now. I have a later one in fact, but I still stick to this one as my favourite. Well, I rescued it from amongst the debris after the bomb, and found a streak of green paint right across the face. How it got there and what it came in contact with in its flight through the air, I've no idea, but other than that it was unharmed, and still sits on the corner of my chest of drawers; even with the green streak it's still the favourite.

I began to wonder whether it was my birthday when I saw all the mail for me last night, for in addition to your package, there were three letters from Don and a package from Jeanne. A couple of Christmases ago, Edna bought the crotchet cotton for Jeanne to make me some table mats, and now at long last they are finished and she has sent them to me. They are truly wonderful. I'd love to be as clever as she is with her fingers, and now I can't wait to see

Picture of Donna, taken in 1940, with the splashes of green paint it collected on the night 23 Dumbreck Road was bombed

them all set out on my polished table when Don and I entertain. Needless to say you just can't buy anything like this in the shops now. The only ones you see are terribly coarse and a fearful price anyway.

Don makes my mouth water with his description of sailing through Venice in a gondola. How I should have loved to have been with him, or better still, how I'd have loved him to have been rowing me in an ordinary little boat on the lake in the park, or around the coast, as he always used to – still, those days are really near at hand again now, we've earned our right to have them back.

Well, Donna, I really have gone on and on, probably told you things I've told you before, I never can remember, and anyway I don't care very much about anything these days, I just go around with a perpetual smile, wanting to hug everyone I see, I'm so happy and carefree – I never thought I'd know how to feel like this again, and it's certainly a wonderful feeling. By the way, I've sent you off another newspaper that might interest you. I'd have liked to have sent the actual V E Day papers and the day following with all the pictures of rejoicing but we can only get one copy and I know you will forgive me when I tell you that I sent them to Don.

Now I really must finish. I've piles of work, heaps to write to that husband of mine, especially with three letters to answer, and anyway you'll probably be feeling a physical wreck if you ever do manage to wade this far through my wanderings. Do write soon, I'm longing to hear all your latest news, and thank you again for the wonderful picture of Gary.

My love to you all – isn't life grand?

Tons of love,
  Win

---

12 July 1945

My Dear Donna

It seems like quite some time since I wrote to you, but actually I have been waiting in case a letter should come from you, as I haven't heard for so long, but I bet now I am writing to you letters will cross.

Isn't it amazing the way time flies? Here life has just been flying by the whole time since V E Day. There always seems to be something on these days and I'm enjoying the pleasure of really having fun with nothing to spoil it, after all these years. I say with nothing to spoil it, but of course there is still one all important factor. Don is still away, and likely to be for years and years, so it seems, but no, not really, it isn't as bad as that. Actually the situation is, that if he doesn't get home leave within the next three months, at the end of which he will have done three and a half years overseas, he will not get any leave but have to wait until his four years is up when he will come home for good. Of course, if he does get leave within the next three months, he will have to go back and finish his overseas service, but this won't be so bad, for his four years are up next March and I'm hoping too that round about that date his 'demob' number will come up and he'll be out of the army for good. However, the prospect of waiting around until then before I see him still seems unthinkable after all this while, but I guess I'll just have to resign myself to the fact if he doesn't put in an appearance very soon now.

He is having a marvellous time though apart from all the routine work which is so very irksome to them when they have seen so much action, but in between whiles he is getting in quite a bit of sunbathing and swimming and has had a week's leave at a really super hotel in Venice. Apparently Barbara Hutton and all the millionaires used to stay there before the war, and he says it would of course be absolutely out of the question for an ordinary person to afford to stop at such a place in civilian life. However, there is no one more deserving of these chances of a good holiday than the men who did the fighting, so I feel as happy as if it were me to read his descriptions of all these wonderful places. I heard on the radio last night that 'La Boheme' is playing in Trieste, and I can hardly believe even yet that Don is able to just walk in and see this if he wants to – what wouldn't I give for an opportunity like that. Of course, though, there is but one thought in all their minds now and that is home, for they've all done enough overseas service to make it certain they are not needed in the Pacific, and they feel that in this case, now that their job out there is done, they could come home, and so say all of us who have waited so patiently all these years. Still, the last little bit is always the worst, isn't it, and I do know it can't be all that long before he is home anyway.

Meanwhile, I've been having quite a good time at home here – now that we can go places again with nothing to hinder us, and whilst it still takes quite a bit of my spare time, I'm afraid the garden isn't getting as much attention as it got last summer when I was forced to stay home all the time.

Win and I have been out and about quite a bit these last few months and seem to have slipped back into a lot of our old habits, as if we'd never stopped. We often go off in the evenings for a tramp through the woods, jawing away like we used to, covering no end of miles and feeling thoroughly good when we get home. We've been to town quite a bit too, and in fact have got through almost every show of every type on our programme to see sooner or later. We saw a really funny farce, carrying the title of 'Is Your Honeymoon Really Necessary?' on my birthday and for my anniversary celebration we saw a really first rate variety show. Last week we saw a really lovely performance of 'Fledermaus'. It was the most polished show I've seen since before the war, the dresses and scenery were really beautiful and every member of the cast had a glorious voice, so for three hours we just sat face cupped in hands leaning over the balcony enthralled by it all. The lovely music of Strauss can never tire, and the ballet was a poem of beauty – I wanted the whole thing to go on forever and never stop. This week we've booked to see a show entirely of men who have been discharged from the forces, even the girls are played by men, and it promises to be worth seeing.

I think I told you about the impromptu party we had in the street on V E night, didn't I? Well, a few weeks ago we had another, but a really organised affair this time, for a boy who lives opposite, who came home after about five years in a prison camp. Boy, did we give him a good time, and ourselves too, for the whole street turned out and we had a really good evening. We started off by giving all the kids a spread, and you should have seen the lovely cakes and fancy things that were turned out – everybody made something and brought it out and added it to the table. This, when that very week the fat ration had been cut to its now laughably impossible level, was a truly marvellous expression of self-sacrifice –

I bet that a lot of people had dry bread all the next week – but it was worth it. We had a collection all down the street too, and bought soft drinks, icecream and prizes. The men had a separate collection to buy beer, and there was enough for them to just help themselves when they wanted it during the evening, and yet another separate collection with which we bought a wallet to present to our returning prisoner, our guest of honour. The kids' tea was followed by a fancy dress parade – they were only told about this the day before, so that all costumes were impromptu, and you should have seen how lovely they all looked parading down the street all dressed up (we put a block across the end to keep traffic out – and for one night it was entirely our street). We got little Alf up as a pirate in an old pair of Edna's shorts, a couple of my scarves, a red blazer, an eyeshield painted with the skull and crossbones, and we made him a hurried sword, finishing the job off with his grandad's last war revolver, which he proudly displayed to all the kids. The biggest laugh of all was the bad boy of the street, a real demon, whose mother obviously possessing a sense of humour had dressed him up as an angel with a large question-mark on him. A tiny tot in her mummy's dress and fur stole got the first prize as Mae West, another in her mother's old curtains made a lovely Indian Prince and got second prize, whilst an enterprising lad in little sister's napkins and mother's stocking dye got third prize as Sabu. Whilst we were washing up and clearing away, they ran races and competitions for the kids, followed by races for all the grown-ups and it was lovely to see all the dads trying to thread needles and the mothers balancing potatoes on a tiny spoon – it should have been eggs.

We presented Len with his wallet and he was almost too overcome to make a speech, in fact the whole affair just left him speechless, and I felt a little sorry for him, he looked so bewildered – folks can alter so in five years, and it took him quite a while to realise who we all were. He remembered us so differently. When he shook hands with me and had to stare hard for a few minutes before he let out, 'Good Lord, it's Win – why you're grown up', I could have told him I considered myself more than grownup when he went away, but I understood what he meant.

As soon as it got dark, we lit the bonfire and started dancing, but every couple of minutes the air was rent with screams as they threw fireworks in amongst us – you just can't be serene with a jumping cracker under your heel. By midnight, the fire had burnt out, we'd exhausted all the rubbish we could muster, all the eats had disappeared from the table, the bottles of beer were empty, and 44 front doors closed again as tired families bade each other good night and retired to bed. What a frenzy it was Sunday morning. Everyone was running up and down the street, returning tablecloths and borrowed dishes, but soon it was all sorted out, and the happy family of the night before became just neighbours again. Still, we've promised ourselves a bigger and better party when the war is really and truly over, and have carefully folded up our flags and decorations again for this event.

Although on the face of it we have done a little towards making up for lost time these last few months, life still has its problems.

Food has become increasingly short since V E Day and I'm afraid it's a rather bad blow to take, for we had hoped that maybe our austerity way of life could ease up a bit with the end of the war with Germany. Instead of which, we have to grapple with even shorter rations and somehow we seem to need them so much more now that we have relaxed. During the war we lived on our nerves and kept going because we must, but now reaction is setting in, and nervous complaints are replacing the digestive troubles which seemed to hit us all whilst the bombs and rockets were about. There were times when I felt so sick I just could not eat, but now, when I haven't had a gastric attack for weeks, I eat like a horse and feel as fit as ten men. The only form my nerve reaction seems to have taken is that of a rash on my arms, but it isn't much, and certainly doesn't affect my good health or spirits. Dad though isn't so lucky. He's been getting a nasty pain down the side of his face and neck, and several other people who have complained of the same thing say that the doctor's verdict is 'reaction' and time and rest will effect a cure.

There are queues for everything these days and the major problem which is on everyone's lips is housing – everyone seems to need somewhere to live, and it will take years to repair all the damaged houses and rebuild those that the bombs knocked completely down, without all the new ones that are so desperately needed. We've little colonies of pre-fabricated houses springing up all over London now, though, on the sites of where there had been heavy bomb damage, and the empty street at the back of us at home now has a row of these in place of the solid brick houses that came crashing down that terrible night. I haven't found anywhere yet but I'm still searching and feel sure something will turn up eventually. I still feel I'm so darn lucky to have Don coming home safe and sound that I can't look on the prospect of us having nowhere to live as a major worry.

Jeanne has just spent a week with us after a week with George near his camp, but she has gone home now and I don't suppose we'll be seeing her until about Christmas. George is still here, although he knows that very soon he'll be Pacific-bound – still let's hope that it will not be long until it's all over over there too, then we can really be happy. Somehow you just can't be, not with the thought of what is still going on out there nagging at the back of your mind, for although with Don nearer to coming home than going away now, I know what it has been like, so I feel for all those wives who are just starting their separation. Still in fairness, they were home when the Desert Rats were flinging them back at Alamein, so it is fair that the fighting which still has to be done should be done by those who haven't already seen so much active service.

The week after I return from my holiday Edna and Bill are coming for a week, and I'm just longing to see Patricia again. I bet she'll be a picture. At the moment the family next door are on holiday and I'm wondering just what Alf and David are going to think of their first glimpse of the sea – poor kids, we built castles in the sand and went into the water right from our earliest years. It must seem rather strange to them to taste these joys for the first time, now they are older.

Well, Donna, I seem to have come to the end of the news from here for a while, so once again I'll close down.

Love to you all,
    Win

19 September 1945

My Dear Donna

Very many thanks for your welcome letter which arrived some weeks ago, but when I explain the reason for my long delay in answering I am sure you will forgive me – yes, you've guessed it, my Don has been home on leave.

It was so wonderful having him with me again after all this while, and he hasn't changed a bit. All his civilian clothes fitted him perfectly as always, and save for the fact that he is a glorious bronze colour all over, and that his hair without grease is practically blonde, he is just exactly the same as he ever was. We've had 28 wonderful days together and now he has gone back to Italy to finish his overseas service, another six months. It was awful having to say goodbye again, but after three and a half years six months is going to seem like nothing, or least that's what we tell ourselves. Needless to say we went everywhere and did everything that is possible to pack into 28 days, and now I am back at the office again, after practically five weeks off – gosh doesn't work come hard – but still it's not for much longer now.

He arrived three days after V J Day, so you see I'd already been off from the office for these two official holidays, plus a day which they owed us from the previous V E holidays, and then that very day he turned up, and I've just not seen a typewriter for the whole of his 28 days plus these others.

I heard about four days beforehand that he was on his way, and a worse four days I've never spent. I was forever rushing to the door every time the bell rang, and just didn't move outside the house, until the day he came, when in desperation I went out for an hour – yes of course, he arrived while I was out. But the neighbours saw him coming and helped him with his kit. We had decorated the house ready for him, with a huge 'Welcome Home' sign, so it wasn't so bad my not being there. And of course I soon made up for lost time when I did arrive. The tanned face and blonde hair struck me first against the khaki, but when next day he got into his dark suit, white shirt and tie, with hair greased down to almost its normal colour, he was just Don again, looking not a day older, with but a very few grey hairs to show for all that he'd been through.

His battle stories were few, he told us mainly only the lighter side and had us all laughing, but putting two and two together we all realised that it hadn't been quite as easy as he'd have us believe, and I for one would have died of worry if I'd really known what he'd been up to, when he used to tell me what a good time he was having. Still he came through, and at least there is no war to go back to, so these next six months should soon pass.

We spent most of our time visiting friends and relations, saw all the old club boys and girls again. Remember Dick and Doris – we spent a lovely weekend with them. They've the sweetest little bungalow in the country just on the edge of town. George and Ida too, now the proud parents of a boy and a girl, we looked up, oh and all our old friends, and had several foursomes up in town with first one couple and then the other, doing a show and having dinner out. We stepped out among the high spots alone too some evenings, seeing all the shows and the latest films – 'I Live in Grosvenor Square', a really lovely film; 'Weekend at the Waldorf'; 'Perfect Strangers' and the very bewildering 'Strange Affair of Uncle Harry'.

Of course, too, we searched for a place to live, without result. The situation gets steadily worse instead of better with more and more men being demobbed – there just isn't an empty room to be had anywhere. Still, I've another six months to try again before he comes home, and I feel something will turn up – if only Jerry hadn't knocked so many of them down. Mostly of course we just sat up late talking, playing cards or looking through old photographs, and too lay in bed in the mornings until past ten, with Mum absolutely spoiling us with cups of tea in bed, and just cooking breakfast for us whenever we decided to get up. We had a grand 'Welcome Home' party with all the family together and all our friends and oh, it was just wonderful having him around to go places with, instead of being odd man out as I have been all these years.

It all went so very quickly though, and before I knew it, I was at the station seeing him off. We met all his pals there, and whilst we waited for the train they kept me doubled up with laughter.

They were all putting on such a brave face, you'd never have guessed how much they all hated it. As yet I can't really realise he has gone again. We slipped so easily into being together again. It was as if he had never been away, and now this being alone after a month is harder to get used to than our being together after three and a half years. On Monday I washed and ironed all his shirts and packed them away, and save for some darning and mending in my workbox, everything is ready for him to come home to again, and I'm back here, tapping away and waiting, as I seem to have spent my whole life doing.

Remember my friend, Win, whom I went on holiday with, well her boyfriend arrived home two days before Don for a month's leave, and he went back two days before him, to finish his time. Actually, he has longer to serve to complete his four years overseas, but his demob number should come up before then, whereas Don reckons on getting home first, and then having his demob come up whilst he is serving in England. Demob doesn't worry me all that much, although it will be lovely to have him home always. But once he gets back to England, there is always the chance of his popping home for weekends and odd days, and isn't the same feeling as having him so far away.

Win and Bill were married 12 days after he arrived, and spent a week on the Isle of Wight again for their honeymoon, spending the rest of the time at his home. We went to the wedding of course, the first occasion I'd been to anything important in all these years with Don by my side – you can't imagine how just having him there made me feel. It went off wonderfully well, she looked lovely in white, and we had a grand party afterwards when they'd left for their honeymoon. Bill had brought about half a dozen of his boys also home on leave with him, and it was a real tonic to be at a party with an equal number of men and girls about, all out for a really grand time. We played silly games and laughed and had fun. It was really like pre-war – really gave us a taste of what we've been missing, and it seemed to do everyone the world of good.

We didn't see each other after the wedding until last night, so we've got each other to console now, and have promised ourselves a winter of going places to make the time go quickly.

So much for all my good news – I could go on for pages and

pages, but you'd be bored to tears. The rest of the family are all well. Edna and Patricia are now living with us, as Bill hopes to be able to get his release to come south and work soon. They too, of course, are searching in vain for somewhere to live, and as you can imagine getting around inside our house is no easy matter now, we are so cramped up, but we get by. We are all here to get things sorted out – we keep remembering that, and I just know things will work out one day.

As yet the fruits of victory still seem very remote to us, with greater shortages of food and everything, clothing coupons having to last longer and promises of a harder, more austerity winter than ever before us.

If we ask ourselves rather bitterly sometimes 'is this what we fought nearly six years for, and endured that awful year of 1940 when we gave our all without counting the cost to give the rest of the world a chance to get ready?', we should not be blamed, but actually we are not really bitter. We think of those poor people in Europe so much worse off and we gladly make more sacrifices that they may be fed and clothed. We believe too, that it is but a matter of time and then we'll get our country going again. We'll make the things we all so desperately need, build the houses, export our goods to get back the money spent so freely that the war might be won. Yes, the people who won the Battle of Britain aren't made of the stuff to lose the peace. We knew it would be hard, but we can fight and win again.

Last week was the Battle of Britain anniversary and we had the most wonderful air display over London. They flew over, almost roof-top level, squadron after squadron, roaring through the air. The noise was deafening, but there weren't many dry eyes as glued to the skies we smiled a prayer of thanks to the boys who saved us then. It didn't seem like five years ago, as we watched them soaring through the air as they did then – we'll never be able to forget them ever – the mere sound of an aeroplane speeding through the air, quickly followed by another, brings it all back.

Wasn't the V J news a sudden and wonderful surprise – it does not seem possible even yet that it is all over, does it? Hasn't the world been a mess for six years? Let's hope we've all learnt our lesson and it will never happen again. Not many of the prisoners have returned yet. They are nearly all too sick but already glad news is coming through for those who have waited so patiently since the fall of Singapore and the other Pacific bases without letters. How wonderful it must be for them. Just to think there is no more killing and all over the world the boys are getting nearer home at last and not farther away.

For us all, things must soon begin to get better, and then we must never look back again. Strangely enough people didn't go as wildly mad here as they did for V E Day. For us at home, we were waiting for Don and that took it off a bit, but generally it seemed that people were just too relieved to go mad. We'd really got our pent-up emotion out of our system on V E Day, and then this other great news so close on top, we didn't want to repeat it all, we just went to our thanksgiving services (Don and I were able to go together to the church where we were married the Sunday after he arrived) thanked God, and told ourselves we'd now have to get on with the job of making the world a decent place again.

Gary seems to be growing out of all recognition judging by the snapshots you sent, all of which were lovely, and all you tell me about him. How I wish I could see him. He looks just my type. I'm sure we'd get along fine. I was so glad to hear the suit fitted him. I was a bit doubtful for I didn't really know if you had different ideas as to style or anything, but most little boys wear suits like that over here.

I haven't heard from Addison since he has been back, but of course we gathered that he must have gone when we didn't hear. If you ever see him, pass on all our congratulations on his marriage. We hope he'll be very happy and we all enjoyed knowing him a lot.

How did you enjoy your holiday? Was the weather kind? We seem to have had no summer at all this year, much the same as you mention. Everything in the garden is all out of gear, and of course it's had little or no attention for a month. However, the tomatoes have been very good and we are getting them bottled as fast as they ripen. Plums and other soft fruits were very plentiful too, so we've bottled what we could, but all came to a full stop when we couldn't buy preserving jars. However Mum and I have done quite a bit between us. I feel that I want to be prepared in case I find myself in a place of my own for the winter, and actually I've got about a dozen jars to my credit. Quite a good effort this and it'll certainly help out in the winter.

I see you've been playing Badminton – that's quite a popular game here, and it gets its name from Badminton which is the Duke of Beaufort's seat – and where I should imagine it was originally played. The shuttlecock is the feathery thing you hit, but the game is called Badminton. I might mention that I am positively hopeless at it, as with any sports that rely on the eye. I just can't have the right kind of eyes, but in any game with anything smaller than a football I miss it by a mile.

Well, Donna, once again I've rambled on and on and it looks about time I did some work, or caught up with this other pile of unanswered letters that have accumulated whilst I've been 'on strike'. By the way, Donna, you shouldn't have sent me more stockings – I feel just terrible keeping on accepting things, and can only hope it won't be long before there can be a bit of reverse lease-lend on my part. You shouldn't do it you know, but when you've written and told me, what's a girl to say with stockings dangling before her eyes. It is enough to tempt a saint. I'll let you know when they arrive, but please you mustn't any more. I'll take the thought for the deed. You've been more than good already.

Do write soon with all your news. I hope Dick is well and that soon he won't have to work such long hours. Lots of hugs and kisses for Gary. I do wish I could see you all – still one day maybe I shall. Meanwhile loads of love to you all.

  Win

17 October 1945

My Dear Donna

I just had to write straight away and thank you for your wonderful parcel which arrived last night. Gosh, once again you've taken my breath away – what can I say? Needless to say I think the stockings marvellous, and the soap, well you must have mental telepathy or something, for it came just as the soap ration was out – no wonder everyone tells me my middle name is 'Lucky'.

I put one of the stockings on at once, and to my amazement Edna just burst out laughing, and when I looked down I realised why – it really was funny. There I was, one leg clad in this, and the other in the awful thick lisle I wear for work, and you should have seen the difference. Edna said it was a good job we didn't realise what a blow to our glamour what we've become used to wearing is. In fact we've got so used to them, it takes something like this to jolt us back into realising what a difference such things make. Maybe the old adage that 'clothes maketh the man' is not so far from the truth after all. Anyway, thanks a million, million times, but don't do it again will you? You know I appreciate it, but I just can't go on accepting things. Believe me though I will make it all up to you one day, and I can only hope that that day is not very far off now.

    It hardly seems possible that Don has been back a month. He is near Rimini now, of all things guarding German prisoners. At least that is their main job but he has got himself a special job, one which he has longed for in all his army career. He is the regimental butcher. I can just imagine how he feels, getting down to the job he really knows and it'll certainly help him over these next impatient months and be much better for him than sitting around.

    It grieves him of course that he could be doing all he is doing for his own benefit, but we've got to be patient for a while longer. His demob group comes up in May, so by then he should be out of the army for good, but as I mentioned in my last letter, we are hoping that he will at least come home to England and get stationed here by about March, for it is then he completes his four years' overseas service. Actually he has been in the army five years next month – it doesn't seem possible, does it, that it was that long ago that I wrote and told you he was going? Gosh, what a lot of water has flowed under the bridge since then. We've been very lucky though, and maybe we have seen great changes in those five years, but we've come through, the two of us, and after all that is the most important thing, isn't it.

    At the moment we are enjoying the most glorious Indian Summer, far better in fact than our real apology for a summer which we had this year. The sunshine has been wonderful, and it really makes you feel good to get out. I've done an awful lot in the garden, got it all cleared up, so that it can rest for the winter. We had 96 pounds of tomatoes in all – not bad, eh, and though we have given a lot away, we've also bottled a great deal – I just love my bacon and tomatoes, or even just tomatoes on toast when the bacon ration is gone.

We've been very busy at home too, on the house, as well as the garden. The biggest job of all was getting the air raid shelter out – they completed this the last weekend Don was home, even if Don did manage to slice the pick right across Dad's rubber boots he wears in the garden (remember how Alf put the pick through George's arm when they put the shelter in six years ago?). However, despite something to remember its coming out by as well as its going in, we weren't at all sorry to see the back of it, and it took several fine Sundays since, filling in the hole and levelling off the ground.

We are all amazed at the difference it makes to the length of the garden. Dad has big plans now for rebuilding his work shed and changing the position of the chicken run, so by next summer we should have a lot of extra ground. He hasn't done anything about repairing the greenhouse, but that can wait until next year now – gradually though we are getting shipshape again.

At the moment we've the decorators in – they've done all the bedrooms, and very nice they look too. It's a treat to really have something to show for your efforts when you clean up now. I just don't know how I stuck those hideous mutilated walls as long as I did. They are on the big job of the hall and staircase now, which should look very nice when it is done. This will only leave the front room, and then every room in the house will be looking something of its own self again. Dad did the living room and bathroom himself, and re-glazed the conservatory some months ago. Incidentally this is the first time we've ever had every room distempered, and it doesn't look at all bad, wallpaper still being unobtainable.

Mindful that Addison once told me that in the States distemper is just a complaint that dogs get, I hasten to explain that distemper is a kind of paint. At least, mind you, I don't know a lot about it, but it is painted on the walls with a whitewash brush and dries with a kind of semi-rough, dull finish, not bright and glossy like paint. Well, my room, for instance, has the background done in cream distemper and then stippled with three shades of green and one of rust. This is done somehow with a sponger and the effect is all twirls and splashes, giving the appearance of paper, in fact you'd never know the difference.

At long last they have decided what to do about the row of bombed houses at the back of us that have been spoiling our view for so long. First they were going to pull them down, then they were going to repair them, but now they really have started to pull them down, for they intend to kill two birds with one stone and widen the road at the same time. What kind of houses they will rebuild there we don't know, or maybe they will just put up pre-fabricated houses as they have in the row that the bombs took completely down. These have been built some months now, and we've got used to the change of scene. Anyway we are not sorry to see these ruins go. It will be much nicer not to see them every time we look out of the window.

For myself, I am still searching in vain for a place for us to live, but it gets more and more impossible every day. In fact I guess it will continue to get worse as more and more men are demobbed and by the time Don comes out goodness knows what the situation will be. I've filled in application forms by the dozen, but as yet everywhere I go they tell me I'm about the 4000th on the list. We tried to get a pre-fab while Don was home, but this is impossible too, for you can't have one if there are just two of you.

I'm beginning to think Don will have to bring that tent home with him after all, and we'll park in the road. However, I'm not giving up, and I feel confident that something will turn up eventually. If I don't get anything it won't be for lack of trying on my part. I've tramped miles and I've made a thorough nuisance of myself. I think they'll have to give me something soon, they will be so fed up with seeing my face at the town hall.

Edna is still with us, although Bill cannot get his release to come down. She doesn't really like being away from him, says it is bad enough when you have to be apart, but she is better in health at home. Somehow Manchester never did agree with her, and of course she has more freedom to put the baby in the garden and much nicer walks and things down here. Manchester is a very dirty industrial city. We'll miss them both very much anyway when they do go back. The baby grows more lovely every day.

Win and I are still making the most of our first and last winter of freedom. First in as much as we are now free to go out where we please, without fear of anything falling from the skies. The lights are up and it's grand to be out at night again, at last. It is also the last winter we will be able to see very much of each other, for after next spring we'll both have our husbands home and be settling down to married life well and truly. She is off to the country to live, so it'll only be once in a while we'll see each other.

Meanwhile, it's making the time fly, getting out and about like we are, and this month that has flown already has been packed every evening with something or other. We've been up to town a lot, sometimes we've gone all high hat and booked the best seats, followed by dinner out, and at others we've queued for the gallery, and done it on the cheap. Funnily enough we always seem to enjoy it more this way, but in any case whatever we see, comedy, drama or variety, it's grand fun, after all the evenings of just knitting needle clicking.

Speaking of knitting, I've managed to get started on some of the children's Christmas presents already – d'you know by this Christmas I'll have ten nephews and nieces – it's certainly as well to start early. I just don't seem to get the time now like I used to though, for when I do get an evening in, there are always mending and washing jobs to be done, but I guess I'll have a bold rush, and just get everything done by the skin of my teeth when Christmas is really on us.

I am enclosing a couple of snaps. They aren't all that good, but the one in my suit I thought your mother might be interested to see. The other one was taken before Don came home, when Edna and Patricia were down here on holiday in the summer. It was a 1936 film which someone gave me, so I guess it didn't do too badly.

Well, Donna, I guess that about covers all the news from here at the moment. I really should be getting on with some work too, for there is quite a bit to be done these days. The firm is closing down soon, just after Christmas as far as we know, and transferring to our other branch in the country. Of course we can all go if we want to, but none of us is as it is too far away. It means therefore that the single ones are getting out already to get themselves good jobs, and those of us that are left have to turn our hand to anything that comes along. I've decided to stay until the end, as I have no desire to go through all the business of learning a new job, when I know it can be but a matter of a few months before Don is home, then I can leave.

As it is, I feel that maybe by the time the actual closing down comes, I may have been lucky enough to find a place, and maybe then too I shall be able to get my release from national service to get a home ready. If on the other hand I still haven't found anything, they may agree to release me, or let me do part-time so as to have time to search more. If your husband is in the forces you can get your release anyway as soon as he is demobbed so I'm easy as to just what I do for the remaining months. I've had just about enough of office work anyway, and won't be at all sorry to leave it all behind, although we all say that we are bound to look back and sigh for the good old days, for we've had fun here, even through the war. Many a laugh has taken the edge off some nasty incident.

At the moment it isn't all that bad, but when on the first of next month still more familiar faces leave us, the old place is going to be very different. I should have preferred of course to have just left when Don was actually home, but maybe it will work out for the best and those extra months will give me a chance to really find us a home.

Now I really must say cheerio, for it is almost time to wash ready for going home, and there is a slight fog coming up, just to remind us not to be fooled by these sunny days and that it really is October. For the first time since the war, we are back to normal time (we've been one hour ahead all through the winters and two in the summer, up until now) and it is difficult to get used to the light mornings and dark evenings.

Hoping to hear from you soon, and again my heartfelt thanks for your lovely parcel.

Cheerio and love to you all, with an especially big kiss for Gary.
Tons of love,
    Win

28 November 1945

My Dear Donna

Your very welcome letter arrived a couple of days ago, having taken just 13 days to get here, which was quite good going, don't you think?

Your new house sounds lovely, and also all the new furniture you've bought. I know just how it is, for I've got all ours during the war and it certainly takes some doing, doesn't it? How different from the old days when one could just walk into a store and buy a complete home. However, I think the way we've had to do it is far more fun and makes it all mean more to you. My only regret is that I had to do ours alone, but Don thoroughly approved of everything I'd bought when he saw it, so that was the important thing. Some of our stuff is new, but in the main it is second hand. Our dining room suite is new, and very lovely, but it cost the earth. We couldn't possibly have afforded everything else at the same price. It is pre-war though and I rather feel it got slightly bomb-damaged in a show room or something, was re-polished up and then sold again. That's how I came to get it at what in comparison with most new furniture is cheap for something so good. Our bedroom suite is walnut and I got this at a real bargain price second hand. It consists of just the double wardrobe, chest of drawers and dressing table. The dressing table is very pretty, Queen Anne style. A week or so afterwards I had the chance to buy a bed to match but in a moment of weakness I turned it down, partly because you can't buy decent mattresses now, partly because it was at the height of the rockets and everyone had told me I was crazy to spend my money. For once in my life I gave way to public opinion and I've regretted it in a way, although we really prefer a divan to a bed with a head and foot. The one we bought when we were married is very useful as you can have it either single or double and has been a boon all these years I've had to be alone. However, we found out when Don was home it isn't practical for permanent use, being much too wide and of course very low as the bottom swings out and the top spring goes down when you have it double. I'm watching all the advertisements therefore in order to get a normal size double one if I can manage it, fully sprung. Then this other one will be very useful for visitors. I told you about the settee and armchairs I bought second hand too, didn't I? The covering is in perfect condition, if a little out of date, but the frame is far better than you'd ever get now, so I plan to get some gay covers made when material comes off coupons. We've several rugs that I've made, oh and a carpet I bought second hand too, in addition to lots of odds and ends. What's more, I am luckier than most, in as much as I have been given things for my 'bottom drawer' for birthdays and Christmas since I was seventeen, so have a lot of little pre-war ornaments and luxuries that you can't buy now, which will offset all the rest of the stuff.

I had heard before that the housing problem is very acute in your part of the world, so you will be able to imagine how much worse it is here with a few million of them destroyed or badly damaged, in addition to other reasons for the shortage, the same as you have. I'm still without any hope of anything and at last we've had to consider very seriously living over the shop. At one time I'd never have even considered it but as things are I feel I've just got to make the best of it for a year or so and count myself lucky that we have these rooms to fall back on. They've not been lived in for thirty years and of course are made to look far worse at the moment due to their very bad bomb damage. All the ceilings and walls have got to be replastered. The staircase leading up was long ago removed when the shop was made larger but we have high hopes that we can get a staircase fitted, if we tell them we intend living there. Things being as they are, they help you to convert anything into living space. There are four rooms, two quite a decent size and two small, so this would make a good-sized living room and a good-sized bedroom, one room would have to be converted into a kitchen as the original kitchen years ago was downstairs where the meat safe is now, and this would leave a little spare room. If they fitted a sink and cooker they could make quite a cosy little kitchen, not the last word of course, but it'll make me appreciate a modern labour-saving kitchen when I get one. Of course I shall hate the feeling of being shut in and not being able to pop out the back door into the garden when I feel like it – in fact I'll miss having a garden – but as things are if we do finish up there I guess we'll have to count ourselves luckier than most. At least it'll be our own. We won't have to worry about people downstairs and we will have our own fireside, a place to put that armchair Don has been dreaming all these years about and a mantelpiece on which to put his feet. Also, as far as business goes, it'll be quite useful for him to be on the spot, as things won't be easy. Anyway, I'm awaiting Don's reply at the moment, to a long epistle from me as to whether or not we should seriously consider the idea. He'll think me crazy when after all these years I've always said I'd hate the idea and would rather go anywhere but there, and even to myself I can't explain my sudden change of heart. Maybe it is because it is something definite to pins my plans around. I don't know, but either way it'll be months ahead, for they haven't started on it yet and it'll take ages completely doing it all up.

The snaps of Gary were lovely. He grows more and more into my ideal man every day. Doesn't he look sweet in his little suit? I was so pleased and really kidded myself he'd put on that shy little smile especially for me. I can imagine how busy he must keep you these days, for he is the age to be into everything – don't you find your entire vocabulary consists of 'Don't touch', 'No' and 'You mustn't'? Patricia is a year old on Friday and the loveliest little pickle you ever met. She is just learning to walk. I think I told you before our babies are never as forward as yours, although she is considered forward over here and finds her way into cupboards all over the place. The stairs are our biggest worry. She got up five of them the other day and Mum is scared to death she'll fall. Jeanne has made her the loveliest little dress for her birthday out of nylon and embroidered it with pink smocking. I've never seen anything so sweet and Jeanne has certainly got anyone I've ever known whacked when it comes to needlework. Patricia has the honour anyway of being the first girl in our house to have anything in nylon. They've just released some and it is on sale in the shops but at this time of the year no one has coupons to spend on it and I have heard it is rather cold for undies. I'm waiting until the stockings come on the market, then there will be a scrum. I knitted her a little coat in that pink wool you sent last Christmas which happens to be exactly the same shade as Jeanne used for the embroidery so she'll look really chic on her birthday. I was keeping it in hopes that I might need it myself but the fates decided that this wasn't to be. I was pretty disappointed at first. It just seemed that everything was conspiring to deny me everything I wanted: a home, my husband and now this. However, I've got over it now and realise it was all for the best, since it is far more sensible to have a home first, whatever it is like, and it would be far nicer for Don not to be miles away.

Imagine if you can though our full house now. It's in a continual uproar with Patricia the centre of everyone's attention. One thing though we've all the interior fully decorated now and boy does it look and feel good to walk in through the front door to a polished hall and to see everything looking spick and span. Dad is still busy rebuilding his workshop at the end of the garden, having made the foundation out of the concrete slabs from the air raid shelter.

Don is away up in the Italian mountains somewhere at the moment — I don't know just how high up, but they are drawing altitude rations, so it must be pretty high, and pretty cold this weather I should imagine. He is worked off his feet, having the job of ration clerk now, and seems to spend his entire day from dawn until past midnight, dividing up the different kinds of food into equal portions for all the different outposts around him. However, he likes being busy for it makes the time pass, and once Christmas is over we'll really be able to count the weeks. It doesn't seem possible that Christmas is almost with us again so soon, does it? It'll be the sixth one Don has been away from home, and the fourth in a foreign country. Thank goodness we can really say it and mean it this time, that this year really will be the last. It'll be still much of an austerity Christmas again this year, but we've planned that next year when all the boys are finally home, we are definitely going to have one of our famous parties, with all the trimmings. It should be possible at least by then. For this year, we are to have a bit of sugar, meat, fat and sweets to help things out, but apart from this with everything so hard to get and the normal weeks before and after on our still low wartime rations, life hasn't become much easier even though the war is over. Lots of things have got scarcer and harder, but I feel that if we can just stick it out this winter again, things should improve next year. Despite repeated warnings that our rations are dangerously low, leaving us more susceptible to common colds and infections, there seems no hope of any increases yet, and I guess we can't expect them, when the whole of Europe is in such a bad way. Maybe we get sick to death of the sameness of the diet and the bulkiness of our food, which makes us all look well fed and plump due to the starch, but at least we never have been really hungry and no one here dies of starvation. When such things are happening elsewhere, it makes you stop and think before you grumble.

We don't really know what we'll be doing at Christmas, whether we'll all be at home that is, Edna, Bill and Paddy, Mum, Dad, Phyll and I, or whether Edna and Bill will be in Manchester. In this case, Mum and Dad will spend Christmas at Jeanne's home in Huddersfield, for George will be there, and it'll be too soon for her to travel. If they do, I'll spend Christmas with Don's people, but either way we'll have a good time you can bet. Turkeys are going to be scarce and dear again, so we've secured a couple of chickens which we are fattening, and Mum has made her Christmas puddings with the aid of some fruit we had from Australia. The extra fat will mean I can make some cakes, and we've all agreed to save our whole month's sweet ration, so when it comes to the point, although there will be no nuts or oranges and apples, there will be a fine spread. We always secure one somehow, and the kids will have their Christmas tree, and their toys in their stockings.

I won't mail this letter today, as I've just remembered, I've got a lovely picture taken in Whitehall on Armistice Day I thought you might like. Show it to any G.I. who has been to London, he'll recognise it as quickly as Piccadilly Circus or Rainbow Corner. I wanted to go up there for the service, but Sunday morning in our house it's impossible to get up and out anywhere early. However, I listened to it on the wireless – that roll of drums preceding the two minutes' silence always makes me go cold all over, but it does make you stop and think what we owe to all those boys who will never come back.

In this changing world with its black spots still, and its little bouts of fighting here and there, its strikes, and now the different future which our new Government promises, the war seems very remote. The immediate problems of where and how to live, seem to over shadow so much of the past, it's as well we stop and remember those that made it possible sometimes. What did you think of our Mr Attlee when he came over? He has gone up many points in my estimation after proving his foreign policy to be the same as we always wanted it to be. The changes at home though are a different thing, and all this talk of nationalisation sounds rather frightening. I make no secret of it, I'm no Socialist, they didn't get my vote at the election. I'm all for private enterprise, and think you can't get anywhere without a bit of fair competition, but they got in by the majority vote of the people, so what I think doesn't count, and anyway, now they are in, in fairness, I'm all for giving them a break and judging them on results. If in the long run their policy turns out to be just what this old country needed, well then I might change my views, but I must confess to being a bit of a diehard when it comes to the old ways and the old traditions. I hate to see so much of what is England to me disappearing, but there, what happens at home doesn't really make much difference, so long as we get along with the rest of the world. It makes me mad to hear the people who blithely talk of 'the next war', that's the thing we've all got to prevent, if there is anything that just ordinary people can do about such a vast problem, and I feel there must be. Surely no-one who has endured the six years of the last war can say with any conscience that another war in twenty years is inevitable, and just dismiss it like that. If there is anything humanly possible to be done to stop wars, it must be done, and we mustn't rest secure, or smug until this is so. Gosh, what started me off that way again? I'd better get off my soap box before I have you as crazy as I am.

    Win and I are continuing to have a good time, and frequently hit the high spots in town for a show or a film. How strange the West End looks now without any Yanks about, and the increasing number of civilian men who are not 'either too young or too old' makes things look a bit normal again. The flags are still waving from many homes, welcoming back prisoners from Japan, and we've had a visit from one of the young chaps from the office, who was a prisoner for four years. To our amazement he looked remarkably fit, and we found ourselves in the rather awkward position of not knowing quite what to say to him. It didn't seem right to say

'How well you look'. He explained it all to us later though, by telling us he had weighed just seven stone when he was released, and he'd put on all the extra weight in a few months in your country. 'The way they fed us' was all he could say, and we heard more about his good time of the past few months than we did of any of the four years. How much better though for his mother to have waited those extra months and seen him like he is today, than to have seen him as he must have looked at first. I think it's a wonderful scheme to feed them up and rest them like that.

Although she isn't properly fit yet, Win has started work again, as she got so fed up being at home, right from Easter is a long while. Still, her husband will be home very early in the New Year so she hasn't much longer to wait.

I've just busted all my money and coupons on a new suit for the spring. A bit previous maybe you are thinking, but I was determined not to spend my coupons on anything for now, as I wanted something super for when Don came home, and I happened to see just the very thing. It's a real super job, non-utility, and it cost me, well I still shudder when I think of the price, but what matters, it's for a special occasion. It's navy blue men's suiting with a faint white stripe and a pale blue stripe running down it. The coat is just that bit different from the utility, having a lovely cut, and sideways pockets, and the skirt has three pleats in the front. It'll wear and wear until I'm sick of the sight of it I guess. I've got a new navy bag and some shoes, so after Christmas I'll see about the gloves and hat, and I'll be all set for that 'meeting at the station'. I've a blouse length of blue lace I bought ages ago, and one of the blouses I had from Lamar last Christmas looks a treat with it, so I'm saving this. Gosh, that husband of mine had better hurry home – I tell you – he doesn't know what he's missing.

I hope your mother will forgive me, but I've had my yellow suit dyed a lovely chocolate brown. I loved it the colour it was, but it just didn't suit smoky old London, and we never have the weather for it over here. I did wear it an awful lot this summer though, so I feel I had a lot of beauty out of it, as it was. Believe it or not, it looks even richer in its present colour and those buttons show up even more to advantage. What's more I'm getting endless use out of it now, all through the winter, under my own swagger. I've left

The yellow suit that came in the parcel from Lamar

the yellow hat, and wear this now flat over one eye, instead of perched on the back as I did in the summer, and everyone wants to know where I got it, it looks so different from the usual run of things. I've a lovely bright yellow scarf which I wear over my coat with a point at the back, and have knitted yellow gloves with some fair isle on the back, so I've a lovely gay winter outfit out of it, as well as a summer one now.

I've managed to get quite a bit of knitting in lately, considering I've been going out much more too, and since Don went back have knitted four pairs of gloves, one for him, two for myself and a pair for his mother. Two little coats, one for Patricia, and one for his sister's baby Keith, a couple of pairs of socks for Patricia, two vests and some things for Jeanne. I'm in the middle of a dress for our Patricia now, which should be just right for her at Christmas.

Well, Donna, I seem to have ambled on in my own peculiar

fashion for quite long enough. Whatever am I going to do when I have to write all my letters? I really don't think there is any more news to impart though, save to say I hope Gary's package arrived O.K. as I sent it to your old address. If this reaches you as quickly as your letter came this way, you'll get it before New Year.

    Lots of love to you all,
        Win xxxxx
        Big kiss for Gary X

1946

1st January 1946

My Dear Donna,

Here's a good start to the New Year, a new typewriter ribbon, a spare hour and the office, and consequently a letter to you. How are you all and did you have a good Christmas? I wonder too just what 1946 has in store for us all, but at least what this year has to offer is something more concrete than we ever dare hope for this time last year.

Looking back, 1945, with all its surprises both grave and gay, will always live in my memory for two important events. V E Day to start with. If I live to be 100 I shall remember those laughing crowds, dancing my feet off in the street, and the load that seemed to be lifted from my shoulders overnight as it were. Even V J day which meant the end of it all, didn't arouse quite the same feeling in me as that wonderful day in May. The other thing that I can never forget is that August day when Don walked in, and the thirty hectic, wonderful days that followed. It was only after he had gone back that I realised that in all the time, we'd never once had an evening alone together, just the two of us, we were either dashing off somewhere, or there were crowds in. Small wonder I went back to the office, looking and feeling a wreck, and that Don says, 'Next time we'll just run away for the whole time.'

1946 promises as many important events as this year just passed, but at least for the first time in six years I really know that it is a definite fact when I say, 'This time next year, Don will be home.' I said it all the other years, but I wasn't convincing anyone, least of all myself. Yes, this year will definitely see us together again, and installed in our own home, these two things at least are certain. The prospect looks a little brighter too for more food and more of those little luxuries we've been so long without. They'll come back gradually, and whilst the politicians and the statesmen argue, we, the little people, sort out our lives, and regulate them back to normal.

It was a wonderful Christmas, as wonderful as a Christmas could be without Don. We didn't do anything terribly spectacular but we were so gloomy about it just beforehand, it came as a complete surprise when things all worked out, and it wasn't quite such an austerity one, as we had at first feared. For months beforehand, food had been the main thought. With everything getting harder instead of easier, the prospects for Christmas didn't look at all good, then, somehow, everything seemed to get started at once. First of all came a parcel from a cousin of Don's I correspond with in Australia, containing all the necessary Christmas dried fruits, jellies, and joy of joys a tin of peaches. Mum made her puddings, and I made the richest Christmas cake I'd ever attempted, just lavishing it with the fruit. Then we were allowed extra rations for Christmas, this extra sugar and fat helped a lot, so we were able to make little fairy cakes which we covered with chocolate or icing. I made mock almond paste with semolina and almond essence for the big cake, then, as we had taken a pound of our extra sugar ration in icing sugar, I gave the top a liberal white coat, with 'A Merry Christmas' in pink. We'd never had such a Christmas cake for years. On the Sunday before Christmas I made blancmanges, topped with the Australian jellies and peaches, and if you could have seen all the good things set out on the huge sideboard in the front room, you'd have known just how it warmed our very hearts just to see it. We had an orange ration too just before Christmas, which worked out at two each, so with our large family, you can imagine what a dishful we had. Then, just as we were saying that we really ought to have someone in to share all our good things – it was the first Christmas we hadn't got anyone coming – the postman knocked at the door with another parcel. It was from those friends in South Africa that Don met on his way out to India, nearly four years ago. We've just exchanged cards other

Christmases, so the parcel came as a complete surprise, but not then as much as the contents. A pound of vitaminised cooking fat, which Mum bore off and used for her mince tarts, almost before I'd got it out of the box. Cream cheese, tea, more jellies, more mixed dried fruit, and a slab of real milk chocolate with fruit and nuts. You can imagine then, the time we had, and why it was no small wonder we were all ill afterwards, our tummies just couldn't take it. It was worth it though, I just ate until I couldn't look food in the face again, and am only now recovering. We had chicken again, turkeys being much too scarce and dear for us to procure one, but we all preferred chicken anyway. We had an extra meat ration for Christmas, and for the first time in years a really decent sized joint of beef lay along side the poultry. For a few days anyway, it was a house of plenty again.

Of course, this week we go back to our normal rations again, but that help over Christmas did an awful lot to cheer people, and we look forward to better times in the year which is ahead. They say it never rains but it pours, and it hardly seems fair for one person to get so much, but I now hear that there is a food parcel coming to me from Denmark. Two of these were allotted to Don's battery, for sending home, and his name came out of the hat. He didn't know then that I'd had the other two from Australia and South Africa, or he might have thought someone else should have the Denmark one, but anyway, I always share them, and all the family get the pleasure as well as me. Our next big 'do' now will be Don's home coming, or Easter when Jeanne and Michael come down, which ever comes first.

As it was our last Christmas before the office closes (it is by the way but a matter of weeks now, but I'll try and get one last letter to you before I say farewell to this old machine for ever) we all went out and had a really good 'do'. A few of us started on the Friday before Christmas – I had a cold, so they kept asking me to have another and another 'for my cold', but they just weren't having any effect on me at all. I lost count of how many cocktails I drank, but I came back to the office and typed back a whole pile of shorthand, so I couldn't have been too bad. I say I typed it back, but herein lies a tale. The boss had dictated it all to me before lunch, and then gone out. Well, I just took it for granted he'd gone for the day and didn't worry. I was back over an hour late, and even then, didn't start work, so you can imagine my face when at three o'clock, when I was calmly drinking a cup of tea, he walked in and asked for his letters. I said, quite truthfully, 'I haven't finished them yet', but when he said 'I'll take what you have done', I had to gulp out 'I haven't done any.' I don't think I've ever had to make such an admission all the while I've been his secretary, but he was endowed with a bit of the Christmas spirit himself, and almost lost for words, just walked away. Maybe it was this that sobered me, but anyhow I got cracking, and in less than no time, had done the lot. Saturday, we all went out again. This time, the whole of the staff from the highest to the lowest, technical staff as well – gosh there was a crowd of us, we practically filled the bar. My cold was really at its worst, and unlike the day before, the first drink just rushed straight to my head, so that after a few more, I seemed to be doing everything in a daze. I don't know how many I did drink, although I remember refusing lots, and leaving heaps on the counter bought by the more insistent who wouldn't believe that I couldn't take it. I told them I could when I felt right, but I had the world's worst head cold. When finally, everyone had kissed everyone else, and wished them a Merry Christmas, we split up for home, and our lovely long four day holiday. Just how I got myself on to the right train, or out at the right station, I don't know, but I did, and soon I was in the armchair at home before the fire, with Mum placing a lovely hot cup of tea in my hands.

 I'd arranged to go out on a similar mission with Win and her family that evening, but I just couldn't face it, and she, being the understanding sort, came to the flicks with me instead. Sunday and Monday I was busy with the cooking, and preparing of all the good things. Christmas Day we just sat in between meals eating fruit and sweets, until they almost rolled out of our eyes, and spent the evening playing silly games. Alf and Doris came in from next door with her sister and husband, who are living with them, as they have no home of their own, so we were quite a crowd. At all our previous parties, we'd acted song titles, until we couldn't think of any more, so this time we went on to film titles. You should see the acting abilities of the Hellewells when we get going. Some titles were acted so well we just couldn't guess them, whereas others brought screams of laughter right from the start, and the correct answer. I got no further than searching around the room saying 'I can't find it anywhere' when they shouted 'The Lost Weekend' at me. Where as Bill's 'I caught a fish thirty feet long' will always be remembered when we think of 'The Great Lie'. Mum and the others turned in about twelve, but Edna and I and the men, sat up until gone four, playing cards on the floor.

On Boxing Day I was due to go to a party at Win's house, but my cold took a turn for the worse, I felt sick, and due to weakness from the very bad cold I had, both my eyelids swelled up – imagine how I looked. I felt so mad, with all the rest of the year to feel bad, I had to go and feel this way at Christmas. I wasn't going to be done though, so I stayed in bed until mid-day, then I got up and got straight ready for the party. I didn't look too bad then, the swelling went down from my eyes, just leaving them bloodshot, so I crawled round to Win's, only to find her family more or less in the same state. They'd all got colds, and had also eaten too much unaccustomed rich food, so everyone looked as though a party was the last thing they were ready for. However, we had to snap out of it, as it was her brother's party for his ex-prisoners of war pals, and when the party got going one by one we forgot that we didn't feel so good, and found ourselves having a good time. The biggest laugh of the evening was when one of the fellows walked in with his eyes just like mine. Some-one said it was quite a common complaint, some germ or other that is going around, but it certainly made me feel better knowing I wasn't the only one who was looking a sight. We played all the usual silly games, ate a lot, drank what was left of the Christmas wines, and then all tumbled home in the early hours, having had a really good time.

I was due to go to the office on Thursday, but just couldn't face it – all the late nights had really told on me by then. The boss was understanding, since he knew I had had a cold before the holiday, but I'm right back to normal now, I'm glad to say. We all sat up last night to see the New Year in, and listened on the wireless to the cheering crowds outside St. Paul's – how happy everyone sounded – it really is going to be a Happy New Year, this one. Other years, as we have raised our glasses it's always been our second wish 'May this year bring us Peace', and when last night we all faltered, trying to think of something new after all this time, Mum made us all laugh by saying the first thing she thought of, 'May you all find your flats and houses'.

We have decided definitely to live over the shop, although it will be months before it is habitable. They have started on the roof, and then the next job will be the bomb damage, which entails new window frames and doors, and the re-plastering of the walls and ceilings. Knowing the rate they work, I guess Don will be home before they get much further than this. It is after the bomb damage has been done though that the real fun will start. Somehow we've got to find someone who will fit us up a bathroom – Don says after six years in the army, and washing down in a six inch bowl, he isn't living anywhere that hasn't a bathroom. Goodness knows how we'll get it done, but we will, somehow or other. The staircase too is another important item – at the moment there are no stairs leading up from the shop, just a step ladder, and Don insists that not only must there be a staircase, but it is to be completely boarded in, so as to cut the flat right off from the shop. When I think of all the painting, decorating and cleaning, as well as a hundred and one other jobs there will be to do, I go hot and cold, but I realise there is nothing I can do until the big jobs are done. I'm confident anyway that once Don gets home, he'll soon get things done. I'm sure it is going to look very nice when it is all finished, and we are more than lucky to have it with so many homeless. I've been longing for this ever since he went back in September, I feel that these next three months are going to pass very quickly, and who knows, before the summer, we might be in there. A home of our own by our fifth anniversary – we've been pretty patient I think.

Win is expecting her husband home at the end of this month, when he will be demobbed and out of the Army completely. It's going to be a pretty lonely couple of months for me after this, but I shall be busy with curtains and things, I'm sure the time will pass quickly. After all, what is but a few months, after four years, for four years it will be, by March.

I almost forgot another important piece of news, Michael John arrived on the 5th December, and according to Jeanne and everyone who has seen him he is the image of George. We haven't seen him yet, and I guess it will be Easter before we get the chance, but George had a week's leave over Christmas, just as Jeanne came out of hospital, and was able to spend it with her and her people in Huddersfield. Of course, he thinks he is the most wonderful baby that ever lived — aren't they all, and calls him 'The Mighty Atom' because he weighed 9-lbs at birth. Edna's little girl Patricia is a real darling, always happy, and about the brightest child I know. She loved her Christmas tree and her toys, but the little rag doll Edna made her, carrying the title 'Raggity Ann', is the love of her life, and she hardly looks at the beautiful doll, dressed in a velvet bonnet and coat, with clothes that come off and on, which her Auntie Jeanne made her. Edna has decided to put it away until she is older and will appreciate it more.

Amongst the grownups in the family we cut presents out this year, as it is impossible to get anything worth buying. The rubbish in the shops at fantastic prices was worse than ever this year, so we just left well alone. However, Mum bought me a gift box of all good things to eat which are hard to get, but not rationed. This contained cake and sponge mixtures, various dessert dressings, junket powders, jelly crystals, and many other things. The box was packed by the makers, and some of the things we just never see in the shops separately. I guess they must have saved them for these special boxes before Christmas, and now perhaps they will come into the shops. I have quite a nice little store of odds and ends like this to start my larder off when I get on my own. It's certainly going to be a blow to me having to do my own queuing after having everything done for me by Mum. Still, when I leave the office, I'll be able to do my share for the remainder of the time I am home, and get used to the idea.

Well, Donna, there doesn't seem to be very much else in the way of news to report, and anyway, I've rambled on long enough. I'm looking forward to hearing from you, how you spent your Christmas — I bet Gary really got the idea of it all this year, didn't he, and I've no doubt Santa was more than good to him. Did his books arrive safely, addressed to your old home — I do hope so.

Seeing that I came here to work, I guess it wouldn't be a bad idea now if I got on with some, having typed away like mad for the past hour or so. The factory is closing in a fortnight, and just how long the office will hang on after that, no-one seems to know, but it doesn't bother me. I can do with a lazy spell, especially this cold weather. Travelling up and down on the railway is no joke when it's foggy, and somehow I don't seem to lend myself so easily to crushing into crowded compartments, and standing on one foot, as I used to. Guess I must be getting old and a bit soft.

I almost forgot to tell you about two lovely presents I had from Don for Christmas. Remember I told you I had bought myself a really super suit, which cost a small fortune, well, the first surprise came in the shape of a cheque for this from Don. He says it isn't a Christmas present though, since he'd have bought it had he been home. The other surprise, no don't laugh, was a mangle. How we've laughed about this, and I've told Don, 'Talk about know you are married when your husband buys you a mangle'. The point is you just never see them in the shops now, and his sister managed to get one somehow, I just don't know how, and wrote and told him about it. He of course told her to get it for me, which she did, and kept it hidden until Christmas. It is a dear little thing, a pretty blue, with dinkie little rubber rollers, and it fits on to a stand which is collapsible when not in use. When I think of the huge, old fashioned mangle my mother used to have, and this dainty little thing, there is certainly some difference. It'll be awfully useful when I have to dry things indoors though – I'm going to miss not having a garden, I know.

Really must dry up now, the boss is getting impatient for his work, can't say I blame him. Here's hoping to hear from you soon, and that you and all your family had the very Happiest Christmas, and may the New Year make your every wish come true.

Loads of love to you all and an especial big kiss for my boyfriend,
 from
  Win xxxxx
  Big X for Gary

Just two weeks after this last letter was finished I left the office, but two days after this, Don arrived home unexpectedly. His elderly father who had looked after the shop for him all the while he was away had been finding it harder and harder to manage, especially with the new lower, postwar meat ration, so Don's sister had applied for his release on compassionate grounds, and this was granted.

He arrived home on 12th February 1946 and on 12th November 1946 our daughter, Christine, who has helped me so much in the preparation of this book, was born.

Don immediately took over, coming to grips with running his shop again, and between us we worked to make those rooms over the shop habitable. My clever father made a wonderful double staircase with a landing in between, in his shed at the bottom of the garden at '23', and when the shop was able to close for a Monday in June when they held a Victory Parade in London, Don and Dad spent two days fitting the staircase in sit. So it was that for the latter part of my pregnancy I could reach our flat without having to squeeze through a hole off a ladder as I had had to do for the first three months.

This was our home for three years, until in 1949 we moved into 159 Minard Road, which has been my home ever since.

Postscript: 15th June 2003

Today marks the 62nd anniversary of the day Don and I were married, on a Sunday in June 1941 (it's a Sunday again this year), and with my 83rd birthday fast approaching in three days' time, it seemed the appropriate day to write this postscript to the book you have just finished reading.

When you think of the nineteen years of my life before the war, and the almost sixty years since, those six years of war are but a tiny morsel in my long life, but I am glad it has been possible to record them. I wanted this for my family, my children, my grandchildren and my great-grandchildren.

After all those long lonely years, I was one of the lucky ones. Don returned to me leaner, fitter, and with his experiences of those years etched forever on his face.

We soon picked up the pieces and had a wonderful life together. In 1946 our daughter Christine was born, and in 1950 Denis arrived. Over the years, good times mingling with bad as in most lives, grandchildren arrived, first Zoe, then Andrew, Michael and Dean. Eight months ago also the most wonderful thing of all happened when Zoe gave me my wonderful great-granddaughter Charly.

It took until 1981 for Don and me to fulfil our promise to visit Lamar and personally thank the wonderful people of the town for their generosity to me during the war. We took a wonderful retirement holiday which involved travelling across the States on a Greyhound bus, from West to East, taking in visits to family and friends, including Donna. So it was that two travel-weary people walked from the Greyhound bus to the offices of *The Lamar Daily News*. After explaining who we were, we were treated like VIPs for the 24 hours we were in the town. A reporter from the paper met us after breakfast the next day and took us all over the place. We were able to meet several people who had actually contributed to those parcels all those years ago, and we were also able to learn quite a bit about the town of Lamar itself. Natural gas had just been discovered in the town, as well as oil. I will never forget standing in that field watching the oil rig in operation. Time went much too quickly and early evening saw us back on a Greyhound bus, waving goodbye to a host of new friends.

The good life Don and I had together came to an abrupt end in 1991 when just a few months after we had celebrated our Golden Wedding, Don had a stroke and died. How well I remember those Golden Wedding celebrations – Donna, herself widowed by then, came over with her grandson.

It's been a very full, active life and these last ten years or so of my widowhood were filled with my activities on behalf of Breast Cancer Care. Breast cancer hit me for the first time in 1959, and proved to be my salvation in the latter part of my life, when I was so suddenly alone. I became even more deeply involved with this charity, and made scores of new friends and acquaintances, which made for an extremely busy life.

Although breast cancer has been a part of my life for over forty years, I can honestly say it has never affected my enjoyment of life and stopped me doing anything I wanted to do.

That is, until recently, for eighteen months ago I learned that secondary breast cancer was attacking my bones, and though I am still able to lead a very full life, look after my house and garden, enjoy my family, and indulge myself in hobbies I enjoy, I know that to a degree time is running out, so I have to get these thoughts down onto paper without too much delay.

I want to say thank you to Christine in particular for all her work in helping to get this book published, to Donna for her friendship of over seventy years, and to Faye Johnson for sending me what I thought were long lost copies of *The Lamar Daily News*, and for her encouragement that the letters should be published.

Win Wyatt